Presented to
Chicago Public Library

by the
Public Libraries Group
of
The Library Association
of Great Britain

on the occasion of the Opening
of
**The Harold Washington
Library Center**

October 1991

For Clyde Pollitt and John Price

When we mean to build,
We first survey the plot, then draw the model;
And when we see the figure of the house,
Then must we rate the cost of the erection;
Which if we find outweighs ability,
What do we then but draw anew the model,
In fewer offices, or at last desist
To build at all.

Shakespeare, Henry IV Part 2

THE ENGLISH SHAKESPEARE COMPANY

The Story of
'THE WARS OF THE ROSES'
1986–1989

'Who won the Wars of the Roses? The crown must go to the English Shakespeare Company. It has been around the world with a cycle of seven of Shakespeare's History plays and triumphed on every field of battle – from Bath to Brisbane, from Nottingham to the Netherlands, from Hull to Hamburg, Chichester to Chicago. The *New York Times* called it a "monumental achievement" yet rarely has something monumental been so much fun.'

Desmond Christy, *Guardian*

'Deep into *Henry VI,* a soldier unknowingly slays his father and another soldier unknowingly slays his son. Sitting on the ground, watching in horror, Henry VI seems to mourn his life, his country and the way of his world. The moment – along with scores of others – illuminates Shakespeare's view of history endlessly repeating itself: a succession of wars, pitting cousin against countryman, nation against nation. Besieged by broken promises and infinite cycles of revenge, the warriors never seem to learn from Shakespeare's words, "Ill blows the wind that profits nobody."

Watching the English Shakespeare Company's marathon performance of *The Wars of the Roses* – presented here this weekend under the auspices of the Stamford Center for the Arts – one is rewarded by a comprehensive overview of English history (as interpreted by England's greatest poet) and of Shakespeare's History plays.

In a marathon lasting more than 23 hours, seven interrelated plays were performed: *Richard II*, followed by *Henry IV Parts 1* and *2, Henry V* and the three *Henry VI* plays distilled to two, followed by *Richard III*. It was, in all senses, a prodigious undertaking, most of all for those theatre-goers who experienced the complete and indispensable Shakespearian event.'

Mel Gussow, *New York Times*

Michael Bogdanov has been a theatre director for twenty-six years. After studying and working in Dublin in theatre and TV for ten of these years, there followed spells at the Newcastle Playhouse, the Phoenix Leicester, the Young Vic, the Royal Shakespeare Company and the National Theatre, where from 1980 to 1986 he was an Associate Director. He has directed in America, Brazil, Canada and Japan, and has four times received awards for Director of the Year, including the 1979 SWET Award for his RSC production of *The Taming of the Shrew* and the 1990 Olivier Award for *The Wars of the Roses*. He is currently Intendant of the Deutsches Schauspielhaus, Hamburg, one of Germany's most prestigious national theatres.

Michael Pennington has been an actor for twenty-six years. He has played seasons with the Royal Shakespeare Company and the National Theatre as well as appearing at the Royal Court, in the West End and on the fringe. He was Hamlet for the RSC in 1980, played a one-man show about Anton Chekhov at the National Theatre in 1984, and was Raskolnikov in Yuri Lyubimov's first English-language production, *Crime and Punishment*, in 1983. He played Oedipus on BBC television in 1985 and was most recently seen on television in John Mortimer's *Summer's Lease*. In 1990 he was Vershinin in the Dublin Gate Theatre's *Three Sisters* and received an Olivier Award Nomination for his work in *The Wars of the Roses*.

Bogdanov and Pennington had worked together on *Shadow of a Gunman* for the RSC and *Strider – The Story of a Horse* for the National Theatre. In 1985 they co-founded the English Shakespeare Company, since when Bogdanov has directed their seven-play cycle of Shakespeare histories under the title *The Wars of the Roses – Richard II, Henry IV Parts 1 and 2, Henry V, Henry VI House of Lancaster, Henry VI House of York*, and *Richard III* – for the theatre and television, with Pennington as Richard II, Hal, Henry V, Suffolk, Cade and Buckingham. To date *The Wars of the Roses* has collected a total of 18 awards and nominations. *The Comedy of Errors* (directed by Glen Walford) was launched in January 1990 and in September (when this book was published) the company was mounting productions of *Coriolanus* and *The Winter's Tale* (with Pennington directed by Bogdanov) and *The Merchant of Venice* and *The Alchemist*.

Michael Bogdanov and Michael Pennington

THE ENGLISH SHAKESPEARE COMPANY

The Story of

'THE WARS OF THE ROSES'

1986 – 1989

N
H
IB

NICK HERN BOOKS
A division of Walker Books Limited

The English Shakespeare Company first published in 1990 by
Nick Hern Books, a division of Walker Books Limited,
87 Vauxhall Walk, London SE11 5HJ

British Library Cataloguing in Publication Data
Bogdanov, Michael
  The English Shakespeare Company:
  the story of the Wars of the Roses, 1986–1989.
  1. Drama in English. Shakespeare, William 1564–1616
  I. Title II. Pennington, Michael
  792.92

        ISBN 1–85459–043–X Hardback
            1–85459–049–9 Paperback

    Printed and bound in Great Britain by
    Biddles Ltd, Guildford and King's Lynn

CONTENTS

APPENDICES

LIST OF ILLUSTRATIONS

Front endpaper: The ESC in Berlin

Plates

The A.I.B cheque
First rehearsal: September 1986
Michael Pennington
Michael Bogdanov
Rehearsals: Henry IV and the Earl of Douglas
Rehearsals: The Boar's Head Tavern
Rehearsals: 'Once more unto the breach'
Rehearsals: Doll Tearsheet and Falstaff
Rehearsals: *Henry IV*

Henry IV Part 1: The Hotspurs
Henry IV Part 1: Gadshill
Henry IV Part 2: Falstaff and Mistress Quickly
Henry IV Part 2: The Coronation of Henry V
Henry V: The Chorus
Henry V: The King
Henry V: Gower and Fluellen
Henry V: The Princess of France
Henry V: The English leave for France

Henry V: The French Court
June Watson
John Price
John Woodvine
Colin Farrell

The Winter of Discontent: Rehearsing at Limehouse
Scaling down the Histories
Henry VI House of York: Cade's Rebellion
Richard II: King Richard
Richard III: Final scene
Henry IV Part 2: Falstaff

Henry VI House of Lancaster: King Henry
Richard III: Queen Margaret
Richard III: King Richard

Acknowledgements
Onstage photographs by Laurence Burns; offstage photographs by John Tramper; line drawings by Jenny Quayle.

INTRODUCTION

Michael Pennington: The mucky stuff first.

In the middle of 1985 I was in a poorish humour. I had been invited by Peter Hall to do the central roles in premieres of plays by Alan Ayckbourn and Peter Shaffer at the National Theatre. I liked working there and had started preparing the parts. However, the view of the NT Contracts Department was that the work was worth £25 a week less than I reckoned. I found the nuance irksome (I knew the National's rates well and was not out of court); they felt that sustaining the marginal difference was crucial to the National Theatre. After many weeks of mutual stubbornness whose pettiness amazes me to this day, the whole thing ground to a most unartistic halt; the two parts went out to two separate actors (presumably doubling the cost), and I flounced off.

At about the same time, the Royal Shakespeare Company came on the line, interested in having me up to Stratford to do Richard II, a part we had often discussed. They promised to get back to me in a few days. A great pause ensued; the next thing I heard of the production was that it had opened.

There will, I hope, be no more sour trade grapes in this book; they are not attractive, though they do sometimes serve to kick-start the engine. A life in the theatre is full of routine screw-ups and small treacheries, but that particular summer they seemed to be piling in rather. Such was the beginning of a long chain of consequences for me; and it would be wrong to embark on an account of the lofty motives behind the launching of the English Shakespeare Company without acknowledging the measly ones as well.

To begin with, I was looking around for a colleague as grumpy as myself to plot with.

Michael Bogdanov: I had been doing mediocre work at the National. After an initial burst of success (and controversy), I was unable to break a run of productions that seemed indistinguishable from A Thousand and One Anonymous Nights that (dis)graced the English stage. A limited success with *Lorenzaccio* (which actually looks better now from a distance), an interesting Revenge figure in *The Spanish Tragedy* (its re-run brilliantly scheduled to play twelve

performances in flaming July). An *Uncle Vanya* of which I had high
hopes but which crashed on the first night. *You Can't Take It With
You* – funny previews, unfunny critics. Something in the building
was stifling me. I was seeking desperately a way of rebuilding my
energy and enthusiasm and challenging myself to break with the
repertoire system. Peter Hall posited a series of new companies. I
put forward an idea for a touring unit. It would initiate projects
outside the building – co-productions – tour them, bring them
into the National. I had lined up two little-performed O'Caseys
with the Abbey Theatre, Dublin. English and Irish actors, rehearse
part London, part Dublin, open at the Abbey, tour Ireland, tour
England, end up in the Lyttelton. A Big Top tour of *Bartholomew
Fair*. A new play about the 1911 Llanelli Railway Strike, to be
performed in an old railway shed in Llanelli in conjunction with
HTV. (Olivier Theatre material.) A link with the country, an
attempt to make the National truly national. I would have my own
Administrator (Ruth Anders, ex-RSC, was practically signed up),
Production Unit, Stage Management team. A pipe dream, of
course. The grant to the National Theatre that year was 2% up on
the previous year, some 8% below inflation in the theatre. The NT
was short £1 million. Peter closed the Cottesloe. My plans went up
in smoke. I was VERY grumpy.

Pennington: The fact was we'd been plotters before. In 1980
Trevor Nunn had suggested that I do Donal Davoren in a revival
of O'Casey's *Shadow of a Gunman* at Stratford. I had hesitated,
feeling the part ought really to be played by an Irishman, and also,
I think, underestimating the play's stubborn relevance to contemporary Ireland. Norman Rodway had agreed to do Seumas Shields,
but the production had no director assigned to it yet. Trevor said
that Michael Bogdanov was a possibility, which surprised me, as
I didn't associate him with either Ireland or with the ruthlessly
naturalistic style I assumed the play would need. Wrong again.
Bogdanov is a graduate of Trinity, Dublin and worked for years in
Irish theatre and as a director at Radio Telefis Eireann; he knew
O'Casey's city by the street. I shouldn't have doubted him
stylistically either.

I'm not sure I'm coming out of this very well so far.

At any rate, feeling rather silly, I had jumped in, and had a whale
of a time, cementing a friendship with Rodway and extremely glad
of Bogdanov's very exacting direction, which took absolutely

nothing for granted. I didn't, however, feel that close to him personally until, after the first night, we found ourselves talking in the pub about how the show had come about; he was surprised to hear my end of it, because he had been told by the RSC when he was offered the production that I had 'insisted' on playing Davoren, so a major piece of his casting had already been pre-emptively done for him. I now understood his reserve. He had thought he was dealing with a snotty Stratford regular who had muscled in on the show. Our appreciation of this managerial fudge cemented our friendship as little else could have done; there are those who would say we are now doing the same sort of thing.

Bogdanov: 'Who, Trevor? How on earth do you think he can play a working-class Dubliner? Yes, I know all about The Voice, but, certes, 'twill be of little use in affecting a nasal Dublin gurrier, methinks.' After all, I had been brought up with Ronnie Drew – 'Seven Drunken Nights', 'The Wild Rover' – a voice like crushed coke. I insisted that if Michael Pennington, whom I had never met, was to play Donal Davoren, then elsewhere *Shadow of a Gunman* had to be strongly cast with Irish actors. After ten years in Ireland, I had a horror of doing Irish plays with anyone other than the Irish. The English try to pin down the elusive Celtic butterfly soul with a sledgehammer. The Irish leapfrog England to middle Europe, the last vestiges of a culture and a language that was once spoken the length and breadth of the Continent. The deep, dark despair, the laughter and tears, story telling and music, the religion, the politics, a sense of the cultural belonging that is once again manifesting itself in Latvia, Lithuania, Romania, Hungary. It is a world strongly alien to the English psyche, unfathomable, deeply mysterious and one which, if we are honest, we are not very interested in. Michael and I prowled warily round each other with Norman Rodway, an old chum from way back, as ring-master and arbitrator. Dearbhla Molloy – Minnie Powell – looked on.

He never made it to Donal Davoren, but he had a damn good try. The last two weeks of rehearsal he went into his shell, but my admiration for him grew as I watched him wrestle with a part he was patently unsuited for, determined to conquer. (I was to think immediately of this dedication when I came to cast *Strider – The Story of a Horse* in the Cottesloe.) That admiration became the cornerstone of a tripartite friendship, Pennington, Rodway, Bogdanov, that met from time to time as an informal dining club dedicated to dirt dishing. I tried to cast Michael as Astrov in *Uncle*

Vanya. Peter Hall was resistant – 'a not very interesting actor'. Michael then emerged sensationally in Lyubimov's *Crime and Punishment*. We clinched a deal on *Strider*. At 8 am each morning he would be in front of the mirror in Rehearsal Room Four, working out, miming the movements of a horse. That same determination. Peter invited him to play the leads in his trilogy of late Shakespeares. 'I thought you said he was uninteresting.' 'I've changed my mind.' A lesson in theatrical pragmatism. More than ever, Michael and I recognised the need to do something independent of the two big institutions.

Pennington and Bogdanov: The English Shakespeare Company and this book are the consequence of our bluff being called. It should be dedicated to somebody. Perhaps to Ed and David Mirvish for the faith, and to the Allied Irish Bank for the fun. Perhaps to the many agents who rang up and asked to speak to Peter Bogdanovitch, or the one in particular who, in answering an enquiry of ours about Ann Bell when we were casting *The Henrys*, said that she felt Ann was a little young for Falstaff; to Robert Sykes, formerly Head of Dance and Drama at the British Council, whose unfailing rudeness and condescension in the early days spurred us on to ever-greater efforts. To Michael Billington, theatre critic of the *Guardian*, bless him, clutching his sheaf of old university notes, peering anxiously under the bed for the red; he still doesn't like us, even though we took him to breakfast at Brown's. Indeed, to most of the critical fraternity, who, interpreting our air of maverick *insouciance* as lack of seriousness, tend to overlook us in their annual round-ups. To Peter Stevens, Howard Panter, Jules Boardman, Board Members who resigned in panic when we announced *The Wars of the Roses*, thinking they were about to lose their shirts. Or to all those whose productions of Shakespeare have left us feeling so short-changed that we started the ESC.

More seriously, it could be dedicated to the company itself, that is to say, to the sixty-odd people who, over the ensuing years, have variously held us to our word, shouted at us, and taken our risks with us. We hope to include them all in this book, and will no doubt fail. They are, of course, the real English Shakespeare Company.

In the end though, it must be dedicated to the memory of two colleagues we have tragically lost: John Price, who died suddenly while rehearsing for *The Wars of the Roses*; and Clyde Pollitt, who died shortly after the end of the final tour. Both men stand for what is best in our profession, and their example as actors and friends continues to influence us deeply. This book is, most decisively, for them.

PART ONE

THE COST OF THE ERECTION

(above) The Allied Irish Bank cheque: was it punts, not pounds?
– Michael Pennington, Joyce Austin, Fleur Selby, Michael Bogdanov,
Niall Gallagher (AIB);
(below) The ESC's first rehearsal – Wandsworth, September 1986 (LB)

'We must all to the wars' – Pennington, Bogdanov,
O'Connell, Jarvis (all LB)

Rehearsals: (right)
The Boar's Head Tavern
– Darryl Forbes-Dawson,
Colin Farrell, John Price,
John Tramper (LB);
(below) Henry V –
'Once more unto the
breach' (LB)

*Rehearsals: (above) Jenny Quayle (Doll Tearsheet),
John Woodvine (Falstaff) (LB);
(below) Gareth Thomas (Lord Chief Justice), Patrick O'Connell (Henry
IV), Morris Perry (Exeter) (LB)*

CHAPTER

1

SETTING UP

September 1985 – September 1986

'Is not this something more than fantasy?'
Shakespeare, Hamlet

Pennington: Because it contains certain rather warming elements in this chilly Age of Feasibility, the story of how a new Charity, the English Shakespeare Company, came about has become, at least in local circles, a good one. Its general outline has over the years been reductively polished by ourselves for a great number of interviews, sometimes with people whose interest was in a good paragraph and sometimes with the genuinely curious. We two adventurers, so the story goes, one serious and classical, the other jolly and irreverent, went to the Arts Council one day with plans to do a production with two actors on a single set with a modest budget, and were immediately sent away with an open brief to think big – £100,000 big – epic, and Shakespearian. The two merry fellows then repaired to a coffee shop near 105 Piccadilly, decided to put on the two parts of *Henry IV* and *Henry V*, went back in and everyone drank to it. All the accomplices who then joined us – the Allied Irish Bank, the Old Vic, Plymouth Theatre Royal and the Association for Business Sponsorship of the Arts – were only too happy to leap onto this confidently speeding bus as it raced towards a degree of fame, if strictly limited fortune.

Not really.

All we knew by the autumn of 1985 was that we wanted to do something, almost any something, for ourselves. We formed a nominal company, membership of two, and called it Mole

Productions, for we were still very much in the dark. Whatever we lit upon, Michael would presumably direct, I would play in, and Mole would be responsible for putting it on somewhere in London. This unsurprising desire had tentatively fastened itself on a single script, *The Gigli Concert* by the Irish writer Tom Murphy, a wonderful play for two actors that had still not been performed in England. If Norman Rodway would come in to play the opera-obsessed tycoon, we would also have the pleasure of reviving the partnership that had done *Shadow of a Gunman* five years before. We started to pay calls on likely backers, sometimes brandishing *The Gigli Concert* before us, sometimes hiding it under our coat-tails. Most significant among these was Andrew Leigh, the Administrator of the Old Vic, who told us that Ed and David Mirvish, who own both the Vic and the Royal Alexandra Theatre in Toronto, were now interested in investing in their own shows for the first time rather than simply buying them in from outside producers; and that they wanted to respond to the deep feeling among English audiences that the Old Vic should be a fairly regular home for Shakespeare. In Andrew's office, we slipped *The Gigli Concert* into our back pockets and reconsidered our burrowing.

We also felt, with some part of our brains, that we should be touring. The tendency to centralise Britain's artistic life in the metropolitan areas (rather like King Henry IV's disdain for the regions) obviously creates two nations, paying one tax. This was a comparatively recent development that neither of us felt sympathetic towards; we were both temperamentally inclined to devolve, and bothered that we hadn't done more. Defeated in his touring plans, Michael was considering giving up his association with the National Theatre. The first thing I had wanted to do when I finished playing Hamlet for the RSC in 1981 was to take the production from the Aldwych – the setting was particularly simple – and elastically tour it to big and small regional dates. At that time the RSC's touring work was usually planned as a self-contained unit with an increasingly tenuous link to its main house activities, and I thought this had unfortunate implications; but my idea wasn't taken up. So unfinished business was simmering away in both of us, a righteous modern impulse to get the work out to short-rationed audiences no doubt combining with an affection for the ancient barnstorming traditions of the trade.

So we now went to see Jodi Myers and Fleur Selby, who were running the Touring Department of the Arts Council in the temporary absence of Jack Phipps, and stepped out on the long and winding road to a first grant of our very own. They pointed out to us what, come to think of it, we already knew, that the precise touring need at that time was not so much for small-scale work to obviously deprived venues – the RSC and Cheek by Jowl were doing plenty of that – but for product big enough to revitalise the old 'Number One' circuit, where managers like Bob Scott at the Palace Manchester (2,000 seats), Judi Richards at the New Cardiff (1,170 seats) and James Donald at Her Majesty's Aberdeen (1,500 seats) would welcome some departure from three weeks of *Jesus Christ Superstar* followed by Alvin Stardust for a night – particularly if it seemed to reconnect them symbolically with the best traditions of classical touring. They would love to hear from us, or at least the Arts Council would love them to hear from us, if we were offering big, popular Shakespeare.

Which suddenly it seemed as if we might be. It was now that we drank coffee, tipping our hats to Tom Murphy – we were either very flexible or very easily swayed – and mentally linking up the Old Vic, the road, and the Shakespearian repertoire. It didn't take long to see that the brief we were being offered extended beyond dutiful ideas of another *Twelfth Night*. We had been invited to think large. Nothing is larger in Shakespeare than the epic sequence of Histories that runs over eight plays from the Deposition of Richard II in 1399 to the founding of the Tudor dynasty by Henry VII on Bosworth Field in 1485. We could hardly do all eight – could we? – but a brilliant self-contained unit lies inside the sequence, in the two parts of *Henry IV* followed by *Henry V*, which deal with the troubled reign of Richard's usurper Bolingbroke and the accession to power of his son Prince Hal, friend of Falstaff, foe to Hotspur, conqueror of Agincourt.* The first two plays, while hardly box-office favourites like the third, anatomise the nation with a quite extraordinary variety and richness, reflecting both its schisms (uncannily like those of the 1980s) and its glories. They belong, in a real sense, to all of us. *Henry V* is a real chameleon: at first sight the most obviously heroic play in the canon, it yields up all kinds of contradictory meanings

---

* **Bogdanov:** *We had both at various times wanted to do the plays. I at the National had put myself in line to do the two* Henry IVs *and, after four other directors, had once been offered the small-scale tour of same at the* RSC.

depending on its surroundings. Olivier had effortlessly turned its heroism to account in his superb, War Government sponsored film in 1944; it had looked like an anti-war play on occasion in the sixties and seventies; and we were now the wrong side of the Falklands conflict, so Henry's self-justifying foreign invasion, drowning discontent at home in its patriotic clamour, looked uneasily different again. All three plays are big, well beyond the means of most repertory houses – and stopping the gap left by the general decline of the repertory movement was surely part of what we should be doing. They also contain a range of parts that would surely keep the hungriest acting talents fed for a length of time, and such great roving plays of the nation would fittingly announce the birth of a new touring company. Michael should direct; I should play Prince Hal/Henry V; and – stroke of strokes – every Saturday we should do a trilogy of all three plays, morning, afternoon and night, at each date on the road and finally, climactically, at the Vic.

Nobody could say it wasn't large. But since that had been the invitation, surely better to start amply and reduce the scale later if necessary. And as we were about to be soliciting funds, the same optimism should apply to our initial budgets. We weren't in the business of cheap six-man Shakespeare – Hotspur doubling with the King and all that – and so we would need a minimum acting company of twenty-five, backed by a full stage management team, and they would need to be paid very much as if we were sending out a major tour from the RSC or the National. With a single set for all three plays that could cost £35,000, and who knows how many costumes and props budgeted at roughly the same figure, with all the fees and salaries and other expenses added in, we reckoned the whole enterprise could cost a capital sum of £350,000 to mount and then, on tour, about £25,000 a week to run, which latter we would hope to recoup through the box office and in committed guarantees from the host theatres. Even though our most promising allies, the Mirvishes, were commercial, we were firmly resting our case from the outset on the principle of subsidy; a commercial management looking for a return would be most unlikely to consider such a budget for Shakespearian history, especially if it were strongly cast in depth as we planned – commercial productions of Shakespeare tend to underpay all but the star, and it sometimes shows. Well, they could only say no. We went back with our idea to Jodi and Fleur, who blinked only a little, and then on again (I am turning the accomplishment of many weeks into an hourglass now) to Andrew Leigh, who introduced us to Ed Mirvish and his son David.

Ed and David are something of a legend in Canadian business circles. Ed grew up very poor in Toronto, the son of Lithuanian Jewish immigrant parents. Working as a boy in the family's grocery store, he watched his father commit commercial suicide by giving out careless credit; and now the cornerstone of Ed's retailing empire — which has grown from tiny premises on Market Street to centre on Honest Ed's Department Store (occupying a full two blocks at Bloor and Markham), also including restaurants and the Royal Alexandra Theatre on King Street — is the slogan No Credit — No Refund — No Goods Exchanged. Conversely, he specialises in occasional loss-leaders, offering, for example, five-cent chickens at Christmas time, to be had from the jewellery department on the fifth floor. You can imagine the rush. His son David is a highly successful art dealer, with a particularly fine collection of modern American abstracts; at a certain point Ed invited him back into the family business, bought the Old Vic in London, and put David in charge of it and the Royal Alex — at just about the moment we went to visit them.

We warmed immediately to their direct and humorous approach to business, an approach which in no way compromises their canny vigilance on detail and feasibility. They are the best kind of family concern, and culture and commerce sometimes seem indivisible. Throughout our first meeting Ed's wife Anne quietly charcoal-sketched us, while David the art collector nagged at us to make savings in our budget and Ed the restaurant millionaire enthused over the fun of the thing and told David not to be so mean. They unequivocally agreed to pitch £125,000 into the enterprise on the not very arduous condition that we play six-week seasons at the Old Vic and the Royal Alex at the end of our UK tour. On these seasons they would also guarantee us our running costs, so they were taking a risk on that too. Almost alone among our backers, Ed and David never wavered from this opening position — though there was a moment not long after when I found myself sitting in some confusion next to David at a performance in Paris of Peter Brook's *Mahabharata*: I had stupidly cleaned myself out in the middle of the weekend and had to borrow £40 from him to get myself through, which must have made him wonder what kind of people Ed Mirvish Enterprises were about to get into bed with.

We now looked around for a theatre to launch the productions from; and if it could be one that could act as partial co-producers by, say, building the set and making the props, so much the better. Andrew Welch and Roger Redfarn were confidently running the Theatre Royal Plymouth, one of the very few touring houses with the facilities to mount original work as well; they were at the time co-producing a tour of Terence Rattigan's *Ross* with a West End management. They were persuaded to put in the equivalent of £35,000 in such production services (measuring the value of them was later to prove a nightmare) and also to premiere the productions for a two-week season at the beginning of November 1986. But if they were to guarantee our playing costs as well they naturally wanted as many paid performances over the two weeks as possible to set against their risk. We believed that if a rehearsal space could be found in Plymouth big enough for us to erect the set, light it and do all our technical work during the two weeks before opening, we could then move the shows straight into the theatre and open *Henry IV Part 1* on the first Monday, *Part 2* on the Wednesday, play *Henry V* twice on the Friday, do a first trilogy on the Saturday and then run the plays in sequence the second week. We would thus be giving the normal average of sixteen performances over two weeks. But Plymouth would only guarantee us for a nine-performance week, so for the first week of seven performances they offered us seven ninths of the figure we needed. It was a rather hard bargain; but on the other hand there was the £35,000 in the pot and a disused aircraft hangar at RAF Mountbatten just outside the city to rehearse in, and so we took the deal.

Sitting on my bed at home, I now rang the managers of some of the great touring theatres. Whatever my sphere of influence might be, I was fairly sure it wasn't strong among these gents, although Bogdanov's name would mean something – *Hiawatha* had been a recent National Theatre touring hit. I explained that we were now in business together, and were offering *The Henrys* for a ten-week tour the following autumn. Their replies furnished a subtle *chiaroscuro* of courtesy. Some were genuinely pleased. Some didn't know what I was talking about, but politely promised to pencil in a booking for us – in pencil so light I am sure it was written over pretty directly. Others registered the choice of plays sceptically, and wanted to know who was to be the Star. I gulped and confessed that apart from myself we hadn't started casting. Well then, would

I let them know when we had our Star booked. I felt a little subdued.

It was now Christmas, and our pregnancy wasn't showing. On the other hand, we had caused some surface agitation. As the year turned over Andrew Welch in Plymouth put in a quiet call to Fleur Selby at the Arts Council. He was worried about the whole project, its speculative, buccaneering air, and wanted to advise her as an old friend that the two of them should perhaps wash their hands of this company which didn't even have a name — after all, they had their reputations to think of. I don't altogether blame him. For in what remote sense were we a reality? We had not only no name, but certainly no Board, no office and no product: we were just a couple of blaggers trading on our reputations. A trio of heavyweight history lessons were being mooted; the 45% financial commitments we had in were all conditional on the other 55% being found elsewhere; and the Arts Council was keeping its counsel. Everyone was waiting to see who would get serious first. Meanwhile, the two of us were going about our individual businesses secure in the knowledge that what was worrying everyone else — was there a horse to back at all? — was the very thing that was keeping us free; our idea was worth fighting for each day, but if need be the whole thing could still be abandoned without shame. On the first day of the new year Michael had been rung by Terry Hands and offered a production of either *Romeo and Juliet* or *The Two Gentlemen of Verona* for Stratford, to be designed, cast and ready to rehearse in three weeks, if you please (it was an interesting approach to planning that had proved the final straw for Joyce Nettles, the RSC's casting director, and she had resigned). Michael chose *Romeo*, got it rolling and went to Montreal to discuss doing a production there; I set about re-rehearsing my solo show about Chekhov for an imminent engagement in Barcelona.

Then, with terrible suddenness, the blow fell. On 17th January 1986, I had a call from Jodi Myers to say that the Arts Council would put £100,000 into our first season. They did indeed want ten weeks of UK touring at approved venues in return, and some assurance that the overall budget was realistic and would be completely underwritten before we started; but basically they were in. They would show further confidence in us. The Council's normal practice with 'project' clients such as ourselves (as opposed to their fifty-two-week-a-year 'revenue' clients) was to hold the money back as an eventual guarantee against losses incurred on tour (up to a certain maximum) and pay it over at the end of the day. Since we self-evidently had no money to put the shows on in the first place, they were prepared to give us the whole sum up front, so that we wouldn't have to borrow against it. They had of course been waiting for us just as we thought we were waiting for them; and now, with £160,000 committed to us elsewhere, they felt able to jump.

There had in fact been a fair bit of poker-playing since we had first gone back to Jodi with *The Henrys*. Initially she had said that £100,000 wasn't impossible, but that £60,000 was more likely. Then, just as we were getting used to the idea of a trade-off, she was expressing doubts on 10th January (a week before the crucial decision) as to whether we had enough experience of touring, worrying also about our administrative structure, or rather the absence of it. (She didn't know that, sitting beside her, Fleur was waiting for our grant to come through so that she could give in her notice and accept a discreet invitation to become our Administrator.) On 16th January Jodi had dropped these objections but was declaring that £60,000 would be the absolute maximum. On the morning of the 17th, just before going in to her finance meeting, she was reminding us that, never mind the £60,000, the Council were in no way committed to us and unlikely to be so even after she came out; now she was calling with the good news very much as if she had snatched the chestnut out of the fires of opposition.

And perhaps indeed she had. We owe Jodi a lot; and of course the Arts Council's processes, like those of any bureaucracy, are easy meat for a satirist. When volatile market forces threaten to take over everything, one feels an illogical urge to kick a subsidising friend. Anyway we now had £260,000, and the moment was decisive. I rang Michael in Canada. We yelped at each other, and then relapsed into awed silence, facing the consequences of all that blagging. We were actually going to have to go through with it.

A week later Fleur Selby came over to our side of the desk. This enticement of the very Arts Council officer to whom we had first made application was a piece of poaching we were very proud of. Apart from the cheek, who better to book and supervise a tour by a brand new company than one who brought with her both credibility and an established relationship with the theatre managers. For her part Fleur, who had been an active member of Timothy West's team at the Old Vic before joining the Council in the hope of positively fostering new ideas, was 'tired of saying no to artists' and wanted to feel creative again. Paradoxically, her support of the ESC was one of the most positive initiatives of her time there, and we now offered her an escape.

So now we were three, albeit three on the hoof, without title or address. We rang up Michael Billington, theatre critic of the *Guardian*, and invited him out to breakfast at Brown's Hotel to leak our news. He welcomed the new company, but I could tell he wasn't happy. What was the trouble? He was fearful that the notorious Bogdanov might be tempted to do the plays in modern dress.

Bogdanov: *We reckoned that we needed a fourth person as an Executive Producer to handle long-term commitments, someone used to the hurly burly of international touring, scheduling, raising money. I had always held a deep admiration for Michael Hallifax, who had recently retired from the National, undefeated, as Programme Controller, Company Manager, Schedule Supervisor par excellence. It is significant that on Michael's departure it took four people to fill the gap that he left. He was extremely interested but had to go to America on a lecture tour until May. Could he think about it till then? Would it be too late? In the event it was too late, and we did not have enough money for an Executive Producer anyway, but Michael became a Board member, stood by us when others didn't, and eventually secured a contract with the Chicago World Theater Festival for us.*

Pennington: Michael and I now began to work out of the National Theatre, where he was still (just) an Associate Director with an office; Fleur, for the time being, from the Arts Council itself. We regarded the slightly enlarged phone bills of both organisations as a well-deserved supplement to our grant, while we struggled to find a base and musingly tried out names on each other.

The London Theatre Company? Upthrust? Downput? The Shakespeare Company?

David Mirvish now helped us towards an identity by suggesting that we use the top floor of the Old Vic Annexe Building, next to the theatre, as our first office; Peter Gill's National Theatre Studio group were occupying the first two floors, but the top was self-contained, and as well as two offices furnished us a roof where we imagined ourselves drinking cold white wine, looking ruminatively across the Cut at the historic theatre that was in a sense our new home, debating with some tremendous catch – actor, designer, writer – some lofty point of policy. However, Peter, though an old colleague of both of us, raised such furious objections to this arrangement – arguing that visitors would become confused as to which organisation they were visiting, and fearful for fire exits and night security – that the idea had to be dropped. David Mirvish fell back in the face of this vehemence and abstained, amazed at the inability of his talented English clients to get along with each other. In the end, my agent, James Sharkey, let us have the back office in his suite in Golden Square at a knockdown rent – the first of many small easements we came to depend on in those days. It was here, on Monday morning 28th April, that I first Went to the Office, arriving on the stroke of ten to sit at an empty desk, looking enviously across at Fleur at hers. She was moving easily about, stacking papers and swivelling in her chair, starting a card index with an air of great experience; I didn't know what to do. Was this an identity crisis coming on? I was an *actor*, albeit a fairly self-organising one; my *agent* was down the corridor; and I was about to telephone other actors to see if they would like to work for our *management*.

What management? Input? The Classic Theatre Company? The New Old Vic Theatre Company?

Within a few weeks Fleur was joined by an Assistant, Sue Evans, who has on occasion in subsequent years held our organisation together alone like a many-handed Shiva.

Bogdanov: *Sue had been working for commercial producers Bill Freedman and Howard Panter for many years and had decided it was time for a change. It was on the basis of our acquaintance during my production of the David Essex musical, Mutiny (one of the toughest shows of my life – it nearly cost me my liver in alcohol) that I persuaded her to join this as yet untested fledgling organisation. (In subsequent years, Melanie Hibberd and Jane Morgan, with Sue the then entire complement of Howard Panter's office, have also worked with us. In the early days, we were better poachers than gamekeepers.) We all now sat down to book a tour of The Henrys. I had had a certain amount of touring experience, first with the Phoenix Theatre Leicester, then the Young Vic, the National, and finally by virtue of an itinerant group of performers who call themselves the New Vic, who were in effect the rump of* *my earlier companies who had dedicated themselves to doing all my old shows.* Canterbury Tales *and* Dracula *would come up with embarrassing regularity. I talked hard and fast to all the managers I knew, indulging in a certain amount of ducking, bobbing and weaving. Among them was Dick Condon of Norwich, who had once asked me to run a theatre with him in Roscommon, Co. Mayo, in the West of Ireland. 'Where will the audience come from, Dick?' 'Ah, they're building an international airport at Knock, so we'll fly them in, in a Jumbo.' It's not surprising that Dick gives no financial guarantees in Norwich.*

Pennington: The outline of a tour soon fell into place as the managers were thus reminded of my harrowing pre-Christmas calls. We could open in Plymouth as planned on 3rd November, and then move on to Cardiff, Norwich, Nottingham and Bath for a week each before breaking up for Christmas. A second block of bookings could start on 2nd February in Hull, but the festive season itself was a headache. British theatres naturally tend to be blocked off from mid December to as late as the end of January with panto; in vain we looked around for a Scrooge who could take us. Under the terms of the nine-month Equity contract we planned to use, our company would at some point be entitled to three weeks' paid holiday, or payment in lieu of it at the end of the job; we could partly solve our problem by providing that holiday over Christmas, in the middle of the tour. But we still had most of January to fill. For any company, especially one as tightly-budgeted as ours, a week off in mid-tour is a disaster: the actors and staff still have to be paid, and there is no income at all to do it with. The only solution was to go abroad, to non-pantomimic Europe. We initiated a series of meetings with Robert Sykes, the then Director of Dance and Drama at the British Council, who greeted us at each one with exceptional contumely. Why should the Council be interested in offering an untried company to its cherished audiences abroad? What did we mean, *financial* support? How many more meetings do we have to have about this wretched project? When, in despair of his assistance, we started ringing local British Council representatives in France, Germany and Spain ourselves, Robert unexpectedly insisted on taking protective charge of bookings himself; and when the shows ultimately opened with some success, we suddenly became his pride and joy. But by then it was November; and it was by the skin of our teeth (much aided by the

recent success of Michael Bogdanov's production of *Julius Caesar*
at the Schauspielhaus in Hamburg) that we managed to put
together two weeks of whistle-stop for January: Berlin, Düsseldorf,
Ludwigshafen, Cologne, Hamburg and Paris. After that we could
see our way through via Hull to Sunderland, Leeds, Oxford,
Manchester and Birmingham into an Old Vic season in March and
Toronto beyond. It occurred to us that we were now giving the Arts
Council twelve weeks' touring instead of ten; with no further
money forthcoming, their rate was now averaging down from
£10,000 to £8,333 per week.

However, there was still a question of £90,000 to be found.
Fleur had come to us with a special interest in the then relatively
young business of commercial sponsorship.*

Pennington: By the end of April Fleur had been introduced by Tim
Stockill of the Association for Business Sponsorship of the Arts to
Christopher Legge, a representative of Addison Marketing, who
had been employed by the Allied Irish Bank to promote its interests
in England. Throughout the 1970s, the Bank had been busily
expanding its UK presence and was now wondering how to support
this activity with an appropriate public relations exercise. What
better than to link their name to a prestigious itinerant theatre
company that was visiting all the cities in which the profile was to
be raised? Fleur and I went to see Niall Gallagher, Group
Marketing Manager, and Declan Mullen, Marketing Services

**Bogdanov: An ephemeral business. The effort involved in chasing a few
pennies is out of all proportion. Small companies often spend more on
wheedling, wining and dining than they finally receive in funds. It is only
the lucky few who succeed in raising any substantial amounts. (Usually the
same few.) And these amounts very rarely amount to more than a point
percentage of the overall budget. And it goes as fast as it doesn't come. I
was responsible, in 1984, for devising an educational project at the
National Theatre, entitled* Orwell's England. *It came under our unofficial
banner of* Low Flying Aircraft. *The only way to get out of the National
without an army of attendants was to pile eight actors in a van, with no
set, props or costumes, and set off.* Orwell *was sponsored by IBM – up
to a point: for £10,000. When they saw the programme, IBM immediately
cancelled four special performances in front of their employees and took
their name off the programme. The reason? An excerpt from* The Road to
Wigan Pier *on unemployment written in 1935, sounded, they said, like a*
Guardian *leader in 1985. 'Nuff said.*

Manager, one day in Old Jewry. Michael was directing *Julius Caesar* in Hamburg by now, but in his absence we were able to expatiate at length on his Irish background: we made him sound like a cross between William Congreve and Brendan Behan, which may have been a decisive factor in disarming objections back in Dublin to the A.I.B. sponsoring such a very English enterprise.

I don't of course mean that it was a pushover, far from it. It never is. Business sponsorship of the arts, that supposed fatted calf of the '80s, is a parlous business, and relations between a theatre company and its sponsor, both initially and in practice, can be fraught, as Michael Bogdanov's experience with IBM shows. The two parties are coming to the table from such very different doors; the one seeking to advertise its business, the other simply to survive. The National Theatre's recent experience with Ladbroke's, when the first night of *Hamlet* was noisily interrupted by various over-watered guests of the sponsors addressing each other down the length of the Olivier stalls, perhaps marks a new low in the much vaunted system. And equivalently, the whole (to the sponsor) delicate process of entertaining potential clients after the show by 'meeting the cast' has on occasion, I fear, been ruined by over-watered actors making it clear that it's not their interests that are being served and they're only there for the beer. We count ourselves extremely lucky to have had with the A.I.B. a sensitive and generally untroubled partnership. During our three years together, Declan Mullen outdanced us at the company hoolies and gradually inched closer and closer to the stage; at first a welcome visitor backstage, by the second year he was to be seen in the wings, watching with a yearning air; and finally, at the Old Vic in 1989, we got him onstage one night in the back of the Boar's Head Tavern, complete with trilby and old coat, for his professional debut.

Now, they gave us £75,000 for our first year. It was the A.I.B.'s biggest sponsorship yet of any kind in Britain, and their first major arts sponsorship here. Their exemplary nerve also qualified us to collect £25,000 there and then under the terms of the Government's Business Sponsorship Incentive Scheme, a sort of congratulatory bonus for such first partnerships. Only when we turned up at the publicity lunch at the Bank to collect the cheque was the boat momentarily rocked; Fleur, Michael, Sue and myself were photographed holding the prize with smiles complicated by the fact that we had just looked down to see that the cheque read not

£75,000, but £65,000. Had we been talking about punts, not pounds?

This wrinkle unwrinkled after an exchange of aggrieved letters, we were now able to announce that our pot was full, and that we were in it, up to our necks. A certain devil-may-care jauntiness disappeared from our step; it has never really returned. We could even make contracts – or could have done if we'd had a name.

The National Shakespeare Company? Laurence Harbottle, our solicitor, didn't say come off it in so many words; but he did suggest that to be a National anything, we needed the Registrar of Companies' special agreement, which he feared in this instance might possibly not be granted. The English Shakespeare Company? Well, he said, for that we would need the Arts Minister's approval, which could hold things up for a month and still not be forthcoming, but he'd try. The Minister replied by return of post, cordially agreeing and wishing us luck.

So, we had an identity. We had also got, if not above, then certainly ahead of, ourselves. What, after all, were we really up to?

Unlike George Devine and his successors at the Royal Court, we weren't committed to developing relationships with original writers; nor were we opening a new building and hoping to characterise it. On the contrary, our repertoire, though ambitious, could hardly be more conventional: *The Henrys* have always held the stage as a trilogy, at Stratford under Tony Quayle in the 1950s, at Stratford in the '60s and '70s, on the screen in Orson Welles' *Chimes at Midnight*, which used material from all three plays. And far from establishing a base, we would be determinedly on the hoof: short-term tenants wherever we went, unified only by our adaptability and our style of work. Still today in many people's minds, the ESC has a fleeting, hit-and-run kind of air to it, largely because we tour all the time – and by then we hadn't even done that. So what was to be our originality?

The productions themselves of course, and perhaps the rather paradoxical partnership of the two of us behind them. The most crucial decisions would lie in our choice of company, the instrument of our innovation and, in the end, the joint creators of the ESC. All of this human tissue would have to be called in with infinite care. Most especially, the actors.

There has always been in England an abundance of classically equipped and inclined performers who for one reason or another aren't to be seen either at the RSC or the National. Perhaps they have done their time there, perhaps they have never been tempted, perhaps they have been overlooked. Many of them are at a highly experienced middle stage of their careers, but they may well have found comfortable ways to live from television and films and be disinclined to live out of a suitcase, even in return for the plummiest roles Shakespeare wrote. Much has been made, after all, of the RSC's recent difficulties in tempting enough weighty actors to reorganise their lives and move to Warwickshire for a year. If they were having difficulties, what would we encounter, trading only on the attraction of a new idea and our own track records as we made our offers? Not only for the leads, either. Most Shakespeare plays depend in the end on the Duke of Exeter as much as the King. Without authoritative casting in these many place-name roles, the machine breaks down, the star pirouettes pointlessly, and the world of the play is lost. On the other hand, many of the parts in themselves look unrewarding. The feel of our enterprise (and our salaries) would have to be attractive enough to tempt the middleweights we needed; and we would also need the right young actors from repertory, out of town and fringe, with a certain flair and fearlessness and an unaffected air: street credibility, in fact. The whole trick would be in the mix.

Certain ground rules came quickly. Our minimal acting company of twenty-five would have to be stretched taut; it would be necessary for the plays and good for us to be busy. Everybody must be prepared to be in every play, without exception: if a leading part wasn't available, a leading actor should walk on; and by the same token everyone must double, treble, turn themselves inside out, and move the furniture. Such a practical sense of company always communicates itself to an audience on the rare occasions it is offered. Less visibly, everyone must understudy everyone else; we couldn't carry 'walking' understudies who wouldn't normally appear, and yet we had to be crisis-proof. Thus actors in big parts should cover smaller ones, as long as going on in an emergency didn't involve them in the obvious absurdity of losing their main part for the night. For example, the Chorus in *Henry V* was in an unique position to cover almost any other role in the play; and, as Hal, I ended up understudying all five of the hapless villagers – Wart, Shadow, Mouldy, Feeble and Bullcalf – in Justice Shallow's recruiting scene in *Henry IV Part 2*, which happens to fall during the one hour of playing time when Prince Hal is in his dressing room. (Over the three years I went on for all but one of them – Shallow's orchard was full of windfalls.)

If an actor had a natural regional accent, a virtue should be made of it. Nothing is more deadly than to hear someone struggling for a received accent because it's Shakespeare and posh: nothing could be less like Shakespeare's theatre or our intentions; and since the plays echo and re-echo with the sounds of Bangor, Northumberland and Southwark, those actors should if possible come from there. Or close by.

Bogdanov: *One of the great joys of the canon is to discover and re-discover the cross-section of British character that lies at the heart of the plays. To trace the paths of fat men, thin men, comics, Welsh, Irish, growing up, growing old, from the* Henry VIs *to* The Tempest. *At a time when Court English was spoken by only a few, and spelling had not been standardised, it is inconceivable that Shakespeare's company was not made up of a rich tapestry of voices sounding from the far corners of the green and pleasant land.*

Pennington: At the same time we shouldn't be doctrinal. One day in the street I met John Price, an old friend and a veteran of Shared Experience, the RSC and just about everywhere else. He suggested himself for Hotspur; he was really from Worcester but knew the Northumbrian country sound well. We jumped at this idea but hesitated for many weeks over Pistol, which he also wanted to do. In the end he was fine as Hotspur but quite marvellous as Pistol. (So we nearly got that one wrong.) A completely unexpected wildness came out of John under Michael's direction; indeed throughout the company new energies were to burst out of actors who were having their base notes cheerfully acknowledged for the first time. John Dougall, who did Hamlet as an audition and whose career might seem to be firmly in the pattern of the classical hero – he did end up playing Clarence and Prince Hal – has a superb streak of vaudeville comedy in him which had never been called on before; his Wart in *Henry IV Part 2* was one of the funniest things in the entire cycle. Sometimes the latent talents were musical. Charlie Dale and Martin Clunes are covert guitarists; Ben Bazell is a multi-instrumentalist of considerable skill; Michael Cronin and Andrew Jarvis are woodwind players; and I count it the proudest of the ESC's boasts that we found in Colin Farrell a definitive Bardolph who also plays the jazz trombone.

In the midst of all this I went to the Barbican to see a Shakespeare – the last, in fact, I was to go to at that address to this day. I thought the show, which was full of old friends, represented, in a well-dressed way, an all-time low. The elaborate set was lit, but not the actors' faces. The lovers, both fine performers, were temperamentally mismatched, and to suit the rationalist tone of the production, their most passionate verse, including much of their parting, had been cut, sexual passion in general being conveyed by a coltish running up and down stairs and the throwing of cushions. Actors loaded with metaphor despaired of their lines and did elaborate gestures of illustration. The show came from Stratford with the highest credentials, and the house was full.

If this company of ours gets going, I thought as the evening stretched on, it will be the best bloody verse-speaking outfit in the country. Playing Shakespeare is one of the most sexually engaging activities there is outside of sexual activity. The seat of speech is also the seat of desire, which includes the desire to share meaning. Our style of playing will be accurate and fastidious, in detail and stress, but it will come from urgent need. There will be no huffing and puffing. We will light the actors as da Vinci recommended and Gordon Craig echoed: from above and the side as you see them in life, lit by the sun. The set will make the imaginary forces work, and not show off.

It was good to feel so annoyed; it made for renewed determination and metabolised some fears. There had been plenty of them that summer, and in their wash certain temptations. Peter Brook had been enquiring off and on if I would like to go round the world with the English version of his magnificent *Mahabharata*, skilfully pointing out that next to such a life-changing experience, Shakespeare's *Henry IV*, even with my own company, was a fairly conservative proposition; I felt like a nun refusing him. I had had a new exchange with the RSC who were asking if I would lead out their annual small-scale tour. What were the plays, I asked. Oh, whatever you like, came the reply: *Coriolanus*? *Hamlet*? I was flattered, but taken aback. Oh, and you will have to be responsible for the company after the play has opened because the director in question has to rush straight back to Stratford to do another show. Well, I asked, why in that case does he want to do the small-scale tour at all? Well, all the other directors have done it by now, and it's his turn. Set against the noble precedents of RSC studio touring defined in 1977 by Trevor Nunn and Ian McKellen, such *laissez-faire* was disconcerting; and following hard on my evening at the Barbican it caused me to feel idealism and bloodymindedness rising in equal proportions.

Michael was already working hard with Chris Dyer on the set, and with Stephanie Howard on the costumes; and we also had, by the end of June, seven actors, including, to our delight, John Woodvine for Falstaff, one of the most difficult parts in the canon to cast. There are perhaps four Falstaffs in England, and three of them don't want to tour. The part calls not so much for the obvious physical characteristics but for a huge vitality, humanity and skill. Within John's slim frame is a fat man bursting to come out and every quality of a Falstaff; as many people now know, he gave the performance of a lifetime. We also had Patrick O'Connell for the King: too often a sententious bore, the part probably has to be played with Paddy's Celtic intemperance; and June Watson, one of England's unacknowledged great actresses, would be Mistress Quickly. By the end of July we had twelve members, including a number introduced to us by Joyce Nettles, who was helping us (since she'd left the RSC, it wasn't poaching this time). Among them were some who, starting lightly, ended up doing big parts – for example John Dougall, Paul Brennen, and Andrew Jarvis. At this point I gave myself a week's holiday and went to Provence. Within forty-eight hours I was back, having been called to the States to play Sherlock Holmes in a CBS Movie of the Week, which would fit in neatly between now and the day of our first rehearsal in September. Technically speaking, the film was the pilot for a series, which meant that had CBS taken up their contractual options I would immediately have had to move to Los Angeles for six months of each of the next five years, making series after series of the things. On the other hand, only one pilot out of thirty goes to a series. I liked the conjunction: to be setting up my own subsidised Shakespeare company with the one hand and shaking hands with what at a pinch could be called the movies with the other. I went off to Arizona and flogged around the desert at Needles Point in a hundred and twenty degrees under an open sky in Holmes' deerstalker, tweed suit and brogues; breaking off occasionally to make long distance calls to London to see if we had got our Earl of Northumberland yet. The fact that for the first year of the ESC's life I was technically under contract to CBS, at their mercy if they exercised their rights, is a tantalising point that at this time need trouble neither their lawyers nor ours; I regarded this commando raid on the commercial world as a just reward for months of celibacy, in which I'd remained faithful to something that didn't yet exist.

By the time I returned we were ready, by a hair's breadth, the goalposts significantly pitched. The acting company were contracted on nine different levels of salary, from £480 a week down to £190, with one at £150. On top of this basic wage, in every week in which we played nine performances (invariably, because of our Saturday trilogy), each of us would earn an additional one eighth of weekly pay, as per Equity stipulations; similarly, everyone would receive a nominal £10.35 per week for understudying and being ready to go on, and if called on would get a performance fee (for a major part) of £13.89. As a company operating under the Provincial Touring Contract we were obliged to pay the minimum of £47.50 a week for subsistence, out of which individual accommodation had to be found; we had decided at the outset that this was paltry, and had decided to pay £100 a week. It still doesn't go far, not even as far as a two star hotel; but if you were prepared to rough it a bit or had well-distributed friends, you could probably save something. Indeed one of the pleasant discoveries was to find that even in these days, £5 – £10 a night can buy a comfortable bed and a big breakfast (at a sympathetic hour of the morning) from the hardy surviving breed of theatre landladies who still offer the best welcome, even if they are not as ripe for anecdote as once they were. So between Equity and our own inclinations, we felt we had come up with a good deal.

That was the company. As for the Company: it seemed (what naïveté) that the knots had been shaken free and we had a straight piece of rope. There was £360,000 to put the shows on. Theoretically this ran out at the moment the curtain went up on the first night. We were then, with nil in the bank, thrown onto our ability to earn income week by week to pay our salaries and bills. When we went abroad, we were safe: our host promoters would cover our fixed costs and so we would, exactly, break even. When we were at the Old Vic, the Mirvishes would do likewise, rounding the figure up a little to give us a friendly, symbolic management profit; and for Canada they were hoping to be decidedly generous. Turning to the UK dates – the reason we were in business – we saw it was not so comfy. Of them, Plymouth, Cardiff, Nottingham, Hull, Sunderland, Leeds and Birmingham would pay us a guaranteed figure of £26,500 to cover what we estimated as our running costs; Bath would guarantee us only £18,000, arguing that their lower potential take (£50,000) tied their hands; and Norwich, Oxford and Manchester wouldn't risk a guarantee at all, offering us instead several varieties of percentage deal: 70% to us, 30% to the theatre being the usual combination. In the case of Manchester this risk was a good one for us, since the Palace Theatre has a high potential yield and a regular audience, and we stood to do better than if we had gone in on a fixed guarantee; but the other dates loomed like migraines: Norwich in particular was uncomfortably early in the tour, before any favourable word of mouth would have had time to spread. Such were the weeks when we could be facing the oldest and most shaming crux of all: how to pay our bills on the Friday. So a windy abyss yawned beneath this ledge of satisfaction.

That was the scenario, and it is a bookmark for all that follows. We were to be alternately held upright and haunted by these precedents for the next three years; the actors would be vexed by a hundred hidden anomalies; and the ESC would veer like a sloop on the high seas between crisis and confidence, from looming deficit towards, finally, a small self-justifying solvency. Now, working late into the night through the weekend before starting rehearsals, cutting scripts, fiddling with lists, checking contracts and imagining Monday morning, we felt astonished, invigorated and dead tired all at once. The whole thing had taken nine months of part-time work, in which I had also made a film and Michael directed two major productions, and a big new door stood open. The only thing we hadn't thought about quite enough was the plays.

CHAPTER

2

THE HENRYS

January – November 1986

> *'Then this guy is going to offer to bet you
> that he can make the Jack of Spades jump
> out of this brand new deck of cards and
> squirt cider in your ear. But, son, you do
> not accept this bet, because as sure as you
> stand there, you're going to end up with
> an ear full of cider.'*
>
> Guys and Dolls

Bogdanov: I was burning with anger at the iniquity of the British electoral system. Eleven million people had voted for Thatcher, fourteen million against. Scotland, Wales and the North were almost totally Labour and only in the fat, green, get-rich-quick Yuppie haven of the South did the Conservative Party hold sway. Moreover, Boadicea had rallied her troops around her with a senseless war of expediency, sailing heroically (in some people's eyes) twelve thousand miles to the Falklands to do battle for 'a little patch of ground that hath in it no profit but the name / To pay five ducats, five, I would not farm it.'

The parallels were plain. *The Henrys* were plays for today, the lessons of history unlearnt. The Grand Mechanism of the Polish critic, Jan Kott, in full sway, the escalator shuttling mice and men up to the top, where the golden crock of Imperialism shone brightly, waiting for the next attempt to snatch it from its podium. We were in the era of New Brutalism where a supposed return to Victorian values under the guise of initiative and incentive masked the true goal of greed, avarice, exploitation and self. Westminster Rule. Centralisation. Censorship. Power to the City. Bleed the rest of the country dry. Bolingbroke/Boadicea/Britannia was in the saddle. The 'rotten parchment bonds' of the fourteenth century were being drawn up again as Britain went into hock, selling herself to any and all who had the money to buy a stake in her and fill the coffers of the fortunate few.

> This land . . .
> Is now leased out . . .
> Like to a tenement or pelting farm:
> That England, that was wont to conquer others,
> Hath made a shameful conquest of itself.
>
> *(Richard II*, II.1)

Carta Mandua, Queen of the Brigantes, did a deal with the Romans while they were sorting out the Welsh. Sold her country for three hundred and fifty years for a few pieces of plate. (Shell?) Maybe the desire to plunder this few hundred square miles of rock and fields runs deep in the psyche of all those who hold power in their hands. (Then again, Marcos, Ceausescu, Noriega, all testify that the latter half of the twentieth century is not going to go down as the greatest example of universal love.) What price humanity, compassion, equality and freedom? Doors were slammed firmly shut on the sixties. The media were belaboured with a censorship stick.

A conspiracy of silence and complicity surrounded shuffles, resignations, rise and fall, crash and takeover – the desperate feeling of manipulation and manoeuvre in the air. One's life controlled by secret forces and the watching eye. Boardrooms may have replaced the Palace at Westminster, Chairpersons (mainly men) replaced monarchs, but the rules were the same. All of which added a spur to the *Henrys* project – provided the passion for portrayal. How could the plays *not* be understood in a contemporary context? The Irish problem still with us; the Scots clamouring for devolution and the desire to assert their own distinctive culture; the Welsh beleaguered in their welcoming hillsides, fighting a rearguard action to save their language, a million people speaking Welsh; the North laid waste by speculative bulldozers and lack of investment; urban decay hastened by the plethora of concrete car parks and high-rise, high-rent office blocks. Nothing had changed in six hundred years, save the means.

There is a story that my French Professor at Trinity College, Dublin, Owen O'Sheehy Skeffington, used to tell, that was told to him by Samuel Beckett (under whom he was a student), who had it from the horse's mouth, so to speak. It was of the French poet Rimbaud discovering that the eyeball could be pulled out of its socket and extended on its stalk and waggled about to get a crazy view of the world. Chris Dyer, the designer, is a bit like that. Whatever we discuss, whatever decisions we come to, things always come out sideways. It is what makes him, at times, a great designer – a completely unique way of looking at things through a surrealist, fish-eye lens. Sometimes the result surprises both of us. We will stand and look at a set or a prop when it gets on stage. Silence for a long time and then – 'Yup': or just as frequently – 'Nope!'

Chris and I met in spring 1986 to discuss *The Henrys*. Chris had designed the two previous productions Michael and I had worked on, *Shadow of a Gunman* and *Strider* and we had, already, a history of successful Shakespeare collaborations behind us. Our partnership began in 1978 with *The Taming of the Shrew* at Stratford-upon-Avon, with Jonathan Pryce in the role of Petruchio. In 1983 we were in Tokyo together to do *Romeo and Juliet* at the Imperial Theatre, a version of which we were repeating three years later at the RSC*.

We have three modes of working – probably shared by most director/designer teams. I know and tell him, he knows and tells

---

*We should have rested on our laurels. The Tokyo version – sixty actors and a stage thirty metres wide by thirty deep – was sensational. Inorganic, scaled down, at Stratford, it lost its motivation, its clarity. I was not to make the same mistake with two further productions with Chris – *Measure for Measure* at Stratford, Ontario, where I think I solved the fiendishly difficult last act, and one yet to come, *Julius Caesar* in Hamburg, June '86, which coincidentally we were also working on at that time. With *Romeo and Juliet*, *Julius Caesar* and *The Henrys* we had our hands full.

me, neither of us knows and we work it out together. With *The Henrys*, we had to establish the common ground. Start with the politics, identify the social structure, the protagonists, the status quo. I had already made a crucial decision – crucial that is, in terms of my own history. From the moment when an *Ur-production* of *Romeo and Juliet*, set in Renaissance Verona, went down the tubes in Leicester in 1976, my work with Shakespeare had been exclusively modern dress. Each production was successively an attempt to relate and clarify the language and open the plays out for new, young audiences. It was the working out of years of bafflement and frustration as I wrestled desperately with my own incomprehension when presented with obscure, effete, literary productions hailed by the critics as 'masterly re-evaluations'.

However, it was clear to me that total modern dress for *The Henrys* was out. Obvious to anyone, you might say. 'Not so my Lord.' There was no way round the fifth act in *Henry IV Part 1* – the battle scenes and the fight between Hal and Hotspur. Arm wrestling would not do, knives were too mini, a chess match inactive, omitting it out of the question. There had to be a final, proper confrontation. After ten years of working exclusively in modern dress, I was about to break the stranglehold it had on me. The last time I faced the problem was in a previous *Richard III* at the Young Vic in 1979. I cut the fight between Richard and Richmond, substituting a metaphor of Richmond (the butcher) splitting open a real pig's head with an axe (representing Richard the Boar). Rather good, I thought. I couldn't quite bring myself to cut the most famous line in the play (the one about the horse) which was relayed inaudibly from off stage. Milton Shulman, in one of his wittier moments, wrote, 'in this production, the least said about Richard's mode of transport, the better.'

In 1986 the challenge took another form. Elizabethan? Medieval? An option. I was put off, however, by the memory of Trevor Nunn's attempt for the opening of the Barbican (the first night impression dominated by the sight of Gerard Murphy as Hal, his armour reversed on his arms, elbows on the inside, flailing like a demented windmill). Here, it seemed, the story and the politics had both been submerged in an effort to bring medieval pageantry and protocol to the stage. The plays seemed hollow.

The Henrys cut a huge swathe across the path of English life at the beginning of the fifteenth century. Yet, of course, the plays are also Elizabethan. Shakespeare analysed the political and social quicksands of his own time, reflecting what he saw as iniquitous and scurrilous in the make up of contemporary *moeurs* and *mores* in the mirror of centuries earlier. Or in the mythical lands of Illyria. Or shifting the ground to Athens, Rome, Verona ... (He was a wily old bird. There was too much at stake to get himself locked up like some of his contemporaries.) In a perceptive book, *Political Shakespeare*, edited by Jonathan Dollimore and Alan Sinfield, the contributors analyse the underlying radical political subversion contained in Shakespeare's work, a subversion that it is important to hold in mind, for example in attempting to scrape off the cloying mud of Olivier's propaganda *Henry V*, a film that involved the cutting of some one thousand five hundred lines in order to make the jingoistic cap fit.

For some reason I had stick and cloth in my head. I was seeing some combination of tunic, greensward and canvas. Tents, drapes, poles, carpets, curtains. It was a throw-back to an early production of *Sir Gawain and the Green Knight* in Newcastle, 1971. Chris drew some sketches; the images were working. The combination of the medieval and the imagination. (The sketches for The Boar's Head Tavern, Glendower's Castle, the Rebel Camp, actually formed the basis for the final production, the Boar's Head looking uncannily like the drawing, even though the stick and cloth idea was soon abandoned.) We modelled up a green thrust stage. We hated it. Although we had a solution, our instincts told us that the plays might look pretty but we would be fudging the heart of them. We discussed again their potency for today's audiences, the central dilemma of wanting to strip away meaningless design clichés from the productions, yet retain that medieval fight between Hal and Hotspur. The obvious was staring us in the face, but we had, or I had, avoided facing up to it.

There is a school of thought that believes Shakespeare should be performed in traditional dress and as Shakespeare 'intended'. Oh yes? What *did* Shakespeare intend? Who knows? Nobody and everybody. It is sometimes hard enough with a living author sitting by your side to know what she/he intends. Many a discussion, argument, alteration to a new play is the result of the spoken word often conveying a different meaning to the intention of the written word. I once heard Harold Pinter shouted down at a university drama festival in Bristol because the students did not believe that Pinter understood his own play. It could be. Writing is a mysterious

force. The interpretation of combinations of words is an industry
in itself. And, of course, finally the responsibility is taken out of the
writers' and directors' hands. Actors can change the meaning of a
line, a scene, a play, merely with an inflection. The old drama
school exercise of a number of ways to say 'To be or not to be'.
Interpretation. 'What Shakespeare really meant was . . .' Who
knows? Thank goodness interpretation is subjective. In the final
analysis, that combination of words speaks to one person, in one
way only. Each individual member of an audience hears the same
words but interprets them in a completely unique fashion. One only
has to read widely differing accounts of an actor's performance on
the same evening to know that this is a truism. With Shakespeare,
due to the volume of received opinion, we are prejudiced before we
begin. Nevertheless, there are, in any story, a set of objective
circumstances, linked to time and place, that are constant no
matter when that story is told. Characters exist in a social and
political environment. What gives them their interest is *how* and
why they relate to each other, given this set of objective
circumstances.

The traditional-dress school of thought does not take into
consideration that Shakespeare himself often performed the plays
in modern dress. Thomas Platter noted in 1599: 'It is the English
usage for eminent Lords or Knights at their decease to bequeath
and leave almost the best of their clothes to their serving men,
which it is unseemly for the latter to wear, so that they offer them
then for sale for a small sum to the actors.' A handful of props, a
cloak, a crown. When a specific costume is called for, it is usually
mentioned in a list of special requirements. That *Julius Caesar* was
played completely in togas or *A Midsummer Night's Dream* in
short skirts is inconceivable. Soldiers' uniforms were worn with
little concern for historical accuracy, if Henry Peacham's drawing
of a scene from *Titus Andronicus*, made in about 1595, is any
indication. In the drawing the leading character is in some form of
Roman dress approximating a toga, while the men flanking him are
clearly dressed as Elizabethan soldiers, doublet, hose, pikes and all.
'Traditional dress' is already a nonsense, because in so saying, we
certainly do not mean uniformly Elizabethan costume for these
plays. Similarly, the Histories would have involved, two hundred
years after the event, armour, heraldic surplices, etc., but certainly
not authentic medieval ware.

It was this eclectic theatre of expediency as practised by the

Elizabethans that provided the first clue as to how to set, first, *The Henrys* and then continue the style with *The Wars of the Roses*. We would provide a space that would allow the plays to range over the centuries in imagery. We would free our, and the audiences', imaginations by allowing an eclectic mix of costumes and props, choosing a time and a place that was most appropriate for a character or a scene. Modern dress at one moment, medieval, Victorian or Elizabethan the next. We would use a kit of props – chairs, tables, a trolley (we thumbed endless catalogues), a ladder, ammunition boxes, kit bags, a collection of large canvas cloths, suitcases, etc., and we would use them in all combinations possible. The kit, as far as was practicable, would remain on stage. The means of transformation from one scene to the next would remain visible. No tricks up our sleeves (until we needed one). We would create a style that was essentially rough theatre, but would add, when we needed it, a degree of sophistication. It was stick and cloth brought up to date. A stick is a stick, is a stick, until it is a flute, a paddle, a pneumatic drill, a bow and arrow. A trolley is a trolley, is a trolley, until it is a cart, a landrover, a carriage. (How many ways can you use a British Rail trolley? . . . Answers please on a post card to . . .) In all this, I should add that there was a degree of expediency – the whole budget for props and furniture was only £10,000. This figure loomed large (or small) in all our discussions.

The setting, we decided, should also reflect the raw approach. We would create a steel structure that would provide a theatre within a theatre, the audience able to see the mechanics of flying, the lighting bridge, the iron-clad framework of the walls of a stage. We developed the idea. The bridge should be able to go up and down and operate at several levels. Two sections of the framework should be moveable towers to provide upper levels. In those days we dreamed of fights and chases up and down the towers. We would hang curtains on the struts, and provide a colourful framework for the Boar's Head. It was silver, this structure, and the floor was white. We didn't like it. They went black. (I was for keeping the moveable towers silver, but they looked silly.) The space looked dead. We added a white border to the floor and a back projection screen with a door to the back. The space came alive. The slatted motif of the back projection framework had the feel of a Tudor rose, but the door was inadequate. The screen needed a large, sliding, centre entrance. We added pulleys and ropes to haul canvases up and down. We thought then that the

productions could be self-contained, with our own lighting, sound
and flying systems, and could therefore play in unconventional
spaces. The touring of what was now a monumental load of old
iron (lightweight steel, actually) was to give us endless headaches.

Henry IV Parts 1 and *2* were looking good, but there was
something not working for us in *Henry V*. The eclecticism made us
uneasy. Our ingrained modernity was asserting itself. *Henry V*,
with its war of expediency, ruthless manipulation, bribery and
corruption, palpable pacifism, the French superior in numbers but
beaten by superior technology, felt modern. It should be modern.
How to break it to Michael P. Michael was wary of what Chris and
I were up to. (He had a right to be.) The stick and cloth approach
had appealed to him. This new eclectic rough form he was not so
sure about, and a further development into modern dress – well,
that might confirm his worst fears, that he was in bed with a
dilettante Shakespearian flirt, who did not take the plays seriously
at all, and used contemporary dress as a slick cover-up. We did not
know each other that well in those days, despite the partnership we
had formed. Chris and I took Michael round the corner from the
office to a sandwich bar where we delicately outlined the idea of
Henry V in modern dress, putting forward all the arguments.
Michael listened noncommitally, prepared to try the idea out. The
first testing ground between the purist and the iconoclast. Horns
not exactly locked, but definitely inclining somewhat warily
towards each other. As he warmed to the style in rehearsal, it was
Michael who favoured Hal in torn jeans and an old denim jacket.
The extraordinary thing is that an eclectic style in form-obsessed
English theatre is (or was then) a novelty. In the rest of Europe,
eclecticism is the norm, rather than purity of concept. Content is
more important. Argument released by a series of conflicting
images, idea joggers, memory aids, etc.

In April, I invited Stephanie Howard to design the costumes.
Stephanie and I had first met at Stratford when I was an Assistant
Director in 1970. We worked together on a dummy project of
Romeo and Juliet to be presented to Trevor Nunn. He didn't like
it. (One of the ideas, Romeo caught up in a nightmare carnival in
Mantua, has survived to be in my three subsequent productions.)
I went to Newcastle as an Associate Director in 1971 and asked
Stephanie to join as a designer. For two years we did some
extraordinarily exciting work together and over the years have
renewed our acquaintance at Leicester and at the National.

Stephanie is a purist, bringing a highly intelligent and sophisticated line to costume design, combined with a subtlety of colour and material. She is also meticulous, a stickler for detail, and sometimes has to be saved from herself when overdesigning. How would she react to an idea that, at best, sounded like the cobbling together of a heap of old cast-offs, culled from the jumble sales of South East London? Bemused? Intrigued? Sceptical? The lot.

The challenge, though, was in making sense of a hundred characters through the ages, turning the idea into an homogeneous whole, bringing groups of disparate characters together in a style that made sense. Stephanie quickly identified the pure design areas – the women, the Court – and decided that areas like the Boar's Head, the street, etc., were bag and rag. It is Stephanie who can claim credit for the punk Mohican hairstyle of Gadshill in *Henry IV*, an image that became something of a symbol for the ESC style. Unfairly, as it happens, because although the final blend was the result of a scramble to find from the National Theatre store anything that could possibly be used, the essential concept was carefully thought through, and costumes selected for period and feel according to the character and scene. Some actors decided that such an approach was a free-for-all and later made attempts completely to rethink what costumes they were wearing, with horrendous consequences. The true nature of a series of eclectic costumes, because the basic concept is *theatrical*, lies in the careful blending and selecting. Just throwing on a pair of wellingtons, a tunic, a football scarf and a horned helmet won't do.

We needed a splash of colour. The Court would have a set of red and blue uniforms, a Royal tunic that vaguely stretches back to the beginning of the nineteenth century, and that, to this day, is worn for ceremonial occasions. Frock coats would complete the political Westminster look, an image that is not so long gone (and in one or two peers is still around). There would be some cloaks for the Coronation Scene. In *Henry V*, the English army would wear modern battle fatigues, the French powder-blue nineteenth-century uniforms, echoing the futile French cavalry charges of the First World War, their battalions mown down by automatic weapons. *Henry V*, left till last (modern dress being, mythically, the easiest to design) suffered in the suit area. As we had run out of money, the smart sartorial image turned into second-hand, ill-fitting appendages, not improved by alterations. *Richard III*, a year later, suffered a similar fate, the suits and overcoats from *Henry V* being recycled and handed down to yet a new group of courtiers. Rebels would be guerrillas in berets, jeans, combat jackets, fatigues. Street and tavern would be modern, Elizabethan (drawers), some fifties, some thirties. Pistol – a Rocker, that John Price clove to and developed into an astounding *braggadocio* performance of comic cowardliness. Stephanie also provided (from the first day of rehearsal) an old greatcoat and a balaclava for Colin Farrell – Bardolph – to rehearse in. A costume he was to wear throughout *The Henrys* for three years.

The simplicity of the final result masked hundreds of hours of agonising and arguing – the frustrations of not being able to provide the quantity and quality of the numbers of outfits required. The entire costume budget was £25,000. (This was eventually stretched, in the final hectic days in the Plymouth hangar, to £35,000 as the figures went wild.)

The accounting was scraps of paper, St Michael our saviour. There was much bitterness, acrimony and many a tear *en route* to scrambling *The Henrys* into production, not least because Plymouth Theatre Royal had underestimated the amount of work that would be needed to launch the shows. (In the final two weeks of our rehearsals, they had embarked full-time on preparing their pantomime – *Snow White* – and all that sailed in her.) Shoes, boots and belts were shared and shuffled from one dressing room to another in the course of an evening, and one memorable overcoat passed through seven pairs of hands, seven name tags on the collar. In the hectic early days, before a routine had been properly established, there was a tendency to grab the first coat that came to hand as you dived in and out of your eighth costume change. Some wonderful combinations (sic) did not help the seriousness of certain scenes. (Roger Booth as Sir Walter Blunt in scarlet tunic and longjohns.) The sheer amount of name-tag sewing demanded an army in itself. The venture was new, high risk and our budgets finite. If the money ran out, it ran out. There was no secret pool of funds to call on; if there was a deficit at the end of our first year, we would either have to carry on until it was paid off, or Michael and I would have to foot the bill somehow, personally.

Old friends and tried-and-tested working relationships were necessary. For the lighting, Chris Ellis, with whom I had worked continuously since Leicester in 1973, and whom I had introduced to the RSC and the National. Lynne Kirwin and Mary Parker to do the publicity. Lynne and Mary are products of that wonderful John Goodwin stable from the National Theatre, indeed old friends, and now running one of the best publicity outfits in the country. Malcolm Ranson for the fights, unchallenged as Britain's leading fight director, known and worked with since the *Romeo and Juliet* days in Leicester in 1974. In the *Romeo and Juliet* in 1986 at the RSC, I had worked with a wonderful stage manager, Stella Bond, who was looking to leave the RSC and move into directing. Stella joined as Assistant Director. I had no stage manager. Stella reminded me of Titus Grant, with whom I had worked on *The Taming of the Shrew* and Michael P., on *Love's Labour's Lost*. I remembered him as a rotund, merry fellow (Tweedledum to my Tweedledee). He was currently concentrating on writing, but wanted to return to the theatre. I dug him up from the depths of Devon and we did a deal. Dominic Peissel, so efficient on *Mutiny*, steering the famous boat away from many a fatal disaster, came as Technical Assistant Stage Manager (ASM), operating the sound. Another *Mutiny* mate, Andy Chelton, who had led the best four-man stage crew I had ever worked with, was to join as Master Carpenter. Stella introduced Nicky Waters as Deputy Stage Manager (DSM) and Loretta Bircham as ASM.

And we had our Falstaff. In 1984 John Woodvine had been involved in my production of *The Knight of the Burning Pestle* for the RSC at the Aldwych (for some 'one of the most hilarious and funniest nights out ever,' 'this play has waited four hundred years for this director', and for others 'a mishmash of juvenile undergraduate rubbish'). John had played Merryweather, a rotund, very mellow fellow, laughing, singing, drinking, in the face of every setback. A wonderful performance. I was convinced that he could give a Falstaff to remember. He had played the part once in *The Merry Wives of Windsor*, so the territory was not unfamiliar. Unconventional casting, but John is an actor's actor, commanding enormous respect throughout the land.

While Michael was away in Arizona, I enthused to him over the phone about Jenny Quayle. Jenny is the daughter of Sir Anthony, in a sense our rival, courageously running Compass Theatre Company, another touring ensemble whose furrow we were about to plough. Michael took my word for her. Paddy O'Connell would come if he could learn the parts now: 'problems with the words, dear fellow'. I rang Gareth Thomas, a fellow Welshman. He would do anything to give his Fluellen. His Fluellen turned out to be incomprehensible North Walian, delivered with machine-gun rapidity. Very, very funny when you could understand it. He was so fast that subsequent versions of *Henry V* without him ran fifteen minutes longer. We contacted Clyde Pollitt, another Welshman, well known to us both: who was, sadly, to die in the autumn of 1989, having gone with us all the way.

Clyde was a lovely, lovely man. His humanity and humility shone through him. A loner, an eccentric. At the interview he stood on the stage at the Old Vic and said, 'No, you see it's the poetry. Shallow is a lovely part but it's the poetry I want. Can I play Morton?' *Instead of Shallow?!!* We offered him the French King in *Henry V*. It was enough, and his Shallow was one of the great joys of our three years together – a forked radish to a gentlemanly tee, where the timing remained as fresh and precise as at the first wonderful run through. The rigours of touring did not suit his frail constitution, but the nomad in him hankered after it. For Clyde, the golden age of the theatrical landlady was ever present. A Merthyr mole, he could scent a burrow at fifty paces – none better to nose out the toast and slippers and the grandfather chair. He lived somewhere (we thought) but finding Clyde was like following a treasure trail of clues from B & B to hotel, to friend, to floor.

He carried his life in a suitcase as if afraid to be caught settling down and yet always gave the impression of having been wrapped up cosy and warm and sent out Welsh and wise to do good in the world. But get him to eat properly? He lived on take-aways and beans and taught himself Russian. Unless to give himself a rare treat. 'I like a good Indian, it cleanses the soul.' And generous to a fault. 'Michael, I was passing a shop and I thought you might like this.' A bottle of Wolfe Blass Cabernet – a reminder of our Australian raid where we drank the wine like fools. He belonged to an era where knowledge was prized, a time of language and books and old style Socialism. His Merthyr Tydfil roots were always present and on a rare occasion he would suddenly unveil his private past, cradling a whiskey in both bony hands and holding a captive audience spellbound and helpless with mirth at his soft, eccentric, story-telling way with language that was like a Celtic corkscrew. To have heard the Clyde at midnight was to have had one of life's most heart-warming experiences.

And then there were last-minute difficulties with John Price. I stood in the garden of Downs Cottage Guest House on the island of St Agnes, Isles of Scilly, the phone cord stretched through the

Henry IV Part 1: (above)
Jennie Stoller (Lady Percy),
John Price (Hotspur) (LB);
(left) Andrew Jarvis (Gadshill),
Clyde Pollitt (Chamberlain) (LB)

Henry IV Part 2: (above) John Woodvine (Falstaff),
June Watson (Mistress Quickly) (LB);
(below) The Coronation of Henry V (LB)

Henry V: (above) John Woodvine (Chorus) (LB); (centre) Michael Pennington (Henry V) (LB); (left) Patrick O'Connell (Gower), Gareth Thomas (Fluellen) (LB)

Henry V: (left)
Jenny Quayle
(The Princess of France) (LB);
(below)
The English leave for France –
''Ere we go, 'ere we go, 'ere we go.'
John Dougall (Nym),
John Price (Pistol),
John Tramper (The Boy) (LB)

window, and argued for three quarters of an hour with John about the principle of understudying, while the families inside pretended not to hear, sedately eating their way through Mollie's roast lamb with six veg. John's determination was an essential ingredient of his talent. He decided finally to join us, and I ate my roast lamb in a sandwich. Morris Perry had written me the kind of letter I can never refuse. 'At my age it is time to take a few risks [he was 60] ... and in passing I also speak Russian.' He was just the kind of actor we needed for parts such as Exeter. His intelligence was initially invaluable, but he was at heart a 'them and us' man, and we parted on bad terms. A pity.

A Board of Management was needed.

I am sorry to say that the initial composition was all my doing. My experience with Boards in Leicester and at the Young Vic (the former a terrific driving force under the chairmanship of Geoffrey Burton, the second, a terrible one, under the chairmanship of Jeffrey Stirling), led me to think we needed a combination of theatre expertise, money, and daring. Once again I called up friends. I started with Peter Stevens, a very old friend, to whose helping hand I am indebted for moves from Newcastle to Leicester, to the National Theatre. Who once upon a time was the best theatre hit-man around, and who, at this point, was a rebel without a cause. He was in. Howard Panter, the producer of *Mutiny* with whom I had struck up a good working relationship and friendship, and who was obviously a coming man, was next. Howard had the advantage of being an old mate of Michael's from the days of Tony Richardson's *Hamlet* where he had been Assistant Stage Manager and Michael had played Laertes. (He cherishes a long-held ambition to get Michael to do a rock 'n' roll show.) Next I contacted Jules Boardman, Peter Stevens's assistant at the National Theatre, now running Ticketmaster, a master marketing practitioner (the fact that he and Howard were also cricket freaks had something to do with it ...) Then came Michael Hallifax (ex-National planning wizard, now freelance consultant). Victor Glynn, once my publicity officer at the Young Vic, the organising brains behind Quintet Films, now working as a producer with Portman International Films, was a must. He had managed to raise money for the filming of my production of *Hiawatha*, and my series for Channel Four, *Shakespeare Lives*. Michael P. weighed in with a profile heavy-weight, Melvyn Bragg, adding a little literary and TV lustre to the group. And there we were. For a time.

May/June 1986 I had been in Hamburg to do *Julius Caesar* at
the Deutsches Schauspielhaus, a production that was so successful
that it set me off on the long trail to the position of Intendant
(Artistic Director/Manager), which I currently occupy. Now, at
the end of July, I went to Tokyo for ten days to finish off a Japanese
production of *The Sound of Music*. I couldn't resist it. I didn't have
time to direct the piece in its entirety, but Malcolm Ranson went
out ahead and rehearsed for four weeks and then we both
completed the production together. I had had an association with
Tokyo for some ten years, having done three productions there. I
took this opportunity to talk to various interested groups about the
forthcoming ESC venture. In between these trips, the pace at home
was hotting up. The budgets were hashed and re-hashed. I booked
the main hall of the Territorial Army Headquarters in
Wandsworth, where I had rehearsed *Mutiny*, for the beginning of
the rehearsal period, and Alford House (Awful House)
Kennington, much smaller, where I had rehearsed many a piece,
including *Romeo and Juliet*. The distance from Wandsworth to our
office in Golden Square was to prove a bind. Sometimes people
trailed backwards and forwards two or three times a day, a total
of five or six hours' travelling if the traffic was bad. Precious time
and precious money, many bikes and taxis for messages and
information. The advantages of Wandsworth were the size, the
ability to set up a running wardrobe in a room alongside, and a
small room upstairs for second rehearsals. And it was cheap. Awful
House was nearer to the office, but devastatingly small.

It too, however, had extra rooms, vital when running two or
three rehearsals simultaneously. We had a series of meetings with
Roger Redfarn and Andrew Welch of Plymouth Theatre Royal, in
London and Plymouth, to beat out a final deal. There were
problems. I betrayed my own instinct, and instead of having our
own Production Manager in control, I agreed to let the whole
project be organised from Plymouth. It was disastrous. The man in
charge was last heard of somewhere in Australia. The set, however,
was in the capable hands of Fred Carro, ex-technical director of
Covent Garden Opera House, who supervised the construction,
building it with an outside firm as the theatre itself did not possess
metal workshops. The 'props', however, were made 'in house' and
were on the cheap. Nothing was built to last. In a short period of
time, before we even got to the stage, renovations were taking
place, and the sandbags defeated us to the end.

August was hectic. Auditions, interviews with journalists, final details hammered out with the Allied Irish Bank. We drafted in Dicky Bird, arguably the best theatre graphic designer in the country, to do the poster and logo. It cost a fortune and we ended up acrimoniously. Now, we're friends again. I contacted Patsy Rodenburg, Guildhall and RSC, to come and do the voice work. Up and down to Plymouth, meetings with Chris Dyer and Stephanie Howard. An expensive meal with Peter Roberts of *Plays International*, that I thought he was supposed to be paying for. And, two days before rehearsals were due to begin, a very fortuitous dinner invitation. Michael Hallifax asked me to his home to meet Jane and Bernie Sahlins, show hunting for the Chicago World Theater Festival. They wanted my production of *Romeo and Juliet* from the Royal Shakespeare Company. Wily Michael Hallifax. 'Don't do that', I said. 'I'll come and do a production of *Romeo and Juliet* for you any time you like. Take the English Shakespeare Company and *The Henrys*.' 'Who?' 'The ESC – same director, different company. Only the 'R' has changed to avoid comparison. Anyway the RSC won't be able to meet your deadline for a kick off, they can't plan more than a week ahead.' They agreed to come and have a look at the shows when they were up and running. True to their word, they turned up in Cardiff for the All Day, had a great time and gave the RSC the big 'E' (elbow – slang term for the bum's rush).

We were ready. Or were we? In all this, after our initial discussions, Michael and I had hardly touched on our roles as director and actor. All idea of romantically rabbiting the night away discussing the nature of kingship, allied to the collapse of oil shares – out the window. We had nine weeks and three plays.

We met that first September day in 1986. The sun was shining over the Wandsworth T.A.H. A good omen. Board members were there, as was David Mirvish. A glass of champagne and a bun, nervously welcoming the group to a new venture. An hour of this, then sit down to deliver an oration on how the company came into being, and on the need to reassess our approach to Shakespeare (a well-oiled wheel, this). Show the set, explain the props-kit theory, make one or two pictures in the model box of the set (Chris was not there, being busy in Canada with *King Lear*). Costumes so far. John Woodvine particularly pleased with his George Melly look, and the combination of his Elizabethan 'man about town' gear. In a rush of enthusiasm (and efficiency), Titus had already provided scaffolding towers and built a sturdy scaffold bridge – all hired at a cost of £500 per week. I pointed out that we wouldn't be needing them for quite a while, and anyway we hadn't got £500 a week to spare. Back they went. Anyway, I had no need of them right at the beginning, because I had decided to risk nearly two weeks discussing the plays, working through the texts slowly, debating the themes, trying to knit together the various storylines.

Certain characters we had linked through – Exeter, for example, was combined with other small parts and followed through all three plays (eventually to be the only character to continue on into *Henry VI Part 1*, to disappear mysteriously, as his death scene was cut). Gadshill reappeared in *Henry IV Part 2*, as did Peto; Doll Tearsheet was around in *Part 1*, etc. Westmoreland appeared speaking and non-speaking in all three plays. In Michael Cronin's hands he was a dominant figure. John Woodvine was justifiably nervous. In such a large part he naturally wanted to get on his feet. However, I needed, after nearly two weeks of brain damage, to involve the whole company in a series of corporate exercises to bind the group together before splitting into what would sometimes be simultaneous four-way rehearsals. For four days we went back to drama school: trust exercises, games, improvisations. Fun. And serious. Probing weaknesses, exploring phobias, establishing a common bond of mutual appreciation of the disparate qualities and individuality of the group, that was to last through the three years. I extended the old drama school 'blind walking' exercise. Paddy O'Connell led Michael Cronin, his eyes closed, never touching him, talking him quietly up and down stairs, across Wandsworth High Street and round the supermarket. The dominant image is one of the parade ground. It was a sunny Saturday afternoon outside. The parade ground was some seventy-five metres corner to corner. The actors hurtled across it one by one, eyes bravely closed. Listening to words of command from their colleagues to ease them gently to a stop without smashing into a wall. We set out markers for Jennie Stoller who ran wildly and trustingly in a complete circle. They were heady days, that autumn of 1986, as we analysed, improvised, proselytised . . .

Now we were really ready. The groundwork had been good. The two weeks' intensive debate paid off. We had matched history with the Shakespearian version and had made our decisions. Actors must have a stake in what they do on stage: they are eventually responsible. Without collaboration, discussion and proper involvement, no actor can have his/her heart in what happens. The excuse 'I'm only doing this because that's what the director wanted' should never pertain.

There is a school that believes that the plays should be allowed to speak for themselves, that directors are superfluous. Just leave it to the actors. True, theatre is organic. Traditionally it has evolved with groups of people of like mind wanting to say something together. Usually, at the centre of this has been a writer/director/actor/manager, a composite figure like Shakespeare himself, Molière, Brecht. Often pieces are improvised, themes and characters reflecting the persuasions and physical attributes of the group involved. Thus, with Shakespeare, we can trace the path of actors who are tall and thin, big and fat, Welsh, have a speech impediment, can play old men, young girls. We watch them grow up, grow old, trace their paths through a series of plays. We can recognise the style of language and the method of delivery. A picture of a rounded figure with a specific personality begins to emerge. Falstaff's is a dialogue with the audience. His method of delivery a personal one. It is inconceivable that actor and part were not inextricably bound up with one another. Richard Burbage, playing with, teasing the audience, improvising on a main theme handed him by William and embellishing and gilding as the mood took him. A true stand-up routine. A collaboration of two artists exploring the common ground of dark, savage satire, the comedy of self preservation, the ruthless mocking of the weak, and the black and bloody comedy of exploitation. But I suspect W.S. had the casting vote.

I rehearsed all three plays simultaneously in storyline blocks. In the space of three hours we would go through three scenes. The Falstaff story, the Bolingbroke story, the Hal story, the low life scenes, the French scenes. Holding the complete picture in our hands was a nightmare. The method was roughly as follows. We re-capped the content and intention of a scene, discussed the staging, then threw it on the floor (theatrical term for 'improvising'), then more discussion. Another improvisation with me refining text, relationships and staging. Further discussion and a third version.

If we were satisfied that we were on the right lines, the scene would be taken away by Stella Bond to be re-worked (when a suitable gap appeared in the crowded schedule) and developed. Roughly an hour and a half for longish scenes, one hour medium

Stella Bond

ones. Big ones – Boar's Head, etc. – three hours. We were producing nine hours of Shakespeare in nine weeks. It was exhilarating and I was exultant. I knew that many ideas would only be sketched in, that often in-depth rehearsal would not be possible. But there was a clarity of intention emerging, a linear energy. The text was spare and lean, winging home to its target with the unerring accuracy of a darter's one hundred and eighty.

There really is no mystery attached to Shakespeare's language. He is a story-teller, using combinations of words, juxtaposed, to tell that story in the richest but often the most economical way possible. And always the language is an instrument of communication, meant to be spoken aloud, one person to another, exploring ideas, giving reasons – telling stories. Written in a rhythm. Strong/weak, strong/weak, etc., or weak/strong, weak/strong. People talk to each other, they don't incant, intone. In a rhythm. Strong/weak, strong/weak, weak/strong, weak/strong.

Observing that rhythm gives the meaning. Modern actors are weaned in the subjective school – plenty of 'I', 'Me', 'Mine' – products of Jung, Hebbert, Adler, Freud, introspective analysis.

And Stanislavsky and method. That's OK. That's right. The basis of all modern acting has to begin with the relationship of one's self and one's personal feelings towards a role, searching for the common ground in one's own emotional experience. Naturalism. However, in the days before the Id and the Ego, the world believed in Fates and Furies, Gods from outside imposed their will; it was not within our power to change the course of events. Those who defied the Gods and Destiny wreaked havoc, sought their own destruction. There was order in the world controlled by an outside force; you did not disturb that order. 'Me' didn't count, 'Me' was an insignificant part of that order. In Shakespeare, the personal pronoun is almost never emphasised. When it is, the man strongly indicates the stress, usually by reversing the verb. The modern obsession with 'self' is the thing that gives the most wrong stresses in a line of Shakespeare. For the listener, this wrong stress brings with it a psychological short circuit. You suddenly receive a fist in the face, the brakes are jammed on while purring along at a smooth seventy. There is a speech from *Henry VI Part 1*. The young John Talbot comes to die by the side of his father who is under siege, surrounded on all sides by the French.

John Talbot. Then let me stay: and, father, do you fly:
Your loss is great, so your regard should be;
My worth unknown, no loss is known in me.
Upon my death the French can little boast;
In yours they will, in you all hopes are lost.
Flight cannot stain the honour you have won;
But mine it will, that no exploit have done;
You fled for vantage, everyone will swear;
But, if I bow, they'll say it was for fear.
There is no hope that ever I will stay,
If the first hour I shrink and run away.
Here, on my knee, I beg mortality,
Rather than life preserved with infamy.

A minefield, if ever there was one, for the modern actor, surrounded by a fruit bowl of juicy *I*'s, *Me*'s, *Mine*'s and *Your*'s. Tricky. I spent hours with John Tramper the following year, taking him through the meaning. Just follow the rhythm, weak/strong, weak/strong, etc. But old habits die hard. John made an heroic effort, but nevertheless the old Ego would come skidding in somewhere. Stanislavsky has a lot to answer for. One line from *The Henrys* haunted me for three years. Try as I would, I could not get a certain actor to say, 'You are their *heir*; you sit upon their *throne*,' correctly.

He would slur the first part of the line, and then hit 'their' with a sledgehammer; then, winding up for the big one, bulldoze his way through the second part of the line, before sending the ball and chain smashing into the second 'their'.

'Youware THEIR heir, you siddon THEIR throne.' In vain I pointed out that an *heir*, for Chrissake, was what every king wanted, a son to inherit the earth, that the *throne*, with the crown, was the ultimate symbol of power. These were the important words in the line. Just follow the rhythm – weak/strong, weak/strong, etc. 'You are their HEIR, you sit upon their THRONE.'

(I was editing the videotapes of *Henry V* in the autumn of 1989 in the Windmill Lane Studios, Dublin, three years after my first – patient – explanation of the way the line worked and up it came. 'Youware THEIR heir, you siddon THEIR throne.' Brian McCue, the editor, looked in astonishment as I leapt to my feet with a howl of anguish and proceeded to beat my head on the wall. That done, I then gave the personal pronoun lecture and spent two hours trying to cut the line out without success. You beat me, baby.)

One scene also beat me. ('Only one?' I hear you cry.) The very opening scene of the whole trilogy. Bolingbroke talking to his Cabinet, beginning, 'So shaken as we are, so wan with care.' Shakespeare was a bugger. So often, right at the beginning of a play, he throws in, in his most complex and complicated language, a monologue giving the vital ingredients of a story – facts and figures absolutely essential to our understanding of what follows. No action. Just words. It is as if he were challenging his audience to follow him. You want something to *really* get your teeth into? Well, listen to this . . . 'so shaken as we are . . .'. The Duke in *Measure for Measure*, the Duke in *Comedy of Errors*. Bolingbroke – 'so shaken as we are'. It is a particularly difficult scene. Bolingbroke appears to be receiving information for the first time, and then seems to know more than he is letting on, suddenly supplying facts that he can only have if he is already privy to the events. Is it a massive propaganda exercise, a wool-pulling act, a 'show' for the media? (Or is this just a dedicated modernist claiming for Shakespeare a psychological subtlety he wasn't interested in? After all, he wasn't concerned with detail . . .) I was convinced, after we had tried it ten different ways, low key, that we would not only lose the story, we would lose the audience. They would not have the requisite information necessary to carry the narrative forward. Somewhere around week seven, we abandoned desks and kingly grouping, and unashamedly stuck a microphone in front of Paddy O'Connell, lined the Cabinet up alongside him and went for the 'show of strength' interpretation. I split the scene in two. The Cabinet exits from the hall, or press conference, or whatever it is, and there follows a small personal scene between Bolingbroke and Exeter. I lifted the lines beginning 'Can no man tell me of my unthrifty son?' from *Richard II* and added them, for clarity, to the speech where Bolingbroke compares Hal unfavourably with Hotspur.

Immediately the story was clear, the text amplified, spoken with quiet control and resonance, accessible. Everything was OK, the country was in safe hands. A few cuts and we were home and dry. Or were we? The staging was a wilful distortion of the intention of the scene (I would submit, the only one in the whole three plays), brought about by the necessity of beginning the cycle with a convention and a clarity that the audience could relate to. There are those who would say that it is precisely this approach, not trusting the language and the situation, the need to use crass modern appliances such as microphones, that desecrates the language and distorts the plays. The defence is simple. People understood. And from then on, the story unfolded with purpose and clarity. I have to assume that an audience has no background, has not read or seen the plays, has no knowledge of the history of England. Unless I assume this, I am being élitist, joining that group who would ignore popular methods of communication, denying that the plays were performed for a whole cross-section of the community, some educated, some not.

The following year the problem was solved by adding *Richard II* at the front of the cycle. The story, if you were seeing the whole sequence, was now known. The audience was following the characters as in a series – a medieval soap opera of murder and

intrigue in the Coronation boardroom. We reverted back to our
original staging of the scene, confident of our approach. 'So shaken
as we are . . .' became a picture of a man confessing in his inner
sanctum that he is having personal problems as well as political
ones, unwell, still yearning for the pilgrimage that would wash the
blood of Richard II from his hands. The traditionalists were
delighted. The scene was returned to its rightful place. (We still
kept 'Harry Le Roy' though, just in case. More of that anon.)

Chaos was building up in Plymouth. It was clear that things were
not under control, and communication was difficult. Chris Dyer
went into his 'hiding' mode (a sure sign that things were not right);
Stephanie into her defensive one. Part of the communication
problem was ours. Information was not being directly disseminated
from the rehearsal room floor. Titus, after an absence from the
theatre of some five years, was not on top of the organisation. (We
were actually too few, and the situation very stressful.)

Nicky Waters, DSM, resigned (or rather, one day just didn't turn
up). We found Graham Lister, a young rock, to take over. Before
the year was out, we were to be grateful a thousand times over for
Graham's presence.

If the organisation and the technical side were heading for the
Needles, the acting and textual work powered ahead. John
Woodvine, whose face, even when happy, is rather like a
bloodhound with appendicitis, was proving every bit the Falstaff
we had hoped for. He and I were rather like naughty schoolchildren
pretending to be grown up. We would discuss seriously the
metaphysical implications of him hiding a 'No Through Road' sign
up his tunic as a shield at the Battle of Shrewsbury. He fitted the
part like a glove – a fat one. The enjoyment of the text, beautifully
pointed, was evident. We savoured moments such as:

> MICHAEL P.   Peace, ye fat-guts! lie down; lay thine ear close
> to the ground, and list if thou canst hear the tread of
> travellers.
> JOHN *(Pause. Think.)*   Have you any levers to lift me up
> again, being down?

and

> MICHAEL P. *(incredulous)*   What, fought you with them all?
> JOHN *(even more incredulous)*   All!? I know not what you

call all, but if I fought not with fifty of them, I am a bunch of radish.

and

MICHAEL P.   We two saw you four set on four . . . Then did we two set on you four; and, with a word, outfaced you from your prize . . . What trick, what device, what starting-hole, canst thou now find out to hide thee from this open and apparent shame?
JOHN *(Pause, look round, slow smile, chuckle, condescending, paternal.)*   By the Lord, I knew ye as well as he that made ye.

And sad ones:

JOHN   Bardolph, am I not fallen away vilely since this last action? Do I not bate? Do I not dwindle? Why, my skin hangs about me like an old lady's loose gown; I am withered like an old applejohn [*a face like Clement Freud's and a voice to match*] . . . I was as virtuously given as a gentleman need to be . . . diced not above seven times [*pause*] a week; went to a bawdy house not above once [*pause*] in a quarter [*pause*] of an hour; paid money that I borrowed [*pause*] three [*pause*] or [*pause*] four times . . .

John would delicately weight a word, and then gently send it winging home to its target. We revelled in comic invention. With John it came easily and organically. I introduced him to the 'six egg in a pint of gin' hangover cure. He stirred it with his sword-stick.
   One Saturday afternoon in October at Awful House, I built the Boar's Head. I had the image of Chris's drawing in mind as I experimented with hanging some old cloths on the two towers, and arranged tables and bentwood chairs. Bentwoods became old pals. One would always turn up in a scene unexpectedly, or go missing, or be one too many. Many a merry moment (Ho! Ho!) was spent persuading actor/bentwood the importance of accurate placing. Sometimes if I have the right feeling for a scene, have absorbed and understood it, and if the actors have been properly prepared, the staging is instinctive, appears to happen by itself. And so it was with the Boar's Head. That very first improvised setting, three

hours on Saturday afternoon, was the basis, virtually unchanged, for three years' playing. And yet it had a marvellous quality of invention and spontaneity. It is often the way. Scenes that I think will give problems turn out to be the easiest; simple scenes on paper, the hardest. I thought I had provided a powerful and imaginative basis for the relationship in the Hotspur/Lady Percy scene. I developed the finger breaking into a world of physical slapstick. The joke, surely, is that this hero of Scotland and a hundred battles, who has carved a swathe through the rebel ranks with the power of his arm, is subdued by a girl who forces him to his knees by bending his little finger (try it) and matches him for temper. 'Gentle Kate' (used twice) is an irony.

> *Lady Percy.* Come, come, you paraquito, answer me
> Directly to this question that I ask:
> In faith I'll break thy little finger, Harry,
> An if thou wilt not tell me all things true.

John Price and Jennie Stoller couldn't get it together. Tears before bedtime. What seemed funny and physical, was leaden and painful.

I'm afraid that finally, impatiently, I had to leave Stella to sort out John and Jennie. There appears to be a fundamental difference between English actors and other nationalities. I was once sitting in a Tokyo pocket-handkerchief theatre watching a production of *King John*, when suddenly fifty actors erupted onto stage for the battle scene and beat the shit out of each other. It was the most frightening thing I've ever experienced in the theatre. The actors in Hamburg hurl themselves around unconcernedly, a few knocks and bruises all part of the game. See Uli Wildgruber, a mountain of a man, fall backwards thirty feet down a flight of stairs in *Lulu*, bouncing all the way. Compare the New York version of *Fool for Love* with Peter Gill's at the National. Not that all English actors are inhibited, but we do have a tendency to act only from the neck up, to rehearse in high-heeled boots, coats, with a cup of coffee in one hand (or cigarette), a script in the other, reluctant to let go the textual umbilical cord until absolutely imperative. One of the reasons why Brook elected to work in Paris with a polyglot group of actors. As it happened, the ESC didn't suffer much from such tendencies – we didn't have time.

And then there were the Jennies – Quayle and Stoller. The Katherine/Alice learning English scene '*Il faut que j'apprenne à parler l'Anglais.'* Absolutely imperative for reasons of state to get my mouth round the mangled sounds of this pagan language. (Beef-eating, fog-bound barbarians.) Once again I thought I had provided a witty, sophisticated political base for the scene, with plenty of opportunity for comic biz *à la française* at the expense of *les Anglais*. No chance. After a flying start, confidence slowly dissolved into a soggy, bog-bound mass, and then slithered and shimmied its way out between the cracks in the floorboards. I cajoled, twinkled, enthused, leapt up and down, tried the scene in a schoolroom, a boudoir, a picnic (used as the basis for giving the news that the English had landed), in a car, in a wood, on a walk. And finally turned them over to Stella.

Meanwhile the other French scenes were progressing apace. I had done a tremendous amount of re-editing of *Henry V* to make sense of the French. The scenes are scantly written and show signs of a lot of improvising and additions as well as being repetitive. I streamlined the characters into four coherent ones and created a running character for Mountjoy, the envoy, the humanist observer, the survivor. He lasted well into *Henry VI*, having published his account of the Battle of Agincourt. Agincourt in *Henry V* is interesting. Everybody talks about it but no battle is ever seen. In fact, the only direct action is Pistol kicking the shit out of a wounded Frenchman.

(Wounded? Is that me or William? I forget.) The braggart, the coward, the bully, the prototype yobbo putting the strong arm on the French aristocracy. Misunderstandings are many in this play, most of them due to Olivier. Those French bastards. How could they 'kill the boys and the luggage,' weeps Fluellen? How shocking. What is often overlooked is that Henry has first given the order to 'kill all the prisoners'. Pragmatic, yes? It's a war, after all, numbers depleted, only reasonable to relieve the extra men from the duty of guarding prisoners. It is quite clear that the French action is a retaliation against the English action. To make it a patriotic play, Olivier had to cut some one thousand five hundred lines. Leave them in and your patriotic interpretation has to cope with the difficult consequences of the above.

> Pistol. . . . Yoke-fellows in arms,
> Let us to France! Like horse-leeches, my boys,
> To suck, to suck, the very blood to suck!   *(Henry V, II.3)*

And who are these brave gallants, these hearts, these lads, this
youth of England who are all on fire? They are Pistol, Nym, and
Bardolph – the scum, the dregs, sell your grandmother for a fire
shovel.

> The French, advised by good intelligence,
> Of this most dreadful preparation,
> Shake in their fear . . .

The Choric ironies are manifold. How do you cope with them? It
seems tradition has not changed much. The English invade the
Continent much like the marauding Celts of old. Imperialism
encourages jingoism. So the Falklands. So Agincourt. 'Fuck the
Frogs.' The banner hung out by the send-off crowd at Southampton
in our production of *Henry V* grew out of the desire to bridge
nearly six hundred years of this same bigoted xenophobic
patriotism. As Pistol *et al.* turn at the end of the farewell to Mistress
Quickly, punch the air to a chorus of ' 'ere we go, 'ere we go, 'ere
we go', 'Jerusalem' swells. The last night of the Proms, the troops
getting the blessing at Portsmouth, football fury, all combined in
my mind to produce this image one afternoon late on a Saturday.
(Do the best ideas come at the end of the week?) For a time the cast
didn't think I was serious until the painted banner appeared. Some
spectators found the moment offensive, others misunderstood,
most applauded. A letter from a member of the public: 'The use of
the word was offensive and the term "Frogs" hardly helps promote
racial harmony and dispel old prejudices. I was ashamed to be
English.' Precisely. The case rests.

Michael and I had known from early on the route we were taking
with Prince Hal. His soliloquy, at the end of his first scene in *Henry
IV Part 1*, makes it patently clear what he's about.

> *Prince Henry.* I know you all, and will awhile uphold
> The unyoked humour of your idleness;
> Yet herein will I imitate the sun,
> Who doth permit the base contagious clouds
> To smother up his beauty from the world . . .
> So when this loose behaviour I throw off
> And pay the debt I never promised,
> By how much better than my word I am,
> By so much shall I falsify men's hopes;

And, like bright metal on a sullen ground,
My reformation, glittering o'er my fault,
Shall show more goodly and attract more eyes
Than that which hath no foil to set it off.
I'll so offend, to make offence a skill;
Redeeming time when men think least I will.

No possible way of misreading his intentions. And he proceeds to do precisely what he promises, straight as an arrow, right through to the final wooing of Katherine at the end of *Henry V*. The banishing of Falstaff is inevitable from that very first moment, never mind the foreshadowing ('I do. I will') at the end of the first tavern scene in *Henry IV Part 1*. The marriage to Katherine, political expediency. *'Il faut que j'apprenne l'Anglais'*. Of course she must, Katherine is his 'capital demand'. It *may* grow into a love story, but at the point where we pick up the relationship, we see a man who has never taken 'no' for an answer, suffered defeat in any sphere (witness his churlish revenge on the soldier Williams) determined to subdue Kate and wring acquiescence out of her. She is 'La Belle France' and must be forced to submit to his will. An iron will, for all that the technique is masked in flattery. Determined. Cold. ('. . . for I love France so well that I will not part with a village of it; I will have it all mine . . .') France is plundered first, then Kate.

> *Henry*. Marry, if you would put me to verses . . . why you undid me . . . I have neither words nor measure . . . I cannot look greenly, not gasp out my eloquence, nor I have no cunning in protestation; only downright oaths . . . What! a speaker is but a prater . . .

What? He never stops talking – The Breach, St Crispin's Day, the joyous horn-interlocking word play with Falstaff. You cannot be *serious*. How can you believe this man? What a dirty rat. Michael and I went for it.

Pennington: *What I was after for Prince Hal (analysing now what was mostly instinctive at the time) was a combination of this chilly political clearsightedness with a wayward, unstable quality in the moment. His humour in* Henry IV *is usually based on wrong-footing those around him – he is particularly disagreeable with*

Francis the drawer – always with his intimidating blood-royalty dangerously sharpening the jokes. He is wayward in emotion, too, in that he falls dangerously in love with the life (Falstaff) that he has committed himself to leaving. There seems to be violence in his humour, in his passionate outbursts to his father, and of course in his bravery in battle – this violence becomes legalised and heroic when he becomes the implacable Warrior King, and an intemperance that had been delinquent becomes official. The humour in Henry V *remains the uneasy same, though – visiting his troops the night before Agincourt and double-crossing the soldier Williams over his gloves is the Prince Hal we last saw in the Boar's Head Tavern. It was good to find this link; since in fact, apart from the obvious narrative connection between* Henry IV *and* Henry V, *there is little in the text to link Prince Hal with King Henry – the vocabulary, dynamics and tone are quite different. What is strong in* Henry V, *and very actable, is that his sense of mission has cost him youth, ease, and spontaneity, since every impulse is now regulated where it wasn't before. When at the end of the play he admits to Katherine that 'a good leg will fall, a straight back will stoop, a fair face will wither, a full eye will wax hollow; but a good heart, Kate, is the sun and the moon', I tried to make the audience remember Falstaff in his high noon, a sense of fellowship Hal has lost in his destiny. The candour of his regret at this point might also make it possible for Kate, his political enemy, to begin to fall in love with him.*

Bogdanov: In his review at the Old Vic the following spring, Mr Billington was still tilting with Tillyard: 'I find Bogdanov's interpretation of England's National Epic wilful, vain and historically dubious. I take Shakespeare's three plays to be complex, ambiguous works about the education of a king; about Hal's immersion in the life of his country in order to become an ideal governor ... Mr Bogdanov often seems to be overlaying Shakespeare with a play of his own invention ... Henry V also looks forward to the Tudor world in proving that kingliness can be achieved ... dynastic succession vindicated ... But my real objection is to the bias that constantly emphasises Hal's ruthlessness at the expense of his humanity.' I think he must be thinking of another Henry IV. Pirandello's, perhaps.

So we worked on, Paddy O'Connell having difficulty with the lines, amazing us with some wonderful linguistic combinations but bringing tears to our eyes with the death scene, moving, emotional, sincere. The panic of a man desperate to impart to his son, in the final moments of his life, all that he knows about governing. 'Busy giddy minds with foreign quarrels'. Deflect attention from domestic problems at home – unemployment, homelessness, the National Health Service – by waging a 'just' war. Just? Any old excuse will do. If one is intent on invading Poland, Czechoslovakia, Panama, Afghanistan, justification is readily to hand.

Our own rock 'n' roll band, Sneak's Noise, was born. ('Go find out Sneak's Noise,' says Francis the drawer, 'Mistress Tearsheet would fain hear some music.') Terry Mortimer, our musical director, composed a rock galliard to cover the horrendous set change into the Boar's Head, giving the 'old farts' (as the older members of the company were known) a chance to jive. The ensemble work of the company was characterised by the Boar's Head scene, in which everyone took part, Michael Cronin and Roger Booth playing eight hundred and twenty-seven rounds of dominoes in the three years. The commitment was total. Both Michael and Roger refused to give up their appearance in the tavern when they changed roles in the second and third year, Michael Cronin doing lightning quick changes between Bolingbroke appearances in *Henry IV Part 1* on the one hand and Roger between Northumberland in *Part 2* on the other. Although Michael 'Moanin' Cronin (as he was affectionately – sometimes – known) would have extreme attacks of bile, and Roger Booth, on one occasion, demanded the management's scalps for not arranging VIP treatment at Heathrow Terminal Four ('Why should we have to check our bags in like everyone else?'), the two were quintessentially a great part of the heart of the ESC. As were the other 'old farts', Hugh Sullivan and Clyde Pollitt. When editing *The Wars of the Roses* for TV in the autumn of 1989, any tension in me would disappear with the appearance of Hugh. Diamond work from first to last. And Clyde's Shallow – tears and a lump still swell as I think of it. Masterly timing, the gentleness, the humour, ostensibly thrown away but cutting like a knife. Frail but unafraid. In the Orchard Scene in *Henry IV Part 2*, I asked Clyde to fall off a bench to be caught at the last minute by John Woodvine, and later to fall backwards in an apple basket to be carried off by Pistol and Falstaff. 'Honest gentleman, I know not your breeding.' But we knew his. The breeding showed.

John Price roared along as Pistol – Rocker, Teddy Boy, Rambo.

Adding a million touches, suddenly turning round with 'Hal's Angels' emblazoned on the back of his leather jacket. (I wish I'd thought of it.) 'Helter skelter, here I rode' – motorbike motion. 'Suttler will I be and profits will accrue' – revealing the inside of his drapecoat lined with packets of hash. All this after a slow start where I battled with him over the language, insisting that it couldn't be just melodramatic. Pistol is not merely a theatrical poseur.

> *Pistol.* These be good humours indeed! Shall pack horses,
> And hollow pampered jades of Asia,
> That cannot go but thirty mile a day,
> Compare with Caesar's and with Cannibal's
> And Trojan Greeks? Nay, rather damn them with
> King Cerberus; and let the welkin roar.
> Shall we fall foul for toys?

'This something's more than matter.' Pistol must communicate through the medium of those strange pilfered phrases, talk as if this were his natural speech pattern. The key turned, and John's performance became one of the great joys of that first year. June Watson moved into top gear as Mistress Quickly almost immediately. A wonderfully soft, hard, romantic, indulgent, Spooner of a character. Her speech on the death of Falstaff was as moving and funny as anything in the trilogy. June's timing, like Clyde's, was impeccable. From first to last, throughout the three years, June recreated person and language, fresh, new-minted and wonderfully funny for each performance.

> *Hostess.* . . . And I have borne and borne and borne; and
> have been fobbed off and fobbed off and fobbed off from this
> day to that day . . .

The innuendo and double meaning that June got out of each of the 'fobs', in a rising crescendo with a holding back of the 'f', would have made a seadog blush.

And what fun as a person, eyes mischievously a-twinkle, a wee doch and dorris at the ready.

Eluned Hawkins had joined us to play Owen Glendower's daughter. Although not a native Welsh speaker, Eluned was born in North Wales and had worked in Welsh-speaking theatre. I wanted to amplify the stage directions 'The Lady speaks in Welsh',

'Here The Lady sings a Welsh song'. There are not a few people in these islands who do not realise that Welsh, for a million people, is a first language. A million people are not wrong. I constructed a scene using the *Oxford Book of Welsh Verse*, stanzas taken from anonymous poets of the twelfth and thirteenth centuries, beginning with a passionate pacifist plea from Lady Mortimer to her spouse.

Eluned Hawkins

Lady Mortimer. Paid mynd i ryfela, f 'anwylyd, paid mynd i
gyflafan ddisynnwyr a ladd gariad ieuanc sy mor ddirodres â
ieuenctid ei hunan. Paid mynd i ryfela!

*Go not to these wars my love, go not to the senseless slaughter
of a love that is young and green as youth itself. Go not to these
wars!*

There then develops a conversation between Lady Mortimer and
her father, Owen Glendower, a passionate disagreement as to the
effect of war, to which her spouse, Lord Mortimer, helplessly
remarks:

This is the deadly spite that angers me:
My wife can speak no English, I no Welsh.

It always raised a laugh.

But the scene is simple and touching. The meeting of two
cultures, a love born of an internal communication transcending all
verbal barriers; a plea for communal harmony and understanding,
for the banishing of bigotry and prejudice. With her Niagara of
Titian tresses, Eluned moved all who saw the scene, the emotion
communicating itself beyond the understanding of 'that pretty
Welsh'. The scene concluded with a song also culled from the
Oxford Book of Welsh Verse, 'Otid Eiry' – 'Snow is Falling',
accompanied by Andy Jarvis and Ben Bazell on flute and mandolin.
Audiences throughout the world responded with a deep respectful
silence, responding to the intention, if not the words. (Full text and
translation are printed in the Appendices.)

I had looked again, as part of my preparation, at the masterly
Orson Welles portrayal of Falstaff in *Chimes at Midnight*. (Our old
chum Norman Rodway as Hotspur, in a bath tub. An idea I half
pinched, setting the same scene with Hotspur shaving.) I think the
version one of the best Shakespeare films ever made. Welles edits
the two parts of *Henry IV* together, takes some of the dialogue and
ideas from *Henry V*, then reshuffles text and story to come up with
some extraordinary insights into the character. The film smells of
sweat, dirt and war in a way I was never able to capture on stage.
(I started on too jokey a level with Falstaff's recruiting scene in
Henry IV Part 2, and was never able to pull it back.) One link in
particular I seized on. Welles reverses the two parts of the last scene

of *Henry IV Part 1* to leave Hal still at odds with his father. The king patently believes Falstaff has killed Hotspur and that Hal's claim to have done so is a lie. Obvious. And brilliant. Shakespeare finishes with an apparent reconciliation between father and son at the end of *Part 1*. But then, at the beginning of *Part 2*, they are estranged again, although it is only shortly after the Battle of Shrewsbury. The problem is that he wrote the second part some time after the first. It is possible, though unlikely, that (a) on completing *Part 1* he didn't know he would write *Part 2* and (b) taking *Part 1* complete in itself, the story had to have a resolution. For us, *Part 2* following *Part 1* on Saturdays one hour later, the effect of finishing *Part 1* with this reversal was electric.

It left the story wide open, with the audience buzzing with excitement to know what followed. It involved no text alterations. Many a member of the audience came back in the afternoon to find out how the story resolved itself, and then couldn't resist staying for the evening as well. (Stories of baby-sitting rows, spouses refusing to leave cars behind, emergency arrangements to get home – or stay the night – filtered back every week.) Of couse, there were always the silly ones who couldn't bear the reversed ending. (As if it matters. And they should be so lucky to know the text in the first place.) Thus John Peter in the *Sunday Times*. Apart from finding some of the comic business 'coarse beyond belief' and that I suffer from 'dogged attempts' to be 'contemporary', and that 'this sort of rabble-rousing rubbish distorts and vulgarises Shakespeare's cool tough line on power politics', he concludes that I feel that Shakespeare needs my helping hand: 'he switches round the last two scenes of *Part 1* for the sake of what he fondly imagines is a psychological insight.' John is Hungarian. The problem with being an exile in love with Shakespeare is that one becomes more traditional than the traditionalists. And then the *Toronto Star*: 'It's all very interesting but it simply isn't Shakespeare. Just by transposing a couple of scenes, director Michael Bogdanov has turned a brilliantly constructed and unified work of art into something that is incomplete and unsatisfying. He could not have said "to be continued" more clearly if he had had a couple of pom-pom girls parade a banner across the stage.' As the story was indeed continued some seventy-five minutes later, I took this intended criticism as a compliment. Something about Shakespeare always brings out the worst in people. John Woodvine, Michael, Paddy and I loved the transposition. It made sense. Thank you, Orson.

We celebrated the end of our rehearsal period in London with some champagne and sandwiches at Awful House and then headed for Plymouth for the last two weeks before the opening. This time our rehearsal space was to be at the Headquarters of RAF Mountbatten, in a gigantic disused hangar on the sea front. (Real helicopters took off and landed during rehearsals of the battle sequences in *Henry V*. The memory of the Falklands was now.) The Theatre Royal had rigged up our set, lights and sound in this vast, cavernous, corrugated and concrete space, where we had to prepare technically and dress rehearse the three shows prior to opening cold, with virtually no time on stage, on a Monday night. In the parlous state of the Arts today, a theatre cannot afford to lose income being 'dark'. I rolled into the hangar late on Sunday night to begin our two-week technical nightmare. The set was up, lights and sound were rigged. Joy – it looked like the model. Round it was a great network of scaffolding. Fred Carro had done us proud to get it there in time. A surge of confidence carried me through the next embattled fourteen days, helped by the relaxing properties of a small barn on the far side of Saltash where I stayed with my seventeen-year-old son Malachi, who was helping with the fit up. We were in . . . a hangar, on the sea front. The rain lashed, the wind howled, the blow heaters blew, the company performed heroically. Crucial decisions were taken here. I decided to start the cycle with all our kit on stage at the beginning of *Henry IV Part 1*, so that audiences could see how clever we were in using it all . . . Then came what many considered a master stroke. If *Richard II* was necessary to understand the story, then we should re-cap the story of *Richard II*. In folk ballad form, a traditional and popular way of telling a story, speaking information. The troubadour tradition.

Taking as its title Hal's name for himself when disguised in *Henry V*, that little known Elizabethan/Victorian/contemporary folk ballad 'Harry Le Roy' was unearthed from the dusty back reaches of Michael's and my imagination. Terry Mortimer put a tune to it. (In America the ballad is already the subject of numerous doctorates. We are refusing to divulge our sources . . .) The background. We are telling the story, in four verses, of *Richard II*. We did not know at that point that we would be doing *Richard II* one year later. 'Harry Le Roy' was launched on the world and I chose the most junior member of the company to sing it: an Acting Assistant Stage Manager, who had the responsibility of leading the company out and introducing the whole cycle.

Skips and skips and skips of costumes, on loan and eventually hired from the National Theatre, were sifted through, tried on, accepted, rejected, as we attempted to fit characters, scene and mood. John Woodvine for the first time in gigantic white pudding padding, more like Michelin Man than Falstaff. The uniforms didn't work with the bentwoods and the collapsible tables. We decided to go more up-market. A heavier table was needed for the king, and a 'special chair'. Rough theatre was foundering on the rock of sophistication. Our splash of colour needed a splash of props to go with it. The sandbags leaked. The sliding screen . . . didn't. The white cloths wouldn't billow, pillow, create snowy landscapes. More a case of the Hesperus crossed with a St Moritz thaw. The tank, collapsible, used for the siege of Harfleur, was divided into two parts. At some venues it had to come from two separate entrances because of space. It was a real wobbly old Heath Robinson affair, the framework held together with pins. Michael leapt on it, staggered each time, regained his balance and began 'Once more unto the breach . . .' with smoke billowing around him, obscuring both face and voice. The tank fell apart on numerous occasions, finally to disappear from the production altogether halfway through the second year, much to my regret.

It was cold, it was wet, it was windy. It was November. The seaspray and gales lashed against the corrugated sides of the hangar. In no time, the props and costumes were filthy as they lay on the floor. The Theatre Royal was stretched to its limit with *Snow White*. An acrimonious battle was fought amongst us all to get the production ready in time, with the funds exhausted. Michael and I put our hands in our pockets (not for the last time) to the tune of £5,000 apiece to help the production get there. A desperate air of panic set in among the wardrobe staff and Chris Dyer and I were hardly communicating any more as we wrestled with great white canvas cloths that didn't do any of the things I wanted. Bits of old curtain and chenille table cloths were cut up to add a splash of colour to the Boar's Head. We had run out of money. Titus was unable to keep up with the changing pace of events. Mandi St Clair, wardrobe, was mostly in tears. I alternated all-night sessions on lights with Chris Ellis with all-night sessions trying to sort out the music. The extracts that I chose were as eclectic as the costumes, sometimes commenting on the action, sometimes complementing it. Schubert, Berg, Mozart, Handel, the

Chieftains, Vaughan Williams, Status Quo ('You're in the army now', No. 1 at the time, seemed to fit perfectly the mood at the end of *Henry IV Part 2*). Elgar, Purcell, Jarre, Bach. Many pieces I chose were used to stir religious and patriotic memories. Functional 'classic' excerpts, *Zadok the Priest*, 'Jerusalem', *Pomp and Circumstance*. Expediency mainly, culled from Dominic Peissel's personal collection, my own, and the Plymouth Theatre Royal sound department.

We were editing bits well into the run. A deal had been done for us to hire and then buy our sound equipment at the end of the run. It turned out to be a bad one. The lighting rig that we were taking with us was planned optimistically to extend to some two hundred appliances. Realism set in, and we ended up with ninety, Chris bending this way and that to achieve the maximum amount of coverage with the minimum number of lights. We bought two Zennon projectors, never used, a legacy of slides that Chris and I were going to throw onto the back screen. The screens jammed, broke, tore, didn't close, warped. Made of wood, made on the cheap. We changed them in the second year for ones made of lightweight steel, but they gave us trouble all the way. White Light, a lighting equipment company, had landed us in the hangar with a bum lighting board, not once but twice. That held us up. Michael P. post-synched the dialogue for his Sherlock Holmes movie into a cassette recorder, sitting in a hotel room with a telephone line permanently open to his worried producer in Los Angeles. Darryl Forbes-Dawson was beaten up by a bouncer in a club, sustaining injuries that would keep him away from the final rehearsals for a week. And yet somehow we moved to the theatre to open with *Henry IV Part 1* on Monday night with a full rehearsal of each of the plays behind us. Wednesday was *Henry IV Part 2*, Friday *Henry V* and then on Saturday, with no chance of a dry run, the plays unprepared technically – all three.

It was chaos.

Costumes and props were A.W.O.L. and no let-up in the afternoon or evening. No breaks for anyone from 8 am till midnight. And of course, the world and his dog were there. The assistant of Hans Neuenfels, Intendant of the Freie Volksbühne Theater, Berlin, where we were planning to perform in January, had been invited by the British Council to that very first Saturday All Day. (Who needs friends . . .?) He left at the interval of *Henry IV Part 1* that morning, saying that it was old fashioned and lacked political bite. I wrote to Neuenfels calling him an arsehole. It is extraordinary that those of us who work in theatre never seem able to understand the process of it. I long ago gave up judging productions at an early stage. Too many shows turn round from one performance to the next, too many actors stand on their heads from one night to the next. 'I wouldn't go and see it if I were you, it runs for four hours.' 'What? Don't be silly. It's two hours and no interval.' Theatre for me, now, is always work in progress. Just get on with it and try and get it better. And yet how many people in the theatre profession leave a theatre after a preview thinking they have seen a definitive version? As I pointed out to Neuenfels (strongly), by the time we reached Berlin the shows would have changed beyond recognition. 'A funny thing has happened on the way from Stratford to London' has written a certain *Guardian* critic on many an occasion. Nothing funny has happened at all. A show has merely played some eighty performances since the first night and is a different production.

That same first Saturday, the annual conference of the TMA (Theatre Management Association) was taking place in Plymouth. Saturday night out and *Henry V* was their treat. And it was. *Henry V* was in the best shape – hard, aggressive, textually like a whiplash, the production technically and visually assured. We stood on the stage that Saturday, having opened all three in five days, and then presented them in the space of twelve hours for the first time. As the cheers rang out I thought, 'How stupid can we get?!' The next year was to show us.

CHAPTER

3

THE FIRST TOUR

November 1986 – March 1987

'We are now again at Plymouth . . . we do
nothing but eat and scarce that . . . the
burghers have either had or conveyed all
their money. Never was extreme beggary
so extremely brave except when a company
of mummers had lost their box . . .'
John Donne, August 1597 (The year of
composition of Henry IV Part 1)

Pennington: At half past seven on the evening of our first trilogy
in Plymouth, John Woodvine made his entrance as the Chorus in
Henry V, all trace of John Falstaff's gross and greasy reality
scrubbed down to reveal a new slim, red-cardiganned profile.
Before he could open his mouth he was greeted with a spontaneous
ovation from an audience still warmed by a morning and afternoon
spent in the company of the Lord of Misrule, delighted to find that
the whoreson round man had in a sense survived Hal's mortal
rejection to return in this trim and reconditioned form. It was a
wonderful boost for John and for all of us approaching the
formidable final lap of the course; and if, that day, he was
momentarily disconcerted by it, even to a fluff, he became used
over the subsequent weeks to riding what became an almost routine
greeting from audiences wherever we went. I always found it
peculiarly moving: partly I was pleased that Falstaff and the Chorus

had indeed turned out to be a canny piece of doubling, and, more personally, it reminded me that I had first seen John Woodvine playing the Lord Chief Justice in *Henry IV Part 2* at the Old Vic in 1955, when he was a young actor and I was a stage-struck eleven-year-old setting a course for life. Naturally I felt very good about it.

In a way, the audience, like children, were glad to see Falstaff come alive again. Respecting the same illusion in an opposite way, I always felt that when Falstaff's death was described a little later in *Henry V*, it was somehow wrong to have John onstage as the Chorus; but perhaps that is taking it too far. Certainly there is a secret magic in the permutations of repertory; in the old days, a popular leading player in weekly rep could confidently expect an entrance round from a loyal audience every Monday, no matter what thin disguise he cared to adopt for the new play. His job security perhaps depended on it. The precedents are long and wide. In the Restoration theatre, vociferous claques, sometimes hired, cheered their favourites and barracked their rivals as they went along. In the 1840s, the French actress Rachel was able to complain to her exhausted *chef de claque* that his efforts in leading the attack – 'three acclamations, four hilarities, two thrilling moments, four renewals of applause and two indefinite explosions' – had disappointed her. In Kabuki theatre today, a hero can be greeted with cries of 'This is what I've been waiting for!' and his rival noisily denounced as 'a radish'. Be that as it may, there is no doubt that an audience anywhere likes to see a permanent company ringing its changes before their eyes and will combine suspension of disbelief with a degree of cheerful recognition. It is part of the human chemistry of the game.

In this sense, the ESC is an archetypal repertory company on the move, albeit working in a style that might have scandalised a traditional rep audience. Perhaps it was this audience that was represented by Mrs Joan Butler, whose letter to the Minister for the Arts on the subject of our work may be found in the Appendices to this book. Dr E.C. Hamlyn ('Speciality: Allergy Testing') wrote more tersely to me after our opening, complaining that having expected to see Shakespeare's *Henry V* he had been 'forced to endure a Pennington play until we could escape during the interval'. Our premiere in Wesley country brought us a few such letters of outrage but also a fan club which has since followed us literally around the world. Jeanette Nicholls works for the Manpower

Services Commission in Plymouth and has seen over fifty ESC performances. She accounts for it like this: 'I heard, and to my surprise understood, every word. No "poshspeak" but accents, regional to match the character's background. You've made Shakespeare accessible to many who would either never have bothered to go or on being forced to go on a school visit would never have returned. So thank you ESC for all that: for giving me back my imagination. I wish I had found you earlier.'

The Plymouth press, our first coverage, seemed to bear Jeanette out. 'The ESC has overnight become a major jewel in the crown of British theatre,' said the *Western Morning News*; while the *Western Daily Herald* declared that 'Mr Bogdanov has managed to fulfil the almost impossible task of making us see the play and hear the words as if it were being staged, for us, for the very first time . . . do not miss these plays . . . we shall not see their like again'; and the local *Guardian* critic described John Woodvine's performance as Falstaff as 'a truly grand portrayal of sycophancy . . . he glows in the part'. It was heady stuff.

As we moved on to Cardiff after the first real weekend off of the tour, the price paid for such an over-excited opening became evident soon enough. The company looked like shadows, shattered and withdrawn, and on the Monday night *Henry IV Part 1* threatened to fall apart. There were severe memory lapses among the principals (the prompt copy had to be consulted at one point); and instead of seizing the play away to compensate I was bland and lifeless as Prince Hal, flat as a pancake. A second night, or in this case a second date, is where the anatomy of a new show is really revealed; no longer blinded by adrenalin, the company can appraise its achievement in a merciless mirror. There were early departures in the audience; some money was handed back. Technically, our act was ragged also. Our mistake in not employing a Production Manager of our own, part of whose job would be the advance briefing of each theatre on our staffing and get-in requirements, was confirmed; our trust in Plymouth's handling of these arrangements was misplaced. In the flurry of getting the shows on, the advance work hadn't been adequately done; and at the Cardiff opening, for which we were barely ready, a benighted resident staff missed cues and, not having been briefed, threw inadvertent silhouettes onto the diaphanous back screen of the set: becoming, understandably, less helpful as they felt the confusion deepen. Michael Bogdanov's productions are unusually rich in outward gesture, and so they need, conversely, to be played with a real depth of conviction. But in Cardiff our acting generally was unconfident and coarse, laborious and rather vacant, and so the attitude struck looked cheap. The company, angered at our own showing, began to demand renewed rehearsal for performances that had obviously been prepared and opened at too great a speed; but on the other hand, the shows were barely lit and technically very unsettled still, so that time would have to be found to finish this work as well. From now on, there would always be a controversy about the best use of available hours. In an effort to steady ourselves, we agreed that we had, in effect, to demote Titus Grant – the first really tough managerial move we had made, and a painful one. With great good grace he remained as Stage Manager, but with Graham Lister promoted to Company Stage Manager over him. Titus was more comfortable and the shows tightened up. But small annoyances bloomed into large issues. The Allied Irish Bank reception on the Monday night in Cardiff was naturally, as we 'managers' thought we had made clear, open to all; perhaps the notice on the board was unhelpful or perhaps people were very sensitive, but a rumour ran round that only certain 'leading' players were really welcome. This first small misunderstanding between 'us' and 'them' would soon lead our company depressingly away from a degree of informal trust into retreat behind the old barricades of 'management' and 'workers'. Where quite that left me personally I wasn't sure.

On the shopfloor, we spent the rest of the Cardiff week recovering our onstage style – in some style: demonstrating that the test of a good company is its ability to recover from a setback. Anybody can rise to an occasion on a first night or give an inspired performance once in a while; the real proof of character is to get your head down and graft even when there is no following wind behind you. By the Saturday some integrity had returned to our work; this was a trilogy which was attended by Andrew Rissik from the *Independent*, the first national critic to be let in. John Shrapnel, with whom I was staying for the Norwich week, woke me up with this review the next sunny Tuesday: I couldn't have dreamed up a better one. For Rissik, 'the three linked productions . . . are a miracle of conscientious ensemble acting and audacious directorial forethought.' Rich in praise of Woodvine, O'Connell and myself, Rissik concluded that 'on this form, the English Shakespeare Company constitutes a daring and serious threat to the RSC and the National.'

He should have seen us earlier in the week.

Bogdanov: *This was also the Saturday that Michael Hallifax brought Jane and Bernie Sahlins of the Chicago World Theater Festival to see us. They were delighted, laid* Romeo and Juliet *with the RSC finally to rest and became enthusiastic supporters of our company. It was also the Saturday that Fleur announced to me that she was six months pregnant. I gulped, blinked, hugged congratulations and thought, 'What the hell are we going to do now?'; then got drunk with the Allied Irish, couldn't somehow manage to get the key in the door of my digs and, at five in the morning, wound up at the Holiday Inn.*

On to Bath. It was freezing. The stage was too small. I had to open the scene dock doors at the back of the stage out into the street and build a platform there to hold the lights set behind our screen and to store some of the larger items of furniture. We erected scaffolding round this, and covered the whole thing with tarpaulin. The iced wind howled through straight into the auditorium. The first ten rows sat huddled in overcoats and gloves, shivering. The constant rattle of chattering teeth provided a percussive background to the action.

Pennington: Meanwhile, we huddled with Fleur in the company office to consider the story so far. The news was discouraging from every point of view except the artistic. Berlin had indeed pulled out of their January date, confirming their disappointment in our politics; Michael B. had flown to Düsseldorf to clinch our deal there, only to be told that, faced with a million-and-a-half mark deficit on their year's budget, the theatre had suddenly cancelled all guest performances. So we now had two incomeless holes in January, with only Ludwigshafen, Cologne and Hamburg, buoyed up with the success of Michael's *Julius Caesar*, holding firm. Meanwhile, all our bills were in, showing that our production costs had gone £20,000 over budget. Weekly running costs over the first six weeks were averaging nearly £30,000: £3,500 above the maximum guarantees we had been able to get from the theatres; and in Norwich, where we had been unguaranteed, we had lost £13,000 – despite the enthusiasm of the *Independent*. The accumulated deficit by the end of the current week could well be £54,000; and we were already in dispute with Plymouth over the value of the production services. Could we make the money up during the rest of the tour? We had our original guarantees in Hull, Sunderland and Leeds, so would at least be losing at a predictable rate; unguaranteed Oxford was a worry; Manchester might make us something. There was to be a built-in profit in Canada of £40,000; the Old Vic was budgeted at break-even. All in, we could be up for a £30,000 deficit by the end of the season — not a huge one as these things go, but we had no means of dealing with it. Might there be other dates we could pick up, even though Berlin and Düsseldorf had dropped out? It was 10th December. Where could we go? Theatre availability aside, we faced a typical crux. If we took a week off we would still have to pay out £14,000 in salaries and other expenses; the moment we committed ourselves to playing we incurred £30,000 costs; so we had to be sure of taking the difference between the two to make playing into the lesser of two evils. None of it looked very good. I suggested going to Chichester for the two cancelled German weeks — in the depth of winter of course, at very short notice, and in no position to dictate terms. We rang Paul Rogerson and John Gale there and were welcomed on a decent 70% – 30% split; a Press Conference was swiftly set up to announce this special late attraction. We would need a bit of luck and we would have to spend some more on extra publicity; but Chichester draws on a big catchment area, in practical terms everything between Bristol, London and the Isle of Wight, and, with seat prices to match the relative affluence of the south, we could be in with a chance.

Meanwhile, could we reduce our costs in any way? Her mind made specially acute by these problems, Fleur thought she had spotted an anomaly, an area of woolly budgeting which we could legitimately tighten. Unfortunately it lay right in the path of the acting company's interests. We were playing nine shows a week, by virtue of the extra performance on Saturday morning, and paying the statutory one eighth of a week's salary to everybody for it. But we were also paying an element of overtime incurred by this morning show, and that in two respects. The Equity overnight break was eleven hours; unless we got a move on with *Henry V* on a Friday night, the break between the end of that performance and the half hour call on Saturday morning was more like ten and a half, so there was an hour's overtime there: that was unarguable. But the issue of overtime on the Saturday itself was debatable. Clearly the long working day exceeded the statutory ten hours; but that was because of the morning show. If we paid overtime as well as the ninth performance fee for this, were we not in reality paying twice over for the same period of work? Did not the extra performance payment implicitly include the overtime? We turned for guidance to the Provincial Theatre Contract, the Equity guidebook under which we were operating; but its overtime clause and its extra performance clause were not qualified by any cross-reference, and it seemed unlikely that it had ever been tested by an arrangement as unusual as ours. The RSC and the National, where such circumstances might arise, had at length negotiated their own contracts with Equity; but as a new company we had had to inherit an existing one and it didn't altogether fit. Our very originality was creating acres of grey area.

But – and here was the mistake – we had already set a precedent. For the first three Saturdays of the tour we had made both payments, pending the moment when we could tackle the question. If we continued to pay them both, it would cost us some £17,000 over the season. Perhaps we were morally obliged to continue; but on the other hand the logic of our present case did seem reasonable, and since the point was at least debatable, we could surely rely on the company's goodwill to reach an accommodation. We called a company meeting and stated our case, dwelling on our financial problems and making gloomy forebodings for the future; we proposed paying either overtime or the ninth performance, whichever was higher for the individual. The company kept its counsel; but the following morning we had an alarmed call from Jack Phipps, Head of Touring at the Arts Council, wanting to know what was going on. One of our company, whose name he wouldn't reveal, had reported to him overnight that we were going bust and would either foreshorten the tour or ask the company to accept a salary cut. Both measures were obviously taboo; despite our hot denials, the Arts Council's newest client was not inspiring confidence at 105 Piccadilly.

We had obviously made a mistake, and had Christmas to introspect on it – and also on Fleur's pregnancy, a joyful event that was going to re-order the New Year somewhat. We should not have linked a contractual point with our own difficulties; it smelt of blackmail. We should not have paid up for three weeks and then attempted to stop, since nothing is more provocative than taking something away. On the other hand, though it had been a bit late in the day, we couldn't really see that we were in bad faith. There was of course another way of looking at it. Morris Perry was Equity Deputy, the shop steward that every company must appoint to protect its interests and liaise with Equity head office; and he has

Henry V: Exeter at the French Court – (foreground) Morris Perry (Exeter), Clyde Pollitt (King of France), Darryl Forbes-Dawson (Orleans), Hugh Sullivan (Constable) (LB)

Backstage: June Watson (JT)

Backstage: John Price (JT)

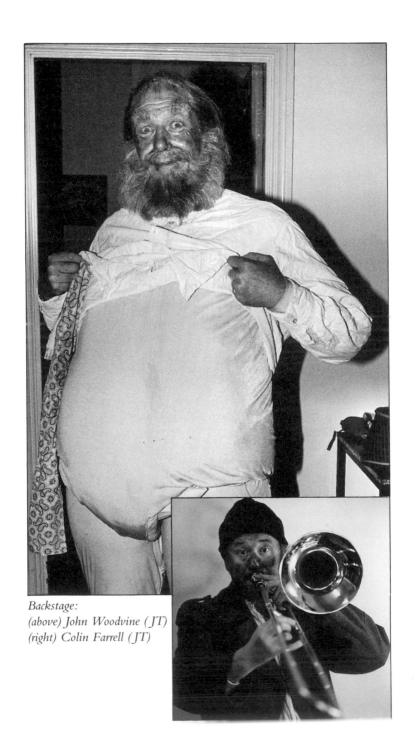

Backstage:
(above) John Woodvine (JT)
(right) Colin Farrell (JT)

no doubts that the contract called for both payments: 'A thorough discussion early on would have brought to light the overtime implications of the contract and the management would not have been caught unawares. Actors who spend a lot of their lives fighting for a decent wage have a strong resistance to giving part of it up after a contract has been signed.'

We felt we had offered a decent wage either way. We took advice from the Theatre Management Association and then, hoping to solve the immediate problem, we rang Equity and suggested a compromise, offering to pay one seventh of a week's salary rather than one eighth and so call it a day; Equity said that sounded pretty reasonable and promised to recommend this solution to the company in the New Year. Meanwhile we – and not only we – sourly contemplated a certain loss of idealism, and felt something congealing within our spirits. Our amiable approach to management, by which we had hoped to avoid traditional mistrust, had clearly not worked. During the vexed meeting in Bath, we had offered to throw the books open to illustrate our difficulty; but the company had not been interested in that, declaring privately that we would probably cook them before opening them. Old patterns die hard; we weren't a co-operative certainly, and perhaps it is in the nature of actors always to distrust managements, deriving a healthy energy from doing so. At any rate we and our company were beginning to feel ambiguous about each other. For me, I was deeply dispirited to find that I was referring to 'the company' as if I wasn't one of them.

However, an incongruous hope had taken shape at this inauspicious moment. Ever since the early days of rehearsal and perhaps before, we had, encouraged by the evident strength and versatility of our team, sensed a possible development of the ESC's work, if it should be spared to fight another day. Then, as if to remind us, Stephen Barry, manager of the Bath Theatre Royal, had stood with Michael Bogdanov outside his box office on the crisp Saturday morning of the trilogy. The queue for tickets was evidently warming his cockles. 'Why don't you add the other Histories and perform all of them in a weekend? I'll launch you here.' Yes, indeed. Lurking beyond the three *Henrys* are the tantalising shadows of the other five plays that complete the cycle, linked to each other as a continuous narrative, though composed at widely varying times. We were tackling numbers two, three and four in the series; if we could add *Richard II* onto the front, and the three parts of *Henry VI* and *Richard III* onto the end, we would have the entire sequence, something never attempted since the famous Peter Hall–John Barton *Wars of the Roses* at Stratford in 1964, and certainly never seen on tour before. All sorts of stylistic, not to say organisational, problems immediately suggested themselves; there was, for example, the question of the rambling *Henry VIs*, early and uneven works which, when they are done at all, are as often as not condensed into two plays. In thinking about it, we had assumed that it would take us two more seasons to add these four plays, introducing two at a time; now, under the influence of a crisis (and Stephen's encouragement), we were inclined to fight our way out of the corner more fiercely. What about doing them all in one swoop, taking thirteen weeks to rehearse, and then two years on the road, here and abroad, to recoup their expense? We tried to avoid using the phrase 'going for broke', since presumably that was what we were shortly going to be. Financial peril aside, the idea would only work if the majority of the company cared to stay with us, so that *The Henrys* could remain intact, requiring merely a brush-up; and clearly John Woodvine was a crucial part of that. We took him to lunch. John applauded the plan, but seemed reluctant to continue with the burden of his Falstaff, joyous as it was: though to be offered Richard III might, he felt, create a new energy in him.

There is an old Sussex proverb that says that when one half of Chichester goes to sleep, the other half goes on tiptoe for fear of waking them up. When we arrived in early January thick snow effectively muffled our footfalls. As it turned out we had new reason to deplore the perfidy of Berlin and Düsseldorf. Considering the lateness of the hour, the box office response here had been good; but of course many people only pay when they collect their tickets. Snowdrifts were beginning to cut Chichester off from the surrounding county; the phones clattered with cancelled bookings. In the end we played to an average 20% capacity, and lost £36,000 in two weeks. The press was fulsome and the happy few delighted; in fact the visit laid the foundation for a visit with *The Wars of the Roses* twelve months later that was as successful as this was disastrous; but that all lay in the abysm of time.

Bogdanov: *In fact, the performances were terrific, utterly against the odds. Chichester was only one of many re-stagings. No* *overhead bridge, no flying, no wings, no storage space. Entrances from vomitoria in the audience – the classical thrust stage, bare, exposed and absolutely the wrong space for the productions. In two days I did a whirlwind re-staging, stripping the props and the action down, placing what furniture we could use around the side in the audience. A complete re-light. (The basis of this staging was used a year later to open the Globe Theatre, Tokyo.) The performances and the texts were suddenly as spare and clear as could be. If anything bound the plays together at this time, it was these bare stage performances in Chichester. Why not perform them like that all the time? Ah ha! Something was missing. The tank.*

Pennington: In the chilly midst of all this the company unanimously rejected our compromise offer on the ninth performance – either Equity Head Office had not recommended it as they had promised, or Morris had not passed the recommendation on, for it seemed that no one had heard of it. Morris: 'Equity did not "recommend" this offer as Michael states. They told me that if the ESC company were in favour, they would agree too, but the company rejected the compromise. The Michaels and Fleur later wrote to me accusing me of not adequately putting Equity's point of view. I was incensed and got the company to support a rectifying statement. I am still waiting for an apology from the Michaels and Fleur.' Fine nuances had thus led to mutually bludgeoning behaviour. Incredibly, the only course now open to Equity and ourselves was to allow the disagreement to go to the Provincial Theatre Council for arbitration, an admission of industrial defeat for both sides, and not the kind of language we had hoped to be talking after only five months of the company's life.

There was nothing warming to do but to dream of *The Wars of the Roses*. Did we have the resources for it? The permanent set would be fine, although Michael and Chris Dyer would have to be extremely ingenious in ringing enough changes on it to justify twenty-one hours on the eye. The acting strength of the company was self-evident, but there was a big range of key parts we would have to be sure of casting strongly. I thought I should play Richard II, feeling well suited and having wanted to do it for a long time; but I didn't think it would be right to do any more front-line work, since the company was now a force in itself and all sorts of talents needed displaying. Much as we both admired John Woodvine, we felt that though he could certainly encompass Richard III in a one-off production of the play, the linking of the piece to the preceding *Henry VIs* calls for a Richard who emerges in his twenties and lives only to his historical age of thirty-five. On the other hand John would be wonderful as Richard's father the Duke of York, the iron man of the *Henry VIs*, if he would consider it. York and the rest of the violent nobles provide much of the energy of these plays, sometimes overshadowing the title role, which both is and isn't the leading part. Pious and politically feeble, King Henry is central to the story, but it is the effect of his weakness on his country, rather than his intrinsic character, that gives the plays their meaning. The part is simply written – compared say with Richard II, the other weak king – but he occasionally has to carry the play alone, as in the great meditation on the mole-hill, where he is flanked on the battlefield by a son who has killed his father and a father who has killed his son. David Warner had had a great success in the part, and Alan Howard too. We were looking at a much less experienced actor, Paul Brennen, a volatile Geordie who had joined the company in an agony of nerves which had disappeared the moment he was encouraged not to speak poshly but to use his own voice. The deplorable mystique of 'how to do the verse' had paralysed him, but now he was in full sail, chafing at not being able to find more in the parts of Peto and Vernon. There's nothing more to be found in them, I suggested one day outside the Body Shop in Bath, both of us swinging our plastic bags. It was frustrating, but on the other hand could it not be a positive challenge to do the same thing in the same way every night? To his credit he didn't believe me, as I wouldn't have done him. Paul is an explorer, pale and arresting, with fine bones, sensitive without being soft, oddly ageless. Henry VI.

But if he played Henry, what to do about John Dougall, who was understudying Hal, playing John of Lancaster and revelling in a variety of comic cameos – we should have known he would turn out to be more like Will Hay than John Barrymore. He did have a certain claim on Henry VI, the rather predictable claim of the classical romantic he in part was. But then, I was already a bit old for Prince Hal and not getting any younger. If, instead of Henry VI, John was now ready to tackle Henry V, perhaps he could pretty soon take it over from me. Queen Margaret belonged unquestionably to June Watson if she would care to do it. The biggest question was Richard III himself, the 'foul bunch-backed toad'.

One of the very longest parts in Shakespeare, probably more demanding technically than Hamlet, Richard calls for a rare combination of temperament, expertise and imagination, and , for what it's worth, enjoys a high pedigree as a 'star' part in the public mind. To play Richard, like Macbeth or Iago, requires of an actor an empathetic acquaintance with evil, belief in a malign principle beyond mere vindictiveness, that lies beyond the limits most people set on their imagination; and he needs an instrument tuned to the part's brain-splitting frequencies. Richard III is an embodiment of what we most fear in ourselves, and can perhaps only enjoy in ritualised form; like Raskolnikov in literature or the Moors murderers in life, he lives in a dizzying area beyond moral restraint, where all values become laughably unreverberative. So there aren't a lot of actors able to take you there. Olivier, using some dark inner resources, had done it, and so had Ian Holm in the Hall – Barton version: terrifying creations in quite different ways which still wrung pity from the part's tormented, dream-riven end. But Richards don't, as Edmund Kean once affrontedly declared in dissociating himself from the Drury Lane management, 'grow on every shrub and tree'.

Among us, apart from John Woodvine, John Price was passionate to play it, having all the credentials – a distinguished classical career, acres of experience, charisma, flair and invention (his Pistol was growing like a mad mushroom), but perhaps not quite suggesting the pure wickedness of Richard. I had a riskier idea and used an understudy run-through of *Henry IV Part 1* – Michael was now in London, putting *Romeo and Juliet* into the Barbican – to check on a dark horse. This was a run that quickly became known in the company as The Audition, since it was obvious by now what we were up to. But we had to do it anyway. A healthy understudy system is one of the infrastructures of a good company, a reserve that, as everyone knows, may have to be tapped at a moment's notice; however, understudy casting is sometimes casual and expedient, and then its victims don't bother much with the work, so that a run-through can often be a rather dismal affair, extended endlessly by dries and uncertainty. We had been determined that this part of the job should feel important; and the company responded in Chichester with a performance that was word-perfect and an exciting alternative to the main show: brilliant. I was watching Gadshill, who was playing Hotspur this afternoon. Andrew Jarvis had joined us to do rather lowly work on the face of it, but he seemed just to want to be a part of it all; and at the last moment before starting we had also asked him, almost casually, to play the Dauphin in *Henry V* – a showy and intemperate part to which he was now bringing physical freedom and neurotic comedy. Andy was one of the many revelations of rehearsals. At a certain stage in his career, he had shaved his head for a part and then left it shaved – an oddly extrovert gesture by the mildest and most self-effacing of men. He is all paradox, looking like a demon and behaving like an angel, and I still can't say I know him; he loyally supports Division Four Chesterfield, his home town, but is obsessed with the violent ambition of Macbeth above all other parts; he is gentle and heterosexual while conveying an arrogant bisexuality on the stage. In other words he is, absolutely, an actor. What is not paradoxical at all is his unflinching devotion to the work in hand. As Hotspur in the understudy run, he was so sure of his lines that he had the leisure to explore the part in some depth, finding in it the expected bravado but also a magnetic, reckless amorality. Obviously he should play Richard III.

With only quickening enthusiasm to back our case – but wasn't that all we'd come in with? – we took *The Wars of the Roses* to our Board of Directors in February. Perhaps it wasn't the best moment to do it. With the accumulated deficit up after Chichester to nearly £90,000, we had gone on to play our January German dates. Our Saturday marathon in Hamburg had been so successful that it had led to an exploratory approach from the Lord Mayor to Michael Bogdanov on the subject of taking over the direction of the Schauspielhaus from Peter Zadek in two years' time. It had also taken place on the day of national elections. The theatre was full, and television screens flickered unattended in the foyer. Some of the politicians were in the stalls; and when the polling returns came through, John Woodvine and Clyde Pollitt incorporated into their basket of pippins in Justice Shallow's Orchard Scene a placard announcing the results. The German visit had made us £7,000 which we had then proceeded to lose in Paris. Our expenses here had simply run ahead of our guarantees. It had been a memorable date. We had arrived at Orly in a snowstorm and had to push-start the bus that was meeting us – the beginning of a relationship with coach travel that never improved much. We were stationed in a hotel on the north edge of Paris, three quarters of an hour from Aulnay-sous-Bois, where we were to play the Espace Jacques

Prévert, a venue quite unused to professional performances. Among other things, this meant getting home after the show on the Friday night after midnight and leaving on the bus at half past eight on Saturday morning for the trilogy. Such arrangements incline a company to tetchiness. If you were at all thin-skinned, you wouldn't want to be the last onto the bus after the show – God help any slow changer at that stage, or, most taboo, anybody who went off a-wooing in Aulnay-sous-Bois without mentioning it to the counter of heads. On the opening night of *Henry IV Part 1* the lights strobed throughout King Henry's first scene; the second scene, in Prince Hal's lodgings, was always staged with two washing-lines of laundry drying overhead, which on this night overstayed into the third scene, which is set in the King's Privy Council. A formidable diamond formation of the King's inner cabinet, all in royal red regalia, thus confronted and outfaced the rebellious Hotspur while Prince Hal's smalls dangled insouciantly over the proceedings, a white sock gently tickling Sir Walter Blunt's head. After the opening our Paris promoters dashed around with coats over their shoulders to usher us into a reception graced by the presence of the British Ambassador and sponsored by Marks and Spencer; the company chomped on not-quite-thawed blackcurrant cheesecake and threw back whiskey and sherry (no froggy wine here) which brought the event to its natural chemical conclusion with some speed; and the Ambassador, in complimenting June Watson on her performance as Mistress Quickly, asked her if she spoke any English.

None of which merriment distracted the gentlemen of the Board, who noted only that we had managed to lose the £7,000. For some reason they seemed to have doubts about the future. Perhaps they had observed that though we had with some skill managed to get back from Paris to Hull (despite ferry strikes and regulations forbidding lorry traffic around Paris after two in the morning) in plenty of time for the Monday opening there (which at one time we feared we might have to cancel – we have in fact never cancelled), the end of the week in Hull had displayed the less acceptable face of the great touring tradition. We had run out of money. All the staggered payments due from the Arts Council, the Mirvishes and the A.I.B. were now in, all the theatres' cheques likewise, and we were turning red. It may be asked why we had no bank overdraft facility. We were in fact banking with the Allied Irish, hoping that there might be some advantage in banking with the sponsors. When we had applied for an overdraft facility the bank had asked us for collateral, and all we could offer was a few sticks of office furniture and a warm and friendly relationship with our sponsors in Old Jewry. No overdraft.* We were still arguing the point when pay day in Hull arrived. A rapid phone call to the Mirvishes elicited an advance of half the profit promised for Canada, we met our obligations, and an already irritated company, in its ignorance, stayed merely irritated. Observing these developments, the Board expressed reservations about our two year 'Megaplan', feeling it was perhaps 'not quite the right development for the ESC at the moment.' We didn't listen.

As winter bit deeper, so did all the realities – geographical, financial, personal.

Bogdanov: *Without Fleur, we were rudderless. We asked Peter Stevens, then a senior producer with Granada TV, if he would take over temporarily as custodian of the ESC finances, Acting Executive Producer. His office at Granada was just across the way, in Golden Square; the arrangement was, on paper, a good one. Peter is one of the best runners of subsidised theatre this country has seen. A hundred decisions will be taken in half an hour, on the basis that two-thirds will be right and the others will return for re-assessment. This hustle is both Peter's strength, and occasionally his downfall. He was opposed to the Megaplan. He produced a set of figures showing that we would need an unrealistic total of £700,000 to finance the productions. At the next board meeting he produced a paper arguing for a period of consolidation the following year, wanting only* Richard II *and then going for the big one in the third year. 'REASONS: (a) The ESC is a very young organisation which should not be pushed too far, too fast. (b) Our current problems arise from an ambitious and innovative policy, quickly realised with inadequate planning, administrative support and contingency resources. Admirable yes; prudent no . . . (c) I do not believe the seven-play cycle can be negotiated and assembled in the short term; its organisation is complex and beyond the competence of our immediately available staff . . .' A vote was forced in which a show of hands of those present supported Peter. Only Michael Hallifax argued cogently for backing our hunch that we had to strike while hot. The meeting broke up with Peter*

---

*We got it later.

assuming that the plan was shelved. He was wrong. Michael and I had not fought this hard and far to be railroaded. If necessary, to raise the funds, we would re-mortgage our respective properties. We had to carry on in any case. Already we were going to accumulate a deficit we couldn't pay off. In a flurry of phone calls, we made it clear that, vote or not, we were going ahead. We were not convinced that we would be able to hold the company together long enough to do all the plays in the third year and I couldn't face the thought of having to completely re-cast and re-rehearse. Peter resigned, to be followed shortly by Howard and Jules. These were indeed dark days.

Pennington: The tour was turning monochromatic, too. By some kind of beginner's luck our two-part schedule had fallen neatly into two sections: the cushy south of England before Christmas, the north afterwards. We had presented this orderly arrangement at the outset to a succession of amazed actors who were expecting to zigzag by the week from Glasgow to Norwich to Swansea to Southampton to Edinburgh. We'd all done tours like that. The ESC's geographical patness seemed miraculous, and we had hastened to pass it off as intentional. Now, coming to the point, it turned out to be instructive in unexpected ways. It's true that you have never really toured until you've changed trains at Crewe in midwinter; more importantly, it was impossible in the late '80s to ignore the acute social and economic divide that stretches from the Mersey to the Wash, gaping wider by the year. In Hull, the pervasive aroma of fish hangs over the city like the ghost of prosperity past; sobered and guilty, we would huddle in the artificial New Theatre coffee bar, which sought to project a sort of cosy southern comfort, or in the cavernous rooms of one of the very few genuine railway hotels left in the country, its towering ceilings looming over the baths and beds, its prices lowered to bed and breakfast rates.* We dropped the prices in Hull to £9 for a best seat, £3 for the cheapest (all three shows for £10 on a Saturday); and the following week at the Sunderland Empire (a beautiful old house opened by Vesta Tilley), £6.50 was the top and £2.50 the bottom; the most expensive seat there was thus cheaper than the

---

*I was, blamelessly, breathalysed outside this hotel by a young copper who then entered me in his report as a 'theatre player', which seemed a noble thing to be.

cheapest seat at Bath (£7 in the gallery). Even if you kept your eyes closed in the street and looked only at the narrow perspectives of theatre business, you could hardly fail to see a thin red line drawn thick.

In Sunderland, the theatre ran out of programmes on the trilogy day, not having printed enough, not having thought there would be a demand. Nevertheless, both they and Hull did manage to guarantee us, which is more than can be said for the Apollo Oxford on our one trip into the opulent south that spring; and they also billed us correctly. At Oxford, the front of house marquee proclaimed us until Wednesday morning as the Vienna Festival Ballet in *Swan Lake*; by Thursday this had been changed to the Royal Shakespeare Company in *The Henrys*. One must look beyond such surface gaffes to the real state of things beneath. The Oxford Apollo was formerly the New Theatre and, together with the Hippodrome at Bristol and the Empire at Liverpool, was a distinguished staging-post on the major tour circuit of the past. All three now belong (together with some smaller venues) to an entertainment chain called Apollo Leisure, who I think interpret the concept of leisure rather freely. It is safe to say that the reduction of overheads appears to be a cornerstone of Apollo's managerial policies: staff, equipment and upkeep are held to a lean minimum while revenue is maximised by the most immediate means, most obviously by rock concerts. All the theatres in the chain are centrally controlled, so that local managers have little authority to take even immediate decisions. There are usually little or no marketing personnel attached (except where the Arts Council in dismay have put their own representative in), so that visiting companies, often based far away, have to depend on their own initiative to sell their shows; there are no established mailing lists of the public available and advance publicity leaflets supplied by the visiting company have been known to sit at the theatres undistributed until the playing week itself; meanwhile box office staff seem reluctant to provide information on advance ticket sales. Double bookings are quite common. Audiences who do get there can find seats with their springs exposed, or plastic beakers rather than glasses in the bars. Backstage an old-fashioned inequitableness prevails: when we played the Empire Liverpool in 1988, I was given a most luxurious dressing-room suite – two rooms designed for Cilla Black, the walls and ceiling satin-draped, no less than thirty glasses on the fridge (which shows that Cilla still gets far more visitors than I do) but the rest of the company climbed many flights to cramped rooms, dubious of their hygiene. During the week, no member of the theatre's administration either said hullo or sent any form of message, a traditional and basic courtesy to a visiting company. It goes without saying that guarantees are not generally offered; the theatres cover their rather low running costs, and the visitors limp away.

Apollo Leisure are at the time of writing one of the subjects of an urgent Arts Council survey into the management of regional theatres; the impact of its findings remains to be seen. Our experience with Apollo accentuates an eerie feeling that the ESC's hopeful baptism coincides with a deep corresponding decline, so that the work we have been created to do has fewer and fewer good homes to go to. Certainly when such conditions prevail in an area as depressed as Merseyside, the chances of bringing an audience back in are disappearing fast. Despite brilliant individual initiatives, there is now no overall repertory movement in this country to speak of; many touring theatres offer a bleak and impersonal welcome; and the Cork Report, reflecting these constrictions, has recommended six strategically-placed 'centres of excellence' in the country to mop up an audience that once found live theatre on its doorstep but might now have to travel many miles to find such a centre. At the ESC our peak of energy has sometimes felt like a simultaneous nadir of hope.

Bogdanov: *I caught up with the shows in Sunderland. By an irony, my production of* Romeo and Juliet *opened in Newcastle the same week as part of the RSC season and was followed in by* Richard II, *the play preceding our sequence. I had followed* The Henrys *through Hamburg and Paris, but the north of England in February/March is the acid test of any work.* Henry IV Part 1 *in Sunderland on that Monday night was probably the worst performance of the whole three years. I set about taking a series of notes and introduced cuts to bring the running times down. The response from the company was pretty surly.*

There was always to be an inbuilt paradox as far as on-going work during our punishing schedule was concerned. On the one hand, the company found it frustrating to play, week-in, week-out, without any artistic feedback. On the other hand, when that feedback came, and rehearsals called, many wanted to sleep in or do other things. All agreed that the shows needed cutting, but when

*it came to losing lines, nobody was first in the queue. I put my foot
down. Cuts there would be. John Woodvine accused me of
favouring Michael P. and penalising himself and Paddy. I added up
the cuts in* Henry IV Part 1. *The totals were as follows: John lost
34 lines, Michael 28, Paddy 27, John Price 17, Donald Gee 14,
assorted others 14. Total 134. Not a lot. And achieved with great
acrimony. It brought the running time of* Henry IV Part 1 *down
from 3 hrs 20 mins to 3 hrs 10 mins. Still too long. But the K. up
the A. had the desired effect. By Saturday, the shows had made an
enormous leap forward. Many chums came over from the RSC in
Newcastle for the day and enthused. Then, after the shows, we all
went back with them to Newcastle, where the RSC threw a party
for the ESC in the Crest Hotel. Whatever sour grapes existed on the
part of the RSC direction ('How can they do that, the RSC taught
them all they know'), the two companies knitted together like old
friends (which many of them are). It was a wholly satisfying union.*

Pennington: We completed the tour with weeks at the Palace
Manchester and the Hippodrome Birmingham, very much happier
dates at which the shows seemed to pull together in conscious
preparation for the undoubted significance of a London opening.
Onstage and offstage life, however, continued to diverge. Onstage
we were now a team working with some considerable ease and
grace, aware of each other, confident and exuding good health. But
offstage we were seething. The Equity dispute was now scheduled
for arbitration in London in March, and each side, God help us,
was preparing its case. More than that, a new dispute was looming.
The company's original contract had included the season in
Canada, for which the standard Equity stipulations on pay and
conditions would be overridden by those of Canadian Equity, and
this agreement everybody had duly signed. We knew that the very
much higher minimums in Canada would improve everybody's
financial position, and we would naturally try to maintain the
salary differentials in some way; but for a long time we had not
known exactly what weekly fee the Mirvishes would be paying the
ESC and so had not been able to finalise precisely what salaries we
could pay. Again, it would be all right, and commonsense would
prevail. On the other hand, time was going on, and the longer it
all remained unsettled the more suspicious the company were
becoming that we were pre-emptively narrowing their options.
Therein lay the misunderstanding: the company certainly felt they

had an option to renegotiate salaries for Canada from scratch, and therefore, if the deal was not to their liking, to decline to go. Morris Perry: 'As for Canada, I have a fat file on that alone. During the rehearsal period in England we were assured that the terms for Canada would be so delightfully generous we shouldn't be able to resist them. The management were reminded throughout the year of our wish to know more. The offer came very late and was in minimal terms. There were many difficult meetings.' The ESC, however, felt that the contract that had been signed was binding in any case, and as long as we were sensible about it and didn't infringe Canadian Equity's terms, there was no real complaint. In Manchester, now knowing our deal with the Mirvishes, the two of us sat down (Fleur being confined with a bouncing boy), and worked out all the deals, observing the Canadian minimum ($890 – roughly £440 a week) and keeping the differentials symbolically intact, though we reduced the size of the 'steps' to keep within our given budget. The higher the salary you drew, the less improvement you noticed. The 'offers' we made – ranging from £550 up to £850, which included an extra 25% in each case for the ninth performance – were rejected. Apart from objecting to the '*fait accompli*', many people were unappeasably worried about the living expenses they would have to meet out of pocket – we countered that Canadian Equity terms had regard to the standard of living in Canada: it is not an expensive country. The whole controversy represented another painful bind for all of us. Unless some accommodation was reached we were obviously heading for another showdown in which we as management would probably rail about breach of contract and the company about breach of faith.

Breached or not, faith was obviously shaken. Dissatisfaction with our business practices was leading to a wariness of Michael's and my general motives and work. Disagreeable incidents followed. One night in Oxford I was 'off' for the opening sequence of *Henry IV Part 1*, when the whole company presented itself to the audience and sang the Ballad of Harry Le Roy. I had in fact been gazing stupidly at my face in my dressing room mirror and hadn't heard the call for beginners, waking up only when I heard the music coming over the tannoy. It was the first time in my life that such a thing had happened, and I was disturbed – what was becoming of me? The next day the company demanded an explanation for my absence, suspecting that I was separating myself from the 'ensemble'. Michael, for his part, was flayed once again, as directors often are, for not being with the production enough and then returning after a long absence to give critical notes.* There were complaints that for all his strictures he had neglected individual performances, although much technical tightening up had been done, and so the shows were in their essence going downhill.

All this accumulated feeling burst forth during the final week of the tour in the following cataclysmic way. In the third scene of *Henry V* a rather unimpressive conspiracy led by Richard Earl of Cambridge challenges Henry's legitimacy to the Throne. His is one of the 'giddy minds' that Henry's father has advised him to 'busy . . . with foreign quarrels'. It is the third such rebellion in the three plays – Hotspur in *Part 1*, the Archbishop of York in *Part 2* – and each carries diminishing force. The final, feeble uprising is bungled and Henry deals with it with a self-righteousness that is rather unappealing in his character, and, in its repetitive zeal, quite difficult for the actor to sustain in performance – I, at any rate, found it a pig. On the Wednesday night in Birmingham, the sentencing to death of the traitors was punctuated by what Peter Shaffer in *Lettice and Lovage* describes with charm as 'an audible personal explosion', emitted by my lord of Cambridge, I think it was. Since we are all children, and to children there is nothing funnier than a noisy bottom, the traitors' arrest was accompanied by broad grins and heaving shoulders from both sentencers and sentenced. I am in a way ashamed to say I was furious, no doubt because I felt the scene was difficult and deserved all the help it could get. Afterwards, feeling uncannily like King Henry, I told the major guffawer that he pissed me off mightily, sensing as I said it the unwelcome musk of head-boyishness filling the air. The actor is an actor of distinction and longer experience than my own and

---

*It certainly can be rather annoying; as an angry young actor I once walked pompously out of one of Tony Richardson's note sessions, resenting any criticism that came out of a face so very suntanned. But a director works for a flat fee and ceases to be paid after the opening night. He must therefore go on to other projects, even if he does not, like Michael, have also to be arguing the ESC's case back in London to a Board and prospective backers. It is only in permanent companies that can afford to retain their directors (perhaps to work on other productions in the same building) or if the director has nothing else to do or is particularly obsessed, that he will be seen more than once in a while.

he told me where to get off. The story got around; a nimbus of deep dislike closed around me, and I walked most delicately all week among dark faces. I was right, but a prig; the company was wrong but had common humanity on their side. I never really got popular again that year, the actor-manager's ambiguous position permanently underlined.

Such was the flatulent end to a tour that had sometimes detonated with real thunder. Where was the eye of all the storms? In some respects, Michael and I had apparently alienated a number of our company, perhaps with the obverse side of the buccaneering spirit that had at first inspired them. Some sense of proportion had certainly been lost, never quite to be recovered; the mistakes were fairly obvious, mutual forgiveness rather limited. Often the only enjoyable place to be was on the stage, where everyone worked with the same passion, united for the most important moment. Every Saturday night we were being cheered by audiences who rejoiced to see what they had long missed: an energetic, committed ensemble working on the best texts in the language. Backstage, the ESC's face was becoming like Bardolph's – 'all whelks and knobs and flames of fire'. Certainly, the Birmingham incident had sealed my own fate for the time being. Unlike Queen Elizabeth I apocryphally greeting Sir Walter Raleigh back from a disgrace occasioned by an imprudently deep bow, our company did not forget the fart.

CHAPTER
4

THE OLD VIC AND TORONTO

April – July 1987

> 'A plum off my tree
> Bit a man on the knee.
> The man had a thirst,
> Got his own bite in first.'
> > Bertolt Brecht, The Good
> > Person of Szechwan

> 'How quick bright things come to
> confusion.'
> > Shakespeare, A Midsummer
> > Night's Dream

Pennington: *On the opening night of* The Henrys *at the Old Vic, or rather the first Saturday trilogy, to which the Press had been invited, Paddy O'Connell dried in his first speech as the King. Later that morning, I inspected my troops at Coventry as Prince Hal, and then hurried off to change into chainmail to fight against Hotspur, forgetting that I first had to report back to base camp and join my father in defying the Earl of Worcester. Neither of us had made such a mistake before in over fifty performances. We thought at our ages we would have known better than to be affected by the occasion.*

Nevertheless, the shows and the new company were enthusiastically received: 'The cumulative effect of Bogdanov's Henrys *is extraordinary in its grandeur and sweep' (*Sunday Telegraph*); 'The* *acting is magnificent' (*London Daily News*); 'This company may be the best thing to have happened to British theatre for years'* (Daily Telegraph*); 'A splendid enterprise stuffed with excellent performances' (*Evening Standard). *Not so Michael Billington, who, not to be bought by our breakfast at Brown's, saw little to recommend 'this dubiously Marxist reading of the Histories'. However, he did 'hail', as the saying goes, John Woodvine's Falstaff. Over the next few weeks he repeatedly declared himself 'worried' about the current state of Shakespearian acting and the* Guardian *once advertised his anxiety on their front page; meanwhile I looked out from my window overlooking the Cut to see exuberant audiences hurrying in to fill the theatre on trilogy mornings, the spring in their step only a little less as they came out for the lunch and tea adjournments, and still with the energy to rise to their feet at eleven in the evening in an unforgettable greeting to the company. It was an 'event' house at once fanatical and fashionable, a cross between dedicated Shakespearians, parental opportunists and the Glyndebourne lot. Bless them one and all.*

Bogdanov: *The Henrys* had originally been designed with the size of the Old Vic stage in mind, and the shows fitted like a glove. I was able to re-light them properly for the first time since Plymouth. The tank was back (still in two pieces) and with a week's work and hard note sessions, the plays were probably in the best shape they had been. The main objective was to stop the actors shouting. The empty, cavernous barns of Sunderland, Hull, Oxford, etc., had induced the desire in all to awaken the sleeping matinée figures of the OAPs lurking somewhere in the hinterland of the upper circles. Rhetoric ruled. Actors would stand side by side, facing out front in true operatic style and, under the pretext of having an intimate conversation, proceed to provide Dr Punt, voice specialist *renommé*, with a gorge full of torn larynxes. Once I had finally induced the company to talk normally, the acting improved by leaps and bounds.

Pennington: *Metropolitan* réclame *thus secured, management and company could now get on with the real business of quarrelling. Each side was getting ready for the Provincial Theatre Council Hearing, where a decision on the ninth performance was to be handed down by the theatrical equivalent of ACAS. I had to leave* *the hearing early to do a matinée; Michael Bogdanov stayed on to argue the case.*

Bogdanov: The issue, in simple terms, was this: while it was silent on the specific point, was it the intention of the Provincial Touring Contract that the same work should be paid for twice over? In the last round of negotiations over the drafting of the Subsidised Repertory Contract, an anomaly had been spotted, and the contract now included, in its conditions for overtime, the following: 'OVERTIME D.4(g). ⅛ of the Artist's salary shall be paid per performance in excess of 8 per week or 2 on any one day, *which shall not be included in the calculation of the 48 hour week*'. In other words – for nine performances you could *either* be paid ⅛ salary extra *or* the overtime but not both. This paragraph was to be the cornerstone of our argument. From the very beginning, we had accepted Equity's recommendation that we should use the Provincial Touring Contract for the company (rather than the Subsidised Repertory Contract), and it had proved, on many an occasion, unsuitable. Why had Equity so advised us? Other touring companies – Oxford, Cambridge, Compass – were on the Subsidised Repertory Contract with Touring Addendum. Why were we the exception?* The contract we were currently using was designed for commercial managements touring commercial product under completely different circumstances. It had never been drawn up with a company such as ours in mind – performing in repertoire, three shows on a Saturday.

The tribunal convened at the headquarters of the Theatre Management Association in Bedford Chambers. We were represented by Andrew Leigh of the Old Vic, who was to lead the case for the ESC, Fleur, plus baby-in-a-basket on the other side of the door, Michael P. and myself. When Michael had left for the matinée and Fleur to baby-mind, the floor was left to Andrew and myself. The actors were represented by Morris Perry and Gareth Thomas. Equity was represented by Marilyn Stoddart, with whom

---

* The following season we switched. Equity tried to stop us. We pointed out that, as a management, provided we offered a proper union contract, we could elect to operate what version we liked. Equity reluctantly accepted this.

we had already done honourable battle on a number of occasions.*
For the PTC, Rupert Rhymes (in the chair), Michael Bramble,
Vivyan Ellacott, John Gardener and Frank Williams. In
attendance, Peter Finch (Joint Secretary of Equity) C.R. Lacey
Thompson (Joint Secretary of TMA), and Veronica Velarde.

Morris put the case for the company; he was cogent and
reasonable. No hint or mention of the pressure the company had
exerted on Fleur to pay. Gareth was emotional. We had 'sold them
down the river', 'kicked them in the teeth'. All they had got for their
pains was 'a slap in the face'. Andrew, for us, was confused. He
attempted to do a Perry Mason. His cross-examination was
faltering, the points not made cogently enough. The hearing moved
into other areas. The stage management representative led an
attack on managements who attempted to get cheap labour in
return for long hours by offering low 'buy-outs', that is, no fixed
hours. I pointed out that our Stage Manager on a 'buy-out' had
been receiving £500 a week, *plus* his £100 touring allowance. The
representative's mouth dropped open. 'Good God, I wish I got
that.' I offered this bit of information to show that our intention
had always been to give our company a reasonable standard of
living. Our minimum wages at all times were higher than the RSC
and the National, the opera companies and the ballet. I brought the
hearing back to the main area of dispute, making the point that we
had taken advice from TMA/PTC and it was their suggestion that
an offer of one seventh of the salaries as a compromise should be
made as a fair indication of the management's good faith. We had
improved on that suggestion and had offered one seventh or the
overtime on a Saturday, whichever was the greater. Equity, we
understood, had agreed. It *should* have been accepted. How had it

---

*It is axiomatic that once a company starts asking Equity for its opinion,
it very soon becomes daily communication. Relations had reached such a
pitch that consultation was taking place about all sorts of extraordinary
things. One such was the hire of the instruments for Sneak's Noise. We
rejected a claim for a hire fee of £10 a week each for two recorders
belonging to a member of the company, pointing out to Equity that for
£500 in the year we could buy a couple of gold-plated ones. Similarly,
£750 for the hire of a mandolin and £2,000 for a basic drumkit was
patently ridiculous. We settled for more realistic sums, ranging from £75
to £150, and dropped Dominic Peissel's drumkit altogether. Our company,
one way and another, kept Equity going that year. Strangely, in
subsequent years there were far fewer problems.

come to this? Marilyn Stoddart said the Provincial Touring
Contract was 'crystal clear'. That is the problem with the contracts
Equity operates. They are so crystal unclear that they lead to
disputes such as ours. The muddy thinking is one of the reasons
why I was part of a five-year battle on behalf of the Directors' Guild
of Great Britain to pull directors out of Equity and form our own
union, which came about in December 1989.

The interests of directors and actors, as far as Equity is
concerned, are sometimes diametrically opposed. As a director, I
want more flexibility of rehearsal hours; representing actors,
Equity wants less. How to reconcile such opposed views? On this
occasion here I was, as a management, fighting with my own
union. It was, and always has been, an untenable position. All
these points I made in a passable speech when called upon to do
so; the bad advice given by Equity, as to which contract to operate,
the confusion of the Provincial Touring Contract itself; that it was
we who had sought the proper advice and had taken the
recommendation of one seventh put forward by the TMA, who had
assured us of their backing. They had agreed there was an
anomaly. It had never been intended by the joint TMA/Equity
negotiating committee that two lots of overtime should be paid.
There were also several examples of three performances given in
one day by other companies where only one eighth had been paid
and this had been accepted by Equity in the past.

We adjourned, leaving the committee to debate the problem.
Later in the evening Lacey Thompson phoned the result through to
the ESC office. Nothing, neither way.

'The Council have failed to resolve the contractual issue involved
in the case of Equity versus the English Shakespeare Company. The
Council feels, however, that certain payments are due to artists
under various headings (including West End work, breached
breaks and overtime amongst others), and directs that each and
every member of the company, both acting and stage management,
shall be paid an additional sum of £10 for each of the twenty-three
weeks [of the engagement] (excluding the first three, for which the
payment has been made), in full settlement of the claim.'

We breathed a sigh of relief. We had the edge on a moral victory.
The hearing naturally had been split. It was quite clear that there
was an anomaly, and it was silly pretending there wasn't. (At the
time of writing, the loophole still exists.) It transpired that the
mood was to concede the acting company something and the first

debate centred on £5 per person for some infringement of breaks. (All of them inadvertently incurred on trilogy days.) But that sum was considered too low and doubled to £10. In total, the payment represented to us a sum of £6,000 instead of £17,000. We paid up, and the most acrimonious chapter in the history of the ESC closed.

We were still without an administrator and a chairperson. Both came as recommendations from Jack Phipps of the Arts Council. David Kay of Goddard Kay Rogers, head hunters, ex-chairman of the Prospect Theatre Company, now disbanded, was interested in returning to the field. I knew him from a small group of theatre 'flutterers' (backers) called 'The Little Angels' organised by Andrew Leigh. He accepted our invitation to become Chairman of the Board, and then watched in amazement as four board members proceeded to resign. It says much for his fortitude at this point that he did not immediately say 'stuff this for a box of tin soldiers'. Melvyn Bragg, who right from the beginning had said he would only serve for one year, thought it inappropriate to leave at this point and decided to stay for another year. Victor Glynn had no intention of deserting. David had a Board of two.

Prue Skene had been an administrator of Ballet Rambert for ten years, retired temporarily to Bath, and now wanted to get back into the action. Prue had seen the plays at the Old Vic and we outlined the future plans and the difficulties. She agreed to join as Executive Producer with special responsibility for forward planning, sponsorship, finding permanent premises for the company, overseeing foreign contracts. She would come on a part-time basis only – three days a week; there being a hand-over period before Fleur finally departed, to link the work through. We were still thinking very much of our original structure of an Administrator and an Executive Producer, but Prue was determined at the beginning to see if she could manage on her own. (This was expediency on our part as much as policy – we couldn't afford an administrator any more.) She soon wished she hadn't. Theatres were excited by the prospect of seven plays all in one week but couldn't wrap their heads round the marathon weekend idea. Even Stephen Barry, so enthusiastic a proponent of the idea, copped out of that one and, in the event, outside of London, the only cycle that we completed in a fifty-six-hour weekend in the UK was for Jude Kelly at the York Festival in flaming June with no air conditioning.

For posterity, we privately videoed *The Henrys* at the Old Vic on one camera from the back of the stalls. Fortuitous as it turned out. The only record there is of John Price's memorable Pistol and John Woodvine's unforgettable Falstaff. It was an initiative on the part of the Allied Irish Bank for whom John Price represented all that was best in the company, an indefatigable ambassador at all receptions. There had been some A.I.B. hoolies on the way round, but none to match the last night at the Old Vic. The bank managers – Brian Wilson (Group General Manager, Britain), Tom Carey (General Manager, A.I.B. Corporate International), plus our old mates Niall Gallagher, Declan Mullen, Joyce Austin and Martha O'Neil – eschewed their normal suits, hired an Irish band and turned up to yelp and hoof the night away in Aran sweaters and pullies.

Somewhere around 4.30 am Niall collared me and extracted a long-held promise to accompany him in what can only be described as an appropriately shaky version of 'Seven Drunken Nights'. It was a fitting end to a triumphant season, and we all tottered into the Cut on a soft May morn feeling the world was alright, alright.

Pennington: *Which, from the company's point of view, only left Canada. Was the money good enough? Were per diems included? How good were these apartments that had been booked? What was the real cost of living there?* A number of people swore they wouldn't come, come what may. We wrote letters of explanation which were disbelieved. I eventually went back to the Mirvishes to beg for $8,500 a week more so that we could satisfy the company's demands, and they gave it to us, still smiling, just. In the middle of all this, Grand National day dawned and we had a sweepstake. The kitty amounted to £75. Some studied the form assiduously, some just fancied a name, some, like myself, carelessly chose a horse without even a pretence at clairvoyance. It was mine that came in. I now had £75 of the company's money in my pocket. There was some pointed singing of 'God Bless the Child' ('Them*

---

*Bogdanov: At one acrimonious meeting, Andrew Leigh produced a comparative shopping list for Toronto and London, solemnly reading out the prices of bread, tomatoes, onions and milk. This was contested with cries of 'Rubbish! Barrie Rutter [from a recent National Theatre visit] says Toronto is the most expensive city in the world.' One member was in tears at the thought of being so poor; another accused us of starving wife and child out of house and home, as he would be unable to pay the mortgage. In the event, Toronto proved inordinately inexpensive and most pockets came home loaded. There were no apologies and no acknowledgements.

that's got shall have/Them that's not shall lose') in the corridors, but really it was impossible not to laugh. The incident probably did more than the PTC Hearing to reconcile both sides. I bought a crate of wine for us all costing a little more than £75 and for a moment all antagonisms were sluiced away.

We flew to Toronto intact: everyone came in the end, except for one – myself; my mother had been taken seriously ill the night before and I postponed my flight till the last moment before our opening. On that night we strode onto the Royal Alexandra stage with our usual air of, we hoped, relaxed purposefulness, for the *Ballad of Harry Le Roy*, guitars cocked threateningly, braces half on, hands plunged in pockets, striking our non-attitude that was itself an attitude. We were faced by a rather unfestive audience of regular subscribers to the Alex, representing the conservative end of a rather conservative city. We had always been proud that a new classical company had announced itself everywhere it went with the unaccompanied voice of our most junior ASM, singing the deathless lines of our Ballad; it declared certain freedoms. We waited for him to arrive. After a pause he strode out onto the stage wearing nothing except a pair of boxer shorts which carried a decorative motif of small pink rabbits in sexual congress. The audience gaped at us, and we at them.

There were two consequences of this inexplicable gesture. One was that we lost the notices and David Mirvish started to get letters from his customers threatening to cancel their subscriptions if he gave them any more of that. So began the graceful decline of our association with David and Ed as far as appearances in Toronto were concerned. The other was of a different order. The ASM, who had thought he was demonstrating the improvisational freedom on which the company prided itself, was tottering on the edge of mental illness from which he has now, mercifully, recovered. Perhaps we could have recognised that his incipient disturbance was being signalled by a gesture which only slightly exaggerated the self-expressiveness that our work was actively fostering. Hm.

Around the still centre of our disapproving audience in Toronto lurked a fringe that was wildly enthusiastic – local theatre people in many cases who would embarrassingly apologise for Toronto audiences. The fact is that for this season we and the Royal Alex were a mismatch. Were it not that the venue was part of our agreement with the Mirvishes, we would have been better off at the O'Keeffe Centre, which is huge but attracts a more general

*audience. Quite aside from the first night incident, David and Ed
had already perceived, though they were too courteous to say it,
that their subscribers might well not like us – I had thought David
looked untypically apprehensive when he first saw the shows in
Hamburg in January. Now he was losing money on the box office
and I was urging him simultaneously to take the entire seven-play
cycle for a six-week season the following year. Over a series of
generous lunches, he extricated himself from what must have
seemed a suicidal booking, reducing the length of our proposed
return engagement to three weeks, then to one, before booking in*
Les Misérables *for eighteen months and politely showing us the
door. But only as far as Canada was concerned; he still fed
£125,000 into* The Wars of the Roses *and booked us into the Vic
in London. These people are really rather remarkable.*

Bogdanov: The problem is subscription audiences. Dead Theatre.
Ed and David rely on their subscribers to provide 75% of their
income. They have thirty-eight thousand subscribers. Their seat
prices are, for Toronto, very high. Therefore what young following
they have is very small, few being able to afford the cost of a ticket.
The average age of our audience must have been closer to sixty than
fifty; some had held seats at the theatre (the same seats) for as much
as twenty years.* They come the first Thursday (or the second
Wednesday or the third . . .) of every month. It was a ritual
performed with Pavlovian precision. People left *The Henrys* both
during the performance and at the interval. I stood outside for the
whole of a performance of *Henry IV Part 1* to eavesdrop and
ascertain the reasons. It was astonishing. Firstly, many people,
passing the poster for *Sweet Charity* displayed at the side of the
theatre, thought that was what they were coming to see. Secondly,
others believed they were seeing three plays condensed into one,
due to the advance publicity of the trilogy day. Thirdly, some
thought the interval was the end! Frankly, many did not know
what they were coming to at all. One man tried to sell me his tickets
half price. 'What's on?' I said. 'I don't know, *Richard and Henry
Get Laid* . . .' Nevertheless, in Toronto (as in many another city
outside of Great Britain) we received some of the most perceptive

---

* Ed Mirvish proudly claims that subscribers have been known to leave
their seats in their wills, and that they are sometimes bitterly-contested
items in divorce cases.

comment on what we were trying to achieve. Alexander Leggatt in the *Shakespeare Bulletin*: 'To a modern audience, medieval dress allows for only a very generalised sense of social atmosphere. Here there was a precision that conveyed the true variety of the text . . . The effect was not so much to add layers as to strip them away, letting the human and political drama emerge with fresh clarity.' And Ray Conlogue in the *Globe and Mail*: 'Bogdanov, for his part, kills Elizabethan nostalgia right off the top by presenting thugs. The comic world of Quickly's Tavern with its fat presiding thief, Falstaff, and the assortment of whores and wastrels who pick merchants' purses by the light of the moon, tends to bring on a severe case of Elizabethan fantasising for most viewers. That innocent countryside full of fat robbers calling themselves Diana's foresters! Ah, those were the days.' Heady stuff, and although one is fond of saying that the critics don't mean anything, when one of them hits what you are trying to achieve right on the nail, no one can resist it. Friends for life.

My own visit to Toronto was characterised by staying two nights (why as many as two?!) in an hotel that is only rivalled in my experience by the one I inadvertently stayed in outside Coventry (England, not Wisconsin). The doorknob came off in my hand, the door fell from the wardrobe, the basin was cracked and the water ran on to my shoes. The bed was at an angle, with one leg missing, and unless you think there is nothing to cap this with, when I sat on the toilet, it fell over. I moved. Gino Empery, the Royal Alexandra press officer, wearing the most wonderful wig I had ever seen, fixed me up with a suite. Sublime to the ridiculous. It was almost a hundred metres end to end. Take a tram to the phone. During the first *Henrys* tour there was one sequence in which in the course of eighteen nights I slept in sixteen different beds, many of them not much better than the one in Toronto. I swore after one such awfulness, in a pub opposite the main station in Manchester, that it was time to raise my sights with regard to accommodation. I was a big boy now. Time at my age to enjoy a bit of comfort. I told Prue and we agreed that the company would at least stretch on these occasions to a Holiday Inn. What joy . . .

Toronto is exploding artistically. When a law was passed making French the first language of the province of Quebec, all the English culture moved out of Montreal, Ottawa, Quebec itself and came to Toronto. Toronto's gain. Arts centres, theatres and galleries are mushrooming. The large number of ethnic communities ensures that there is a polyglot cross-fertilisation of ideas, cultures and energies. Which made the kind of audiences we were getting all the more disappointing.

Pennington: *So we revelled in a minority following, the Mirvishes appeased their subscribers, and the four actresses in the cast – Eluned Hawkins, Jenny Quayle, Jennie Stoller and June Watson – worked through the Toronto heat to put on* Other Voices, *a cycle of writings by women such as Virginia Woolf, Charlotte Keatley, Coretta King and Olive Schreiner, mostly on the subject of the warlike male – in other words what Lady Percy or Doll Tearsheet, gifted with tongues, might have said to their belligerent mates. The show, which was directed by Sue Hogg, played with great success at a theatre club called the Place Muraille, raising £2,000 for the self-help programme run by the Women's School in Tigre, Ethiopia. The more idle of us looked at the moose in the beautifully protected Algonquin Park, churlishly declined to visit Niagara Falls, or sat eating the best Caesar salad in North America, which comes from the deli next to the Royal Alex – even better than at Ed's Italian. I peered across Lake Ontario to the States wondering how we would get on there the following spring – Jane and Bernie Sahlins from the Chicago Festival had arrived with Richard Christianssen, theatre critic for the* Tribune, *to confirm our booking once again – and waiting for the phone to ring from home. I finally got the call the morning after the last performance to say that my mother was worse. It was as if she had waited till then, and now was only waiting for me to get back. This time I travelled a day ahead of the company.*

I sat packed tight into a Wardair flight back to London, trying not to listen to the compulsive talker next door telling me about her Saskatchewan childhood, sometimes nudging me out of sleep to make a point. I was obviously only just going to be home in time. Able to achieve nothing for the moment, I warded off my neighbour as best I could by thinking about what The Henrys *had meant, as if settling a small account before confronting the real matters of life and death. I felt we were in credit. The productions certainly had offered the plays up to the 1980s – they were perhaps as good as anything Michael had ever done. The acting was classy, though I suspected we were longer on smelly reality (the Boar's Head) than on darker emotional resource. June Watson's Mistress Quickly seemed to me definitive: devoted to Falstaff, still enough of an old tart to brandish a practised bosom in appeasement to Pistol, garrulous, soft-hearted but unsentimental; and, superb comedienne that she is, I still couldn't grasp after a year how she got some of her laughs. Paddy O'Connell had revealed Henry IV as a great part, not the usual boring old stick but a violent, passionate Celt whose cunning is so deep he believes it doesn't exist. John Price's Pistol was a magnificent creation, swaggering and farouche, alcoholic, and, by the end of Henry V, with the toxified vacancy of a traumatised war veteran. Jenny Quayle's alleycat Doll Tearsheet and proud, highly-strung Princess of France were the work of a leading lady for all seasons. Clyde Pollitt's exquisitely timed Shallow; Gareth Thomas's marvellous Fluellen, loyal and verbose; Colin Farrell's mournful, gently swaying Bardolph; and above all John Woodvine's magnificent Falstaff, in many minds the best since Ralph Richardson's. Michael Cronin, Hugh Sullivan, Roger Booth, John Dougall, Andy Jarvis, Paul Brennen and Charlie Dale were all bursting the seams of parts that were now too small for them. And that's to ignore half the company. Loretta Bircham, Titus Grant, Graham Lister, David Hall, Andy Chelton, Mandi St Clair, Dominic Peissel and Terence Hayes had got us everywhere, we'd always opened on time and never cancelled. We had ambitious plans, but we were broke. In front of us, apart from our own sad affairs, lay more board resignations, financial crisis, eleventh-hour casting, perfidy and momentary despair. For the moment, though, the case rested.*

PART TWO

Draw Anew the Model

CHAPTER
5

THE WARS OF THE ROSES

July–December 1987

'I am Taliesin.
I sing perfect metre.'
                    Taliesin, sixth-century
                    Welsh poet

Bogdanov: We were to move from the office in Golden Square by the end of May 1987. James Sharkey was expanding. He gleefully invited me one day to share a glass of champagne and said, 'Congratulate me, I've got the new James Bond.' He had just signed a contract for Timothy Dalton. It reminded me of a round-table rabbit in February, when Michael P. had sat down to dinner with three old friends from the RSC. Norman Rodway, it transpired, was filming in China, Mike Gwilym likewise in Spain, and David Jones was off to direct a film with Robert De Niro. Michael gallantly owned up to opening *Henry IV Part 1* in Sunderland the following week.

Giles Webster at Pineapple West Studios, Paddington Street, had heard a radio interview in which I had posited an ideal rehearsal space for the company – video facilities, gymnasium, three rehearsal rooms, office space. 'Come on over,' he said, 'We've got what you want.' He had indeed – of a sort. Two offices on the second floor were split by a small dance studio and our ears were split by the noise. The only compensation for the male chauvinists in the company was the sight through the glass door of leotarded female bodies, sweatily working out, in all positions. There was the

advantage of a coffee bar and a large rehearsal room on the ground
floor big enough to house the *Wars of the Roses* company for the
duration. I did a deal with him, £13,000 for the offices for the year
and the use of the large rehearsal space for thirteen weeks. Other
rooms we would pay for on a pro-rata basis. We moved in at the
end of June.

We were in deep financial trouble. Glumly we contemplated the
battle to raise the money for the next leg. We were £50,000 down
from the first season and clearly there was a ceiling to what we
could expect to recover from English theatres during the next year.
Our weekly operating costs for *The Wars of the Roses* were to be
£31,000 – £32,000. Against which, five theatres out of ten in Great
Britain were offering varying guarantees of between £18,000 and
£26,000. (Our deficit was mainly due to theatres with no
guarantees failing to achieve the minimum box office requirement,
offset against the budgeted shortfall.) It was clear that if we were
to survive in England, we had to make money abroad. I got on the
phone. This time it was international time. Calling in all my
contacts – Keith Statham (an old friend from Newcastle days)
running the Hong Kong Arts Festival and Nick Jones,
Administrator of the Hong Kong Arts Centre. Martyn Naylor,
English businessman domiciled in Japan who acts as go-between
for foreign theatre imports; Jane and Bernie in Chicago; the
Schauspielhaus in Hamburg (now showing a second successful
production of mine, *Reineke Fuchs*); Nele Hertling, in Berlin, a
contact from the Young Vic touring days, who was now in charge
of the Berlin Festival for the Eight Hundred Year celebrations.
Anthony Steel from the Melbourne Spoleto Festival, who had seen
the shows in Toronto. Miraculously, it started to take shape. There
was one new problem.

Abroad we could charge handsome fees, to offset our inevitable
losses on the UK touring circuit, and we now had potential
contracts worth £1 million. But we had to survive until March,
when they would be realised, with a cash flow deficit of, at the
worst, £175,000 due to the lack of income from UK touring. The
Allied Irish Bank were refusing to give us an unsecured loan. I went
to my own bank, the Royal Bank of Scotland. They were amused
at the thought and politely declined. To add to our problems, the
Arts Council had a change of Financial Administrators. In a burst
of brilliant bureaucratic bungling, they reasoned thus: we had a
cash flow problem; therefore at some point, if we could not meet

(above) The Winter of Discontent –
Roger Booth and Michael Cronin rehearsing at Limehouse (JT);
(below) Scaling down the Histories – Michael Bogdanov (LB)

Henry VI House of York: 'First thing we do, let's kill all the lawyers'
– Jack Cade's Rebellion (LB)

(above) Michael Pennington as Richard II (LB);
(below) 'Now civil wounds are stopp'd; peace lives again'
– the final scene of Richard III (LB)

Henry IV Part 2 – Barry Stanton as Falstaff (LB)

the bills, we would have to cancel the rest of the tour; therefore if they gave us all our new grant (£110,000) they might lose it all; therefore it was wise to stagger the payments over the year, giving us £25,000 every quarter. Therefore they increased the amount we had to borrow at the beginning, increased our cash flow problem, increased the interest we were likely to pay by £25,000 *and* thereby increased our unsecured overdraft by the same amount. Through this crazy piece of financial logic, they almost guaranteed that the company would collapse. Brilliant. With everybody making ominous noises, Michael and I prepared to put up our respective houses as guarantees of security. We signed no contracts and postponed September rehearsals a week as we desperately fought to put the package together. It was at this point that David Kay, our Chairman, showed his mettle and extracted a grudging agreement from the Allied Irish Bank to put up the loan. We breathed out. The tour was a reality. We were exultant, confident. We had learned much from the first year. We had masterminded our brainchild past the Board, past the Arts Council, past the theatres, and were up and running again.

A number of team changes had taken place. I had invited Titus Grant to rejoin us, not as a Stage Manager, but as a Deputy Stage Manager, running three prompt books for the seven plays. Loretta Bircham was also to do three books and the ASMs were to share the final one. We also had, in Rosy Fowler, someone to look after the props for the first time and, in Philip Rees and Simon Elliott, two recruits to share the load of Stage Management and understudying. Best of all, we filched Janet Morrow from the RSC for Press and Publicity. Janet bombarded the world. Among the actors, Paddy O'Connell did not feel he could take the rigours of touring for a second year and reluctantly was no longer with us. John Price – not without the usual round of argy bargying – would be the new Bolingbroke and continue to do Pistol (it would be a strange double in *Henry IV Part 2*) but would cede Hotspur to Chris Hunter, a punchy young actor of growing reputation whom we were delighted to have alongside. I don't think John was too unhappy at losing Hotspur – the fiery, whipcrack temperament of the character was not his natural rhythm and on the days when he was down, he was unable to supply the attack and aggression needed to sustain the part. Many a black Monday was the result, in that first year, of *Henry IV Part 1* always being the start of the week.

Martin Clunes and Darryl Forbes-Dawson were leaving; Charlie Dale was taking over the part of Poins from Charlie Lawson, whose wife was having their first baby; Jenny Quayle needed to look after her son rather than tour him worldwide; and Mary Rutherford, a veteran from my days on Brook's *A Midsummer Night's Dream* in the early '70s (she was the original Hermia) took over a mixture of Jenny Quayle's and Jennie Stoller's parts. Lynette Davies added a touch of elegance to various female roles. Siôn Probert took over from Gareth Thomas, Phil Bowen from Donald Gee (a lovely actor, but one so homesick that he had changed hotel rooms continually, travelled with his own microwave oven from home, and on one occasion tried to plug his own handset into the phone socket in his dressing room at the Oxford Apollo: Apollo Leisure were on to him in a flash). John Darrell, Stephen Jameson and Michael Fenner completed the male line-up. John Dougall would begin taking over from Michael P. as Hal/Henry V by playing selected performances this season. Saddest of all, John Woodvine hung up his touring boots.

John had brought a sophistication and quality of elegance to the acting of the company and, with Michael, had led the tour in gentlemanly fashion. On one occasion he had called us into his dressing room, and said we were the worst management he had ever worked for. We invited him to be an Associate Artist of the ESC. He generously accepted. Barry Stanton, also a veteran of Brook's *Dream* tour (Bottom) would replace him for two years and bring a new dimension to the part. Ian Burford, once a performer of light operetta, had replaced Morris Perry, and with the women all swapping round, it was really a question of complete re-rehearsal.

Michael and I had jointly pasted up a version of the *Henry VIs*, condensing the three parts into two. The plays sprawl and brawl and they are clearly early works. It is conceivable that the three parts were written in the wrong order. They are probably the result of improvisation and have been tampered with, edited, and the best writing is in *Part 2*. We called our two parts *House of Lancaster* and *House of York*. The first being dominated by the former, the second featuring the rise of the latter. We decided to wrap up the rather rambling Joan of Arc story in the first half of *Lancaster*. It is clear that the original story is weighed down with a fair amount of sixteenth-century English patriotic propaganda, Shakespeare's or otherwise. We took a crucial decision here to balance the English belief in her as a witch with the French (and her own) as a divinely inspired saviour.

The second half of *Lancaster* would begin with Henry meeting Margaret for the first time and would finish at the death of Suffolk (Act IV, Scene 1 of Shakespeare's *Part 2*). *House of York* would begin with the Duke of York's return from Ireland and the Jack Cade Rebellion; we would condense the battles and finish the first half of this play with the famous 'Son who killed his father, father who killed his son' scene. The second half would see the rise of Richard Duke of Gloucester leading to his accession as Richard III in the play to follow. We wrote linking lines and passages where necessary to clarify the story and straighten up the loose ends (of which there were many). This became known as 'Bogspeare' although I probably provided only about one half of the three hundred odd lines that were re-written, Michael P., the company and Sue Best supplying the rest.*

As rehearsals and the tour progressed, Sue, who had joined Stella Bond as a second Assistant Director, emerged as something of a genius at composition. It is worth noting that the Hall – Barton *Roses* included some 1,500 new lines, so we were quite modest really. Our work included such gems as:

King Edward IV. We'll drive the quondam queen into the sea,
And make her swim the long way back to France.

and:

Suffolk. Fret not yourself my Lord for this reverse.
Somerset. Fear not for that, I will not brook this sneap.

and:

Warwick. Let Richard be restored to his blood,
So shall his father's wrongs be recompensed.
Somerset. His father was a foul ignoble traitor.
Shall he reap honour from his father's shame?

*__*Pennington:__ I began to understand why John Barton had got so involved in writing his own 'Shakespeare' in the Stratford version. When I heard my first pastiche Shakespearian metaphor: 'The turncoat Burgundy will soon turn tail' confidently declaimed by Hugh Sullivan, I felt myself puff up with an unholy pride. So this is what the writer feels . . .*

The final version in performance differed radically from our first
paste-up job, although the skeleton structure remained much the
same. We are rather proud of *House of York* which turned out to
be a stirring piece of political and psychological narrative. Any
similarities to any other versions are purely coincidental. *The
Plantagenets*, a compilation of the *Henry VIs* and *Richard III*
directed by Adrian Noble, opened at Stratford in the summer of
1988. In 1989, Elizabeth S.C. Brandow, in 'History, Royal or
English, a Study of the Royal Shakespeare Company's *The
Plantagenets* and the English Shakespeare Company's *The Wars of
the Roses*' said: 'It will be noted that the conflation of the three
parts of *Henry VI* into two followed a very similar pattern in both
productions. I have not attempted to determine the reason for this,
but various possibilities suggest themselves. The overall shape
broadly matches the RSC's 1963 *Wars of the Roses*. This may be
simply because common sense suggested the same arrangement to
all three directors. Alternatively, the directors of both modern
productions may have chosen deliberately to adhere to this and
study the text, which is freely available. Another possibility is that
Michael Pennington, a very junior crowd filler and spear carrier in
1964, may have been influenced by his memory, assisted by Hugh
Sullivan who played Burgundy and Hastings in 1963/64 and
Reignier, Hereford and the Lord Mayor for the ESC. The ESC was
touring *The Wars of the Roses* for a year before the opening of *The
Plantagenets* so details could have been noted by the RSC. Darryl
Forbes-Dawson, who was in the ESC tour of *The Henrys* and
subsequently played Stanley in *The Plantagenets* at Stratford, may
have taken his new colleagues to see the work of his previous
company. Only one hypothesis is untenable; that the ESC may have
been influenced by the RSC *Plantagenets* as implied by Michael
Billington (the *Guardian*, February 13th, 1989).'*

The question of the design style was now vexing Stephanie
Howard and myself. Chris Dyer had virtually abandoned the set
and props, leaving the re-drawing in the hands of a young assistant,
Colin Peters. The productions this time were going to be supervised
by Simon Opie, late Production Manager for the Royal
Shakespeare Company, and Ted Irwin, ditto of Covent Garden,
who had formed themselves into a new company called PMA –

*Thesis submitted to Birmingham University for the degree of M.A. in
Shakespeare Studies.

Production Management Associates. The rear screen was rebuilt (to work, this time, we hoped), the flying bridge reconstructed, to go down to ground level, which it hadn't been able to do before.

We custom built the scaffold 'zip-up' towers in lightweight steel to make them easier to negotiate (and more stable). Two sets of steps for ground-level access to the bridge were wheeled on from off-stage. And I introduced a white (grey actually) circle motif to the glazed floor for *York* and *Lancaster*, reduced the sandbags from two to one and, sadness of sadness, lost the tank.* We had started eclectically with the costumes and yet there *was* a sort of chronology to be found. Stephanie proposed that we start *Richard II* in the Regency period, which would then allow us, with the advent of Bolingbroke as King Henry IV, to retain our Victorian frock coats and scarlet tunics for his court. The *Henry VI*s would progress through the Edwardian period, the First World War, the twenties and thirties, the Second World War, until we arrived at *Richard III* which I wanted modern and 'computer'. This left *Henry V* as something of an anomaly, as we had already used modern dress in the original production. Accordingly, the suits were replaced with late Victorian frock-coats. The political arena of the plays thus spanned a period of one hundred and fifty years. Street life, battles, etc., retained their eclecticism, though *Henry IV Parts 1* and *2* remained the best examples of this. I concluded the *Roses* cycle with a conceptual juxtaposition: a fight between Richmond and Richard III in full medieval armour and long-swords, immediately followed by Richmond's address to the nation from a TV studio. From where territorial aggression starts with a one-to-one combat for the ruling of a country, to where it is currently at, with the media recording events as they occur in Eastern Europe.

We rehearsed on 10th September. The pattern of work was familiar to most people although this time I did not allow myself the luxury of two weeks to read the texts, or lead the company in a round of exercises. We had thirteen weeks for what would now be seven plays and I was not as well prepared as I had been for *The Henrys*.

Although I had attempted to go away to the Isles of Scilly for ten days, and then to my own home in Wales for a week to prepare, much of the time was taken up with phone calls and paper work, making sure that we (a) had a tour at all, and (b) had the money for it.

---

*Pennington: *Goal!*

Our relief was visible as we finally made it to the first rehearsal, albeit a week later than we had intended. Our versions of the *Henry VIs* were greeted with enthusiasm although the originals were soon brought out as the company culled stricken couplets from their folders with, 'There's a couple of lines here that you've left out and I'm not quite sure why . . .' The deal was – anything could be re-inserted provided an actor was prepared to lose the same amount in exchange. To be fair, most of the company adhered to this side of the bargain. (There *are some* one has known . . .) Although there were themes to follow as in *The Henrys*, it was naturally far harder to rehearse seven plays all at once and to keep the strands in one's head, and *House of Lancaster* and *House of York* were, in effect, two new texts started from scratch.

The first problem we confronted was in the very first scene of the series. The reported murder of the Duke of Gloucester, Thomas of Woodstock. In *Richard II,* Bolingbroke accuses Mowbray of being responsible, thereby indirectly accusing Richard, on whose orders Mowbray was acting. In the second scene, the Duchess of Gloucester, his widow, pleads with John of Gaunt, Woodstock's brother, to do something about her husband's murder. John of Gaunt refuses to touch King Richard:

John of Gaunt. God's is the quarrel; for God's substitute,
His deputy anointed in His sight,
Hath caused his death; the which if wrongfully,
Let heaven revenge; for I may never lift
An angry arm against His minister.

Clear as daylight. Except when played on the stage. The language is complex, the nuances sometimes oblique. In the Duchess's scene, Richard is never mentioned by name, yet knowledge of the King's participation in the crime is crucial to our understanding of why Richard has to get rid of both Mowbray and Bolingbroke. Mowbray covers up for Richard – *this* time. The duel is not the answer. If Bolingbroke wins, as is likely, he becomes all powerful, proved right. His next tilt could be at the King himself (in fact, it is). He has to go. In the unlikely event of Mowbray winning, he has a strong hold over Richard. He *definitely* has to go – for ever. You cannot have a courtier hanging around with grounds for blackmail. All this hinges on our recognition of what lies behind Bolingbroke's challenge to Mowbray. We discussed it endlessly. Despite a common understanding of the issues involved, and the need to show, through reaction, the danger of the situation, we never solved this most tricky of starts. I scoured an old play, *Thomas of Woodstock* (anonymous), to see if there was a scene I could lift. There wasn't. I suspect the answer lies, as one would do on film, in creating a pre-scene showing the murder and the people involved. I don't know why I didn't do it.*

Thomas of Woodstock was also a valuable source of material for the characters of Bushy, Bagot and Green, notoriously under-written in *Richard II*, yet held by John of Gaunt, Bolingbroke and others to be the authors of Richard's being led astray, and his concomitant misuse of power. Bolingbroke has two of them executed. The problem is that these 'caterpillars of the Commonwealth' are so sketchily drawn that there is very little evidence of their crimes against the state on which to pin a convincing death penalty.

The problems pile up. The Aumerle sub-plot, which we retained to fill out the female roles, I later cut in the TV version. Both Lynette Davies and Ann Penfold, who inherited the Duchess of York the following year, performed with humour and passion. Yet

*Pennington: *I do. Think of the blank verse we'd have come up with.*

the scenes, coming as they do at the end of the play, between
Richard on his way to the Tower and, then, his murder, are
palpably a dramatic device to hold the audience in suspense while
waiting for the dénouement. The problem is in asking the
onlookers, suddenly, at that stage in the play, to involve and
interest themselves in characters who only play supporting roles,
merely to demonstrate a conspiracy against Bolingbroke; although
we do have the chance to see the Duke of York willing to sacrifice
his son, giving Bolingbroke the opportunity to demonstrate
clemency.

The play appears to be static, the action determined by the
relentless rhyming couplets, doggerel. But if ever there was a part
that Michael P. was born to play, it is Richard II. Some days in
rehearsal he would float the language, tease, it, bend it, send it
soaring skywards and then back down to earth again. The younger
members were spellbound. They were receiving the best lesson
possible in the use of language from one of the undisputed masters.
The use of colour and sound, the picture building and imagery that
has to be discovered anew each time the words are spoken. One
morning we were improvising the Deposition Scene in Act IV,
where Richard relinquishes the crown.

Bolingbroke. Are you contented to resign the crown?
King Richard. Ay, no; no, ay; for I must nothing be;
Therefore no no, for I resign to thee.
Now mark me, how I will undo myself:
I give this heavy weight from off my head,
And this unwieldy sceptre from my hand,
The pride of kingly sway from out my heart;
With mine own tears I wash away my balm,
With mine own hands I give away my crown,
With mine own tongue deny my sacred state,
With mine own breath release all duteous oaths;
All pomp and majesty I do forswear;
My manors, rents, revenues, I forgo;
My acts, decrees, and statutes, I deny;
God pardon all oaths that are broke to me!
God keep all vows unbroke are made to thee!

He played with Bolingbroke as a cat with a mouse. The crown
was dangled like a carrot, it was held high, gently offered, snatched

away, the anguish of the virgin, refusing yet knowing ultimately the prize would have to be given away, determined to tease and frustrate, delaying the moment as long as possible. And the language to match. I wanted to keep it all, every intricate, exquisite moment, but time was to pare this sequence down to a spare minimum.

Pennington: *In the end, though, I think I failed as Richard II. I was sad about it, because I had loved the part since I was a teenager. The problem was partly 'the context of the show and partly a miscalculation of my own. It was important, in the opening movement of a seven-play sequence, to emphasise Richard's disastrous qualities as a king and, in his egotism, indulgence and greed, how much he is slashing the fabric of his society. Bolingbroke's putsch is urgently needed: Richard is, publicly and personally, a sort of monster. But the whole of the second half of the play turns on his agony as, in losing a 'divine' identity he has never questioned, he fumbles for a new one. When he calls for a mirror in the Deposition Scene, it is not simply to pose but to seek anxiously who the stranger is in its reflection:* Alack the day / That I have worn so many winters out / And know not now what name to call myself. *He is re-inventing himself in the most painful way, and the audience must feel for him. But I had established the petty tyrant unusually firmly in the first half, and often found it difficult to turn the audience round for the second. As with all great parts, there were nights when it worked, by force of* ésprit. *But it depended a lot on leaving a seed, in the first scenes, of a kind of innocent destructiveness, the Sun King's joyousness in power, the image of an artist without a calling, that would turn into pity. But too often I was too closed off, too cruel. R.I.P.*

Bogdanov: The Regency style, Beau Brummell dandyism, suited our purposes; a profligate, dilettante Richard. I suspect that were we to embark on a one-off production of the play this is not the period we would ideally choose. (Don't ask me which – I don't know, never having thought about it any other way.) Michael and I decided that we wanted Richard surrounded by music and artists, a contrast to the puritan austerity of Bolingbroke Rule. (1960s to 1980s?) It would be colourful before turning dark and Victorian. Attempting a setting for this sumptuous scenario within the framework of our steely black structure was a poser. I added three

sets of net curtains – all we could afford – sprayed the back set
purple and left the two front sets white. We 'rouched' them. This
allowed for a certain amount of softness when properly arranged,
but did not quite match the velveteened volumes of the
imagination, great swathes of silk and satin festooned liberally in
the great hall surrounded by gilded oils and Louis Quinze. What we
did have was our (my) bits of chenille tablecloth, that we had used
to drape the tavern in the Boar's Head. They would have to do. I
draped the throne (symbol of misuse), an easel, the card table, three
chairs and a cushion. (Later we bought a few off-cuts of velvet.) It
did. Just.

Meanwhile Andy Jarvis as Richard III was justifying every bit of
our faith in him in offering him the role. With his impressive shaven
head, Spock ears and blue eyes, Andy looks the quintessential
villain. Inadvertently. In fact, he is one of the gentlest of men and
given to an inordinate amount of sensitivity. In the first year, Andy
had volunteered for everything. You could rely on him, you knew
that a prop, a set change, a line here, a line there, was safe in
Andy's hands. Now, where in the not-so-distant past he had
followed Antony Sher's Richard around the stage at Stratford and
in Australia as Lord Stanley, here he was moulding the text to his
own rhythms as if born to play the part. I worked with him on the
humour, asked him to challenge the audience to find him
audacious, outrageous. Not to hate him. To be drawn into his
charm. Corporate flies entangled in his black psychopathic web.

> *Gloucester.* I'll have her – but I will not keep her long.
> (*Makes to exit with a halting limp. Stops, thinks, turns,*
> *comes back to the audience, eyes wide.*)
> What! I, that killed her husband (*Go to turn away, turn*
> *back, smack head with palm of hand*) AND his father . . .

And partnered by Michael P., his smooth-talking Buckingham
crowning a remarkable display of classical kings with a
consummate piece of TV acting.

The *Henry VI* rehearsals were fast and furious. Discuss a scene,
improvise it, set it. If satisfied, send it away with Stella and Sue to
be worked on. And so many fights. Malcolm Ranson, knowing the
problems having worked on the plays for the BBC, had cancelled
all other engagements to remain available for the duration. There
is always a problem with suspension of disbelief in staging medieval

fights involving large numbers. Mostly, elephantine cavorting in suits of armour, wielding balls and chains and swords too heavy to lift, makes me laugh. In this frame of mind I had no wish to be hoist with my own petard.

Finally, I condensed all the big battles into ones of single combat, the sole remaining large one, known as 'the *York* rumble', finding its way into performance before being cut on the return from Australia. However, there was still quite a lot of running on and off stage and obligatory smoke. The death of Rutland (in reality supposed to be a young boy, but here played by a somewhat larger Stephen Jameson) was particularly gruesome. A rifle and bayonet in the hands of Charlie Dale playing Young Clifford was a lethal weapon.

The choices of music were mainly from earlier periods with a few exceptions. Harsh, atonal bars from Berg's *Violin Concerto* introduced the rose-picking Temple Garden scene in the *House of Lancaster*, an indication of future disintegration; a jagged electronic theme from an unknown horror movie helped decapitate Suffolk. Henry VI's piety was emphasised by the use of a solo choir boy singing Psalm 121: 'I will lift up mine eyes unto the Lord'; a Gregorian chant accompanied Henry V's funeral and the deaths of Mortimer, Lancaster and Beaufort. All the battle scenes echoed to cannon fire and Byrd's *Mass for Four Voices*, emphasising the religious justification voiced by the participants. Simon Elliott played live accordion music for the French victory at Orleans and Henry VI's Coronation in France was introduced with Mozart's *Coronation Mass*. His wedding to Margaret was celebrated with Handel's *Music for the Royal Fireworks*, various other court scenes in England were accompanied by Monteverdi's *Vespers* and Pergolesi's *Stabat Mater*. The same themes were used yet again in *House of York* but became more modern with *Glassworks* by Philip Glass and Louis Armstrong's 'Alligator Crawl' which was used as background for Edward IV's Cocktail Party, beginning the second half. The long-sword/armour fight between Richmond and Richard was fought out to the strains of Samuel Barber's *Adagio for Strings*. It was a trick picked up from the film *Platoon*. (Yes, Michael Coveney, Samuel Barber, *not* Mahler's Eighth.)*

Believing in the divinity of Joan of Arc was proving a problem, and Mary Rutherford and I worked on the mysterious ethereal

*Financial Times, 21st January 1989

aspect; difficult, given the lack of text to do it with. I don't think
I helped by loading down her supernatural powers (the encounter
with Michael Fenner as Talbot, for example) with Peruvian pipes
reminiscent of the film *Picnic at Hanging Rock*.

Lois Potter later wrote in the *Times Literary Supplement* (in a
review otherwise extremely complimentary): 'The one failure to
confront the text is the treatment of Joan of Arc ... No devils
appear to her. La Pucelle is played as the dazed recipient of an
incomprehensible magic; the music that accompanies her
throughout her success suggests fairy land, and when it abandons
her, the effect is of a performance of *Peter Pan* where no one claps
in order to save Tinkerbell.' It *was* kitsch, though liked by many.

In fact I was struggling altogether to find depth in *House of
Lancaster*. The downfall of Gloucester hinges on witchcraft. His
wife dabbles in the occult in an attempt to find out whether her
husband will be king or not. The predictions of the medium come
true, in point of fact. The trap is to burden this scene down with
a lot of comic mumbo jumbo. I fell right in. As with the Gads Hill
fight in *Henry IV Part 1* and the Recruiting Scene in *Henry IV Part
2*, so far in that it was difficult to pull the scene back. The seance
table won the Naff Prop prize for the tour. An empty goblet was
to spill and run blood, a knife was to up end itself suddenly and
sink into the table, an empty glass to fill with water. Passing
through the surface was a network of tubes, wires and strings,
leading to squeezy bottles ... Derek Scriminger, Stage Manager,
the tallest of tall, for some reason elected to crouch under the table
and work it all and succeeded only in soaking himself with water
and diluted ketchup. Ditto, in turn, Rosy Fowler, Loretta Bircham
... our attempt at ectoplasm resulted in Barry Stanton as
Bolingbroke the Conjuror winding his head and arms in white
bandages like some Frankenstein emerging from his operation. The
thunder and lightning emphasised the silliness of it all. Impossible
after all this to take seriously the Hawking Scene that follows,
where a blind man has to have his sight restored and then recovers
the use of his leg by another 'miracle'. The problem with rehearsing
such scenes so fast is that it leads to easy options, humour being
the road of least resistance. It is easier to invent comic business
quickly and leave the actors to develop it on their own, than to
painstakingly (and painfully) build up the truth and reality of such
skimpily written situations. Nevertheless, when so much 'real'
action depends on the consequences of these scenes, the time must

be taken. I didn't, and the result was always an uphill struggle to make the plot hang together in the second half of *House of Lancaster*. That we did, on occasions, succeed, given no time to re-conceive or re-rehearse, is a testimony to the actors' belief that they had to sacrifice the laughs in the service of the story.

Another road of least resistance, I suppose, was the developing of the hooligan, National Front theme in *House of York* in the form of the Cade Rebellion. Could one believe that this drink-sodden, totem-twirling, Union Jack brigade of Doc Martened bovver boys could ever take over the running of the country?

In Shakespeare's version, this Kentish rebellion is also somewhat unbelievable. (There has always been a pocket of insurrection in this plummy heartland of English garden conservatism; in 1985 the Kent miners, all six thousand of them, were the last to capitulate.) The original Cade Rebellion, born of genuine grievances, had the support of the landowners and gentry. In Shakespeare's version we are confronted by a man gathering to his standard the illiterate and uneducated under the pretence that he is the rightful heir to the throne. The measures that he would institute would warm the cockles of the New Brutalists. The lawyers would all be killed, there would be no more reading and writing, and henceforth the laws would all come out of his mouth. Thatcher would have loved him. Home Secretary in no time. The only thing a bit *de trop* maybe, would be having the 'pissing conduit' run with red claret. Michael P. turned Jack Cade into a machete-twirling tornado, with spiky red hair and a Union Jack vest. The chant of 'you're gonna get your fuckin' 'eads kicked in' rang out weekly on stage as pitched battles raged on sea ferries to the same cries and the Heysel stadium went up in flames. Europe certainly doesn't believe such groups could never take over the country.

In week six, tragedy struck. On Saturday afternoon I had been rehearsing with John Price. He had a fight call with Malcolm and Ian Burford on the York – Clifford duel in *House of York* and then we proceeded to have a marvellous Bolingbroke rehearsal. We also worked on an idea for a Dave Allen style introduction to the whole cycle. Before the beginning of *Richard II*, we would set a table, a glass, John sitting there casually, a cigarette, lights down, then: 'Edward III, my Lord, had seven sons – are you with me so far?' and then he would go through the whole rigmarole of the royal succession, taken from the second part of *Henry VI*. John was in great form. We laughed and joked and finished at six o'clock with John enthusing about the idea and taking it away to develop it.

I was never to find out if it was a good idea or not. The following day I had a call to say that John had slipped and fallen while in the bathroom, had knocked himself unconscious and was in hospital. The next day was to reveal that in fact John had suffered a stroke. At that stage there was no cause for alarm but, as the days passed and John showed no signs of recovering consciousness, the awful truth of the situation began to dawn on us. When the news came that the doctors had switched off John's life support system, the tears flowed unrestrainedly. He had come into my life as an actor only one year before. We had fought, argued, discussed, laughed and enthused together and had become the firmest of friends professionally and personally. He was like a wolf, lean, lank, dark, gangling. But friendly, benign, his soft brown eyes quizzical, questioning. Hal's Angel.

Rehearsals with John were a riot of invention, or an intellectual challenge – a quest for detail. Memories of him: in a sandwich bar, his huge frame squeezed into a green plastic booth built for pre-war flyweights – 'I come from Worcester' spoken in a Geordie accent – his audition for Hotspur. Paddy O'Connell, etching fresh nudes nightly on John's forearm – 'Saturn and Venus in conjunction'. A bar in Hamburg, 2 am, writing up his diary, not drinking – 'I am rather bad at being a Celt.' Not to the Allied Irish Bank. He was a hero, a star of the A.I.B. receptions; the flag-flyer, the ambassador, mentally jigging the night away, the indefatigable energy of the rehearsal floor, recreated verbally over the salmon and the Sauvignon.

Talking to people, wanting to know. No 'side'. Humane. Equal. We would have gone with him anywhere. He and Michael Pennington clasped in each other's arms, their frames panting with the exertion of the fight – 'Fare thee well, great heart!'

My final memory from that last Saturday: a rehearsal gag as Pistol – removing a bench with a huge screwdriver and manhandling it off stage. It took five minutes. The room convulsed. Sometimes his voice a whisper, hoarse from the day's exertions. Helping others as much as himself. Asking questions, analysing, writing, asking, helping, improvising – the energy and invention flowed from him. A risk taker, a creator, an innovator. I knew him a bare fifteen months. Others knew him better, longer. I store the memory of those months. 'Never mind the bollocks, here comes Pistol.' It was 23rd October, 1987. It was many months before I could believe that this flowering of artistic compatibility was at an end.

With a critically short rehearsal period, we were now in deep trouble. John Castle, with whom I had coincided at Trinity College, Dublin, agreed to take over the roles of Bolingbroke, Pistol and York. It would take him all his time to learn the words. How would I ever be able to fill in any detail for him? We both agreed that I was to carry on with my normal schedule and he would catch up as best he could, as long as there was somebody available to keep taking him through the lines. Often he would prefer to have a word call instead of a rehearsal. This was to become a *Catch 22* situation, one that he would throw back at me in later arguments, maintaining that he had had no rehearsal and no guidance from me as to how the parts were to be played, often accusing me of having withheld crucial information that would have unlocked a scene for him. In these hectic last few weeks, with a massive hole left in five plays by the death of a leading actor, direction was indeed down to a minimum, and woe betide anyone who wasn't listening at the appropriate moment. John also did not make things any easier for himself by refusing to inherit the props and business that John Price had created for Pistol.

An actor's reluctance to accept a role at second hand is understandable, but in this situation it was impractical. Barry Stanton stepped into John Woodvine's clothes and comic business, added timing and invention of his own, and made Falstaff inimitably his personal creation, as different from John Woodvine as chalk and cheese. Take-overs always have this problem, but it was impossible for us, at this stage, to have full-scale re-rehearsal from scratch of every scene. John Castle would not accept this, and it led to much acrimony, with me trying to accommodate him as far as possible, but without John supplying any real re-assessment of the role on which I could usefully build.

Pistol was a mess, and remained so right up to his last performance. Not so his Bolingbroke. Here was an intelligent, cold usurper, a real threat to Richard, a marvellous still use of the stage and a brilliant match for Michael. Due to his youthfulness, believability as Hal's father was stretched somewhat in the second part of *Henry IV*, although his emotional depth and sheer stage presence carried him through. Despite the addition of a beard, the age discrepancy was wider and he never reached the desperate heights that Paddy had achieved in the same part.

John Castle: The interesting thing about taking over eight roles in

seven Shakespeare plays, in six weeks, is that you barely have time
to learn the lines. I was frightened. Fortunately the company were
a tremendous help. John Dougall, Phil Bowen, John Darrell,
Terence Hayes and others took me through the lines. I had only one
artistic problem. Pistol. It's a small and badly written part and
unfortunately I'd seen John Price in the role and hated his 'star'
performance. I'd found him raucous, unmoving and incomprehensible. Michael wanted me to repeat this performance. I found it
impossible.

Bogdanov: The last week in November. We moved into our end
phase, for technical rehearsals. This time, it was to what was
laughingly called a 'studio' in Limehouse. It was an old storage
warehouse, barely large enough, measuring some fifty foot by
seventy. One end had a huge entrance, obviously for container
lorries, and no doors. It would have to be blocked up. So would
the holes in the roof, the holes in the walls . . . It had been the
mildest of autumns but, as luck would have it, the weather turned
nasty for the two weeks that we were there. Rain, wind, snow,
sleet, we had everything the Thames, ten yards away, could throw
at us. We had underestimated and underbudgeted the extras.
Simon Opie put two Portacabins outside the dock doors for
emergency dressing rooms (the main ones were some several
hundred yards away across the compound). They had to be heated.
The familiar sound of propane blow heaters filled the air in the
'studio'. But whereas in the hangar at Plymouth they were some
way away from the action, here we were right on top of them. They
could not be kept going during rehearsal. We froze. I set up a small
electric blow heater under my chair. This I relinquished for long
spells to Clyde Pollitt, who was turning purple in the cold. I feared
for him. Clyde would never complain unless absolutely necessary.
We rehearsed in overcoats, gloves, mufflers . . . at one stage a
chunk of the roof blew in. Simon hired a heater that pumped air
in through a tube from outside; it was fiendishly expensive. Prue
Skene was feeling panicky about the budget, believing that Simon's
expenditure was out of control. Quite rightly, Prue was worried
about the Allied Irish Bank who were monitoring our control
mechanisms in the light of the unsecured overdraft that they were
providing.
   We had, in fact, tightened up our act considerably. We had
ditched our accountant John Catty, with whom in the first year we

had had an arrangement to do our book-keeping. Unfortunately I think we were something of a nuisance to him as we didn't have a proper system for supplying him with information. For whatever reason, he didn't do the work and we refused to pay his bills. I brought in Lynne Ash with whom I had worked for the New Vic. She introduced a new system of book-keeping with monthly and quarterly updates. In vain I pointed out to Prue and Lynne that Simon had ten years' experience of budgetary control at the RSC. (Now that I'm writing this, I don't know how much of a recommendation that is.) If anyone could pull the production together, it was Simon.

They didn't believe me. The problem was that the system of invoicing that we were trying to force on Simon was one that he was not only unused to, but was also, for him, impracticable. At that level, production management in London is a Mafia activity. Call in all sorts of favours, do deals, trade in one small job on one production against a big one on another. Grease palms, scratch backs, turn blind eyes, etc. Sometimes it is a very close wind-sailing job. Simon is a master mediator. True, we *did* overspend. Michael and I dipped into our pockets yet again. This time it was to supply the armour and video camera for the end of *Richard III*. As I had pointed out to Prue, there wasn't anything else in *Richard III*, just modern suits. The armour and video were the only real props and without them the production – indeed the whole cycle – had no climax. The acrimony between Prue and Simon reached fever pitch, with letters of accusation and defence flying backwards and forwards. I had to call in my personal relationship with Simon to ensure the shows reached Bath, where Simon left them to Ted Irwin, and went off to do the musical *Carrie* for the RSC and Broadway – the most expensive flop in history. Simon was having a great year.

We had the same scramble on costumes as the year before. Stephanie is also not one of the greatest book-keepers the world has ever known and, in her turn, pulled down the wrath of Prue and Lynne on her head. Derek Scriminger was a hero. He is one of the great busking stage managers of all time, relying heavily on what is practically a photographic memory, very rarely writing anything down. One of our ASMs finally walked out in Limehouse. He disappeared and could not be found. We replaced him with one week to go. Through Rick Clarke, who supplied our sound equipment in the second year, we found Brian Beasley. Brian is a wonderfully calm and gifted sound operator who took everything I threw at him and supplied the crucial Varèse – a modern composer whose *Arcana* and *Ionisation* formed the entire basis of the music for *Richard III*. Mark Henderson had taken over the lighting from Chris Ellis, who was heavily engaged in his home theatre, the Haymarket in Leicester. Unfortunately Mark was only partly available, working at that time at the National Theatre. His schedule had been tight anyway, and due to our postponing the whole production a week, he was going to be unavailable in Bath.

In Limehouse we were sitting too close to the action. The subtlety of the lighting from that distance was to prove useless when we got onto the big stage. I was to start re-lighting the seven shows from the beginning, a situation that I never properly caught up with.

If there was acrimony between John Castle and myself, it was worse between him and Michael P. John had already put the backs of the Yorkies up. The three sons of Richard Duke of York in *Henry VI*, Andy Jarvis, John Dougall and Phil Bowen, all had adopted Yorkshire accents, as had Michael Cronin as Warwick. John found it pretentious, refused, as Richard Duke of York, their father, to do the same. 'There's nothing worse than actors doing bad accents.'

Now, he quarrelled daily with Michael until one moment during Act III Scene 2 of *Henry IV Part 1*, John suddenly lashed out at him and caught him a stinging blow on the cheek. In the heated discussion that followed, with me trying to act as arbitrator, it transpired that John believed that Michael was sneering at him. Michael pointed out that, as the character Hal, he was looking at his father disbelievingly. John said that if a son of his had looked at him like that, he would slap him hard, but that anyway he didn't believe Michael: it was Pennington, the actor, who was being arrogant towards him, John Castle, not to King Henry. If Michael looked at him like that again, he would hit him again. Michael said he didn't mind being hurt if he knew it was coming but that the least John could do was (a) warn him (b) rehearse it and (c) pull the blow a bit. John said no, he would hit him when he felt like it and as hard as he liked if Michael continued to behave to him as he had. Michael objected to having to alter his performance through physical intimidation, and found the whole affair a bad case of one actor trying to exert pressure on another. We managed to arrive at a certain amount of common ground with Michael agreeing to modify his sneer and John agreeing to be a little less violent. Some time later we re-did the scene. It happened again. Slap! Even harder. Michael walked out. John shouted triumphantly after him, 'There you are, you see, you can't take it. Be a man!' There then followed another argument with me as to Michael's abilities as an actor, and mine as a director. I wondered if we would get through the next five days to Bath, never mind the next year . . . The strange thing about John was that in other areas he could be the most accommodating of people. He is a great giggler and laugher, a warm and compassionate colleague. And no nonsense. Not for him petty union regulations. He was always the first to help move props, set up, sweep the stage and, on form, a stunning actor.

John Castle: I felt very strongly that Michael P. as Hal was being intolerably rude to his father, King Henry. In a rehearsal I slapped his face. We played the scene without interruption, through to the end. In the rehearsal break, I went up to Michael P. and half apologised for the slap, telling him why I had done it. He said maybe he'd have to rethink the scene. Michael Bogdanov did not mention anything about the scene, let alone the slap. His sole contribution was to read out a small piece about himself in the *Evening Standard*.

Due to the appallingly brief rehearsal time, it was ten days later when we rehearsed the scene again, in a run-through of the play. Michael P., as Hal, was even more rude to his father, and so I slapped him again, harder. Probably to avoid 'decking' me, Michael walked out. When he came back, Michael Bogdanov, Michael P. and I discussed the slap.

Michael Pennington and I never quarrelled. We had one big and violent disagreement, and that's all. After being out on the road for eight months with him, I came to have great respect and some affection for him. He'd been at the sharp end all the time and had borne all, stoically.

Michael Bogdanov and I never 'quarrelled' for that matter either. We had a lot of disagreements and a couple of barnstorming rows, but I never bore him any grudges and he embraced me on my last night and thanked me for my work. I told him then what I still feel now: that I wouldn't have missed any of it for all the tea in China.

Bogdanov: We froze on. Coughs and colds notwithstanding, we managed to get some sort of a run of all seven plays. There was an awful lot left to do in Bath. The pattern for the opening there was as follows:

Tuesday, 8th December: *Richard II*
Wednesday, 9th: *Henry IV Part 1*
Thursday, 10th: *Henry IV Part 2*
Friday, 11th: *Henry V*
Saturday, 12th: *Richard II*, and *Henry IV Parts 1* and *2*
Monday, 14th: *Henry VI House of Lancaster*
Tuesday, 15th: *Henry VI House of York*
Wednesday, 16th: *Richard III*

I don't suppose we can claim a world record, but opening seven shows, twenty-four hours of Shakespeare in nine days, is not bad going. Don't boast, don't complain. Why bother? What's the point? What are you trying to prove? A familiar argument ran: 'If the circumstances are so rushed, and the compromises so great, what's the point of it all? Why fuck up a great set of plays just to show you can get them on? Anyone can do shoddy, ill-prepared, technically unsound work.' It *was* an achievement just to get them on. But the reasons for doing it ran much deeper. Despite all the obvious drawbacks, there was paradoxically one great advantage.

Artistic freedom. Even if the compromises at times seemed unending, in another way the line was straight and true. The release of the language, the quality of the story-telling, at its best, was exhilarating. Nobody can get a production right. As a director, you do one good one, one bad one, one medium. You spend your time trying to eliminate the bad one. Then with one good and two medium, you're pretty good. With two good, and one medium, you're world class. And here we were with seven on offer. It's a very simple equation really. If you get 90% of a production right (What is right?) you are a world beater. At 75% it is a great production and about the most that any self-respecting director can hope for. The problem with getting even 75% of *The Wars of the Roses* right, however, is that while out of twenty-four hours eighteen might be passable, that still leaves six whole hours that are naff! That's two whole plays! ('Which two?' I hear you cry. Opinions vary.) And if Bath Theatre Royal was too small the year before this time it was pretty catastrophic. We knew the routine, however. Build a platform out the back for the lights, to store the props, etc. The weather in December this year was mercifully mild, no repeat of last year's audience deep freeze. For some unfathomable reason, known only to the gods of theatre statistics, the year before, the turnover had been sensational. This time the public, if not exactly staying away, were not exactly besieging the box office. From being one of the most successful venues, Bath turned out to be almost our worst. Why? It was the same time of year, the weather better, four new plays on offer. Was it an omen? *Richard II*, the first one in, was certainly pretty shaky. Very long, that first performance, three and a half hours. (Amazing the number of people who, having seen that opening night, were to say two years later, 'Funny, it's changed beyond all recognition.') Technically none of the shows was up to much, and *House of York* and *Lancaster* were very messy. Each of them contained twenty-four fast-moving scenes. They needed tightening. The best was *Richard III*. It was clear that Andy was going to deliver all that he had promised in rehearsal, and the two scenes at the end were sensational. Andy's armour only just arrived in time for the Bath opening, and when he donned it we discovered to our horror that the hump had been built on the wrong side of his back. In a series of frantic phone calls, we ascertained that there was just enough time to get it changed. We had done it on the cheap. Straps and buckles were to break, and bits fly off – one of the penalties of tight budgets. The 'quick changes' in and out of costume on that first performance took an eternity.* *Richard III* ran four hours. I had written *à la* Jan Kott a staged introduction to the central characters.† The company was split as to its necessity. To the end, opinion was divided. I thought that maybe it was necessary for single performances, but for trilogies and cycles . . . Barry Stanton had not had time to learn it and carried a folder as if he were a 'Miss World'/'Come Dancing' compère.

The Introduction, effected in elegant thirties cream outfits to the background of a cool modern jazz number played by the company, went down sensationally. Not that the laughter was all intentional. As when John Darrell stepped forward, bass guitar strapped to his

---

*Pennington: Finally (almost) I flopped down in my room at the end of House of York, *relaxing in a tasty beige suit. Hugh Sullivan burst in, immaculate in collar and tie, waistcoat and jacket, cream shoes – and no trousers. Framed in the doorway, he demanded mine off me. I'd forgotten. They were one of the pairs that were to be shared.*

†*Shakespeare our Contemporary* – the chapter on the kings. See Appendix 7.

white suit, to be announced as Earl Rivers . . . 'And there you have it, the Woodvilles, the Plantagenets, the Politicians, the Ladies.'

It was an exhausted Allied Irish party that saw us off for Christmas. We were patently unprepared. What would a three-week break do? The next time we would perform this ridiculous feat would be in Hong Kong.

CHAPTER
6

THE SECOND TOUR

January–March 1988

> *'I liked Hong Kong very much – roads,
> buses, railways; I even travelled on a
> rickshaw. Everywhere in Hong Kong you
> can see how solicitous the English are to
> their employees. There's even a sailors'
> club. Of course the English exploit the
> Chinese, but they do bring them roads,
> museums and Christianity, whereas we
> Russians, we exploit people but what do
> we give in return?'*
>
> *Anton Chekhov*

Pennington: *The Wars of the Roses* called for a formidable list of
weaponry: ten M.16 replicas, Sterlings, Lee Enfields, grenades and
handguns, to look only at the mechanised element. All these items
naturally had to be accounted for on a Customs carnet when they
were to travel abroad, and we always expected them to attract the
interest of some diligent officer who might ask what a
Shakespearian company were doing with such things, side by side
with the more predictable medieval broadswords and breastplates.
What was the decoy for what? It would then fall to Derek
Scriminger, Stage Manager, and his Props Supervisor, Rosy
Fowler, to interest the officer in an aesthetic of stage design that
sought to reflect the development of warfare across the centuries
from heroic hand-to-hand conflict to advanced technology; the

officer might then take on the sceptical look of one of our national theatre critics. Fortunately the question never got asked; and as the company rose from their beds in January, aching not so much from the aftermath of Christmas but from the shock of opening seven plays in Bath immediately beforehand, to take the long flight east for the Hong Kong Festival (where we were to open forty-eight hours after touching down), we also managed to get away with carrying one more gun than was itemised on the carnet, not for any wicked purpose but because pre-Christmas panic had damaged Derek's arithmetic. Once there, he had to take special care to conceal the deception from the Hong Kong police as well; it is quite illegal to possess firearms of any kind, and so the entire armoury plus one had to be deposited at Wanchai police station for safe keeping after the show each night. Thus it was that Derek, who has in himself a little of the glamour of Warren Beatty playing Clyde Barrow crossed with the piratical leanness of the rock 'n' roll gipsy he used to be, and Rosy, whose demure bespectacled prettiness irresistibly suggests the latent violence of Baader Meinhof, could be seen each midnight trudging through the streets of the Crown Colony with kitbags full of the things, terrifying their taxi drivers and indeed any new desk sergeant at the station – and climactically, after the closing night, taking a short trip on the Star Ferry to ditch the rather large remaining quantity of blank ammunition off the top deck into Hong Kong Harbour.

All this provocative behaviour would perhaps have gone down even worse at the time of writing, when 1997 looms large on everyone's agenda; but the Hong Kong Chinese were angry with Britain even then, dreading the secession to mainland China of what someone has described as the paste jewel in her ear, and repeatedly pointing to the example of Portugal, who, by contrast with Britain, had handed out passports to every member of their (much smaller) community on Macau. In the remote and misleading world of showbusiness, however, the Chinese showed up in surprisingly large numbers for our very British entry to the Festival, drawing unmistakeable pleasure from it and doing something to balance out a predominantly expatriate audience. Perhaps our manner, dressing by character rather than chronology and feeling able to let ten years pass with a flick of the wrist, is not so very far from that of traditional Chinese theatre, in which an upturned table may stand for a wall, an oar for a dinghy on the ocean, and all finally depends on the actor's expressive physical sculpture *en plein air*.

Bogdanov: *I was one of the few who knew what to expect from Hong Kong. Some three years previously, in January 1985, my production of* Hiawatha *had visited the Hong Kong Festival from the National Theatre. We had played in the Queen Elizabeth Hall, a sports stadium. This time we were in the spanking new Arts Centre. The set and props now, as then, had been built out there. For* Hiawatha *it had been a bamboo lash-up job, and the painters, thinking our own colour scheme a bit drab, had decided that things needed brightening up and had added their own imaginative touches. Flowers and dragons sprouted everywhere and Hiawatha's chums all sported rainbow tom toms. We had pointed out as kindly as we could that this was not exactly what was wanted, and tried not to look as the hurt faces turned what had been a proud manifestation of eastern individuality back to grey western conformism. For* The Wars of the Roses *there were no such problems. The steel set was a bit heavier, glossier, but only the great sofa and chair shrieked 'I am bright red' at you. This was the set that was to take a slow boat to Chicago for our date there. The shows were rocky. Moments that had not had any cement to solidify them in the first place fell apart. And yet something was happening. We started the fortnight with a noticeable preponderance of expats. By the end, the balance had changed. Chinese audiences were finding something in the plays to relate to. Certainly it would appear that their prejudices were not confirmed. We had feared that Shakespeare would represent to them all that was inaccessible in our minority culture that, for a hundred years, had dominated six million people. There does arise, of course, the debate as to why one should be arrogantly exporting that culture to Hong Kong in the first place. However, there we were, and grateful that we were at least not confirming their worst fears.*

Pennington: Nevertheless, a guest at the British Council reception after the opening night felt able to come bounding up to me, moist of eye, and declare his joy at seeing an *English* company out here for a change, neatly splicing together as he did so the fervent home-sickness and simultaneous parochialism of any expatriate community anywhere. The occasional awkwardness of overseas touring was underlined. In Britain one may try to go beneath the guard of the cultural establishment to some degree, or at least that element of it that would annex you as an asset rather than enjoy you as a sustenance, and hope to solicit a rawer response from a more unguarded public. Abroad you cannot avoid something of an ambassadorial profile and a certain proprietorial friendliness from the Brits; this accompanies the sense, usually correct, that you are resented quite deeply by local groups who are fighting for a mite of the $150,000 that, for example, the Hong Kong Festival's sponsors had cheerfully dished out for our two-week visit, counting the eventual loss as $20,000 worth of prestige. We found this local anger openly expressed sometimes in Australia and the U.S., and more covertly so in the rickety context of Hong Kong, where we were playing sometimes to English people who after forty years in the Colony were proud of speaking no word of Cantonese, side by side with Chinese who spoke no English.

Bogdanov: *At the end of the first week in Hong Kong, Ted Irwin (who had now taken over permanently as Production Manager from Simon, much to Prue's relief) and I flew to Japan to set up our Tokyo visit in April. Due to the prohibitive cost of air freighting or shipping our set by sea, we were having yet a third version constructed in Tokyo. What that meant, in fact, was a set of mobile towers and a cantilevered bridge. In general, we would use the 'thrust stage' version now 'perfected' at Chichester.*

On arrival we were met and wined and dined by our promoter, Mr Seijo Tamura. The meal was a perfect example of the insidious western ways that are slowly invading Japanese culture. It was a strange mixture of eastern and what passed for western food, enormous quantities of shellfish being served up alongside bits of liver, raw chunks of pineapple, eggs and whole raw aubergines which we were invited to bite into. I arrived back at the Imperial Hotel at 3 am to find an urgent message to ring home. My mother had died. She had spent Christmas with us before moving to a nursing home. She had lung cancer. There was nothing I could do. I decided to cut short my stay by one day, but to finish the job we had come to do.

The pink and grey theatre – which became known to us as the 'Tokyo Grobe' – was a Japanese artist's impression of what the Elizabethan version might have looked like if it had been fed through a 'modern living' computer. It had patently been designed by someone who had no practical idea of how a theatre functions at all. (This is often the case with contemporary architects. Many would say the design of the National Theatre and the Barbican are perfect examples of architectural ignorance.) It was the end of

January and it was only half built. They assured us it would be
ready in time for its April opening. In England, one would have
said, 'You mean April next year?' There was initially no access to
the stage whatsoever, and no storage space. There were huge fire
doors everywhere. The two 'Juliet balconies' on either side of the
proscenium were purely decorative; there was no means of getting
to them. 'What are they for?' I asked. 'For sound speakers.' 'How
do you get them there?' 'Up a ladder.' We persuaded them to
construct a walkway behind, with a door to make them practical
and also to construct two openings underneath the balconies to
give access to the forestage. (Otherwise it meant opening one of
the great fire doors at the back to get onto stage at all.) We opened
up two entrances at the back, constructed a new corridor to
provide access to the stage from the side, and re-allocated the
space underneath the stage for dressing rooms and storage. At the
point of inspection it was planned to cram twenty people into one
small cubicle with only one shower. When I say 'constructed',
what I mean is that Ted and I argued with the architects and
planners about alternatives before Ted drew up a set of plans in
three days, virtually re-designing the space as far as was possible.
The solutions were rough and ready but the best we could do in
the circumstances to make the stage usable at all. We had got there
just in time.

Pennington: Back in Hong Kong, reflecting on the wide divergences
of the visit, our company reeled back from Chassagne Montrachet
receptions up on the Peak and Government House lunches to purge
themselves for two weeks in the mercantile sulphurousness of
Aberdeen Harbour or Nathan Street in Kowloon, where on the
pavement cafés you can refresh yourself on raw liver swimming in
a watery broth among other livid and nameless entrails, or buy
bad-bargain suits from Sammy the Tailor: choose your cloth, get
measured, pay and wait until, just as you finally leave your hotel,
or even at the airport, Sammy will arrive with your finished suit;
at which point you are too relieved to make much of the fact that
its cloth, though similar in pattern, has a certain soapy shininess
that you don't remember from the tweed sample you so carefully
chose. Beyond the approximate length of Sammy's sleeves could
also, on the outgoing flight, be seen a variety of dollar watches –
but not on the wrist of Siôn Probert, who, as soon as he had got
back from the market and into the bath, had watched the whole

face of his ('waterproof to nine fathoms') gently lift off, the lettering wobbling dreamily up into the soapsuds.

Striking some sort of mean between these extremes of tone, the legendary Sir Run Run Shaw invited us up to his studios for lunch one day. Sir Run Run has moved on from Kung Fu movies – instead of the forty features a year (yes, forty) with which he used to ply his huge chain of South East Asian cinemas, he now delivers 3,000 hours of television to a hungry network from the fifteen stages of his production village, which also incorporates an acting school and apartments for many of his 1,200 employees. Here, at the other end of a dizzyingly beautiful drive into the New Territories, he looks down from his mountain peak onto the pacific blue of Clear Water Bay, lamenting the holiday homes that have begun to obscure his view in the last few years like breezeblock toads in his paradise. Sir Run Run, an unlikely ascetic at 82, rises religiously each morning to perform Tai Chi Chuan and rigorous breathing exercises, and he takes an equally disciplined view on entertaining: turning my eyes to him from a barely-begun dessert, I was surprised to find him on his feet, myself and my colleagues beginning to be borne by an urgent and invisible wind towards the door, where two maitresses d' were already in position like usherettes to bow us out, wiping our mouths in surprise. It was ten past two, and apparently we had done well to get past two o'clock. I hope Run Run didn't punish himself too hard the next day.

Recovering from Run Run's Bum's Rush, we sat in the bars of the Harbour View International Hotel – which may by now have changed its name, since (land reclamation from the harbour being still in fullish swing) it will by now be cowering behind a new waterside skyscraper; or, in the case of Colin Farrell, making dour trips to the Telegraph Office next door, whence, having made nice judgements about time differences and the dollar against the minute, he would return rather more lonely than before, since the satellite disharmonies of the long distance phone – are you pausing or just catching up? – had made him feel if anything slightly further away from his family. We headed out to the Buddhist mountain monasteries of Lantau and Castle Peak Hill in cold so violent that a contemplation of golden Buddhas now always provokes in me a longing for cappuccino and bathfoam. Far more to the point for myself at least, I kept an appointment with Jackie Pullinger, the extraordinary Christian missionary from England, who, following God's voice off the boat, armed only with an unshakeable faith and therefore a belief in the miraculous, has achieved it in reclaiming many of the hoodlums and junkies embedded in the infamous Walled City. This square mile or so of tenement was preserved as a Chinese enclave when the island was ceded to Britain in 1842, and soon it became an asylum for villains where the Hong Kong police, even had they had the jurisdiction, might have feared to tread. During the Second World War the Japanese tore down the walls and used them to build the runway for Kai Tak airport a few hundred yards away; peeled of its shell, the livid body of the place hurts to the touch. Those tourist guides that refer to it at all recommend it as an interesting spot to 'peer into'; anyone who looks at its misery and squalor in that spirit deserves to be rooked by the illegal dentists whose windows, stuffed with grinning plastic jaws, form a cordon around the huge slum. The City lies directly under the flight path of one of the world's busiest airports, and once inside the enclave you could look up and read the writing on the undersides of the incoming planes – or would be able to, but for the fact that virtually no light enters the place from above; the upper stories lean in to join each other, allowing only excrement and skeins of garbage to fall on any unwisely upturned face. It is like a huge, highly populated, open sewer.

Jackie's upturned face, as many people now know, moves like a light through this blackness in which the Triad gangs murder and mutilate, where prostitutes can be eight or eighty, and opiate addiction is as universal as the rats that scurry across your feet. The deal she has struck with the gang bosses – give me your smacked-out operatives and I will cure them and return them to you more efficient – is one she seems able to renege on, since, once clean, they are more likely to become honorary Triad members than active ones. Jackie uses as cure not a gram of methadone but the fervent ecstatic experience of the prayer meeting, where speaking in tongues is quite common; she, something between Joan of Arc, a hot gospeller and a sensible sports captain, induces in them an equivalent but healthful ecstasy. She is, of course, re-addicting them – to life; but that truism does little to explain the demonstrable fact that the physical symptoms of withdrawal are almost entirely absent from the process. Looking into the brightly serene, cheerfully proselytising faces of young men who have murdered and robbed and never had clean blood in their own veins either, it is impossible not to feel on the edge of the miraculous.

One of the boys who had lunch with us at a stall on the edge of the
City, sensibly sterilising the chopsticks in hot tea (God is needed for
more important tasks) had recently run away from her insistent
fervour and now come back afraid; you could sense the darkness he
had re-entered for a moment. The T-shirts Jackie's huge 'family' print
and sell declare: 'Love always perseveres, always protects, keeps no
score of wrongs, never fails'; and of course it is the experience of
unconditional human love that has reclaimed them. Like many
people certain of a large mission, Jackie is tremendously at ease,
approachable and friendly, and in fact the pleasant blandness of her
immediate personality makes sense: all her character has gone into
her mountainous work; logical too, when you think of it, is her
fanatical intolerance not only of obstructive bureaucracy (she is not
generally mentioned in dispatches) and organised Christianity, but
of any other religious creed at all (Buddhism is a particular demon).
Such is the price paid for such extraordinary curative success.
Nobody in the Walled City greets her without a smile; accepting our
hospitality in return, she issues out of her tiny room (she lives in the
Walled City full time) where she plays Mozart and paints her nails, to
come gaudily uptown to see *Henry V*. Sitting in a dressing room that
could house two or three of her families, feeding themselves on the
price of a ticket, I am hoping that the ambiguous but persistent
identification of the play's hero with God will interest her; but in fact
she just enjoys her evening. The three of us who had plunged hungrily
into her world for a moment, gobbling up its horror like advanced
tourists, performed that night in a state of inner exhaustion
somewhat similar, I remember, to the evening after playing the
maximum security prison at Long Lartin some years ago: a fatigue
brought on, I dare say, by the effort of holding a certain revulsion at
bay for long enough to reflect on what we were seeing. We were also
noticeably nicer to each other that evening and more than usually
offended by the smaller preoccupations of our colleagues, who had
been out striking bargains all day.

Climbing narrowly above the Walled City, banking and tilting to
avoid high buildings on either side (is it true that pilots get danger
money for landing here?), skimming the sea at the start of the long
journey home, merry touring faces suggest that rich pickings of all
kinds have been had.

Bogdanov: *On the negative side, though, I was struck down in the
middle of the first week by a bout of food poisoning contracted*

through eating mussels at an English establishment called Bentley's: receiving, as a consequence, a life-time invitation to eat there for free. Andy Chelton, our Master Carpenter, in turn was struck down with a collapsed lung. Monica McCabe, our new Company Manager, and I took him some books in hospital and I was shocked to find him on a drip feed, isolated, with no one around him who could speak English. He seemed cheerful enough, but the doctors were concerned about the effect flying back to England would have on his lungs and he was left behind to follow on some weeks later. Phil Large, his companion on many a fit-up, would step into the breach in Chichester. Not only that, he would step into the lift shaft in the dark, fall twenty feet and break his leg. He had been trying to find his way round the back of the stage by way of going over the top of the theatre in the dark. The only other way was to go outside. He opened a door that should have been kept locked and stepped off into the blackness. He was lucky to be alive, and to be found.

Pennington: Back on the plane, Adam Daly (Assistant Electrics) has fallen in love in a night club with a Japanese girl who speaks no English; a year later he was to go back and marry her, but for the moment he is heartbroken. Simon Elliott has a thirty-piece crockery set; all those unworn suits sit fetidly in the hold; and Hugh Sullivan has been told by a fortune teller who took him for a businessman that he can look forward to a full life with many men under him – and since Hugh is well out of the closet by now he is a happy man. With the sense of not quite having caught up with ourselves since Bath, with memories of tediously duplicitous tailors, rabid diplomats, unlikely love, and the abiding faith of an extraordinary woman, we thus went home to Chichester in the rain. There the miracle of faith was to be sorely needed by Colin Farrell, who had been so frustrated by the long distance phone; for during the second Monday there, news reached him that his adored daughter Madeleine, a popular and gifted student at the Bristol Old Vic Theatre School, had been mown down by a car as she crossed the street. Raced by Ian Burford to Bristol, along roads familiar to him from when the family lived in Brighton and visited Madeleine at the School, he was, with his wife Ann Penfold, at Madeleine's bedside by midnight; but she never recovered consciousness.

The theatre often seems to mimic life and death in a banal and frivolous way; and yet without it we might be lost. When John Price died and the unbelievable thought dawned on all of us that we would not see him come loping through the door of this rehearsal room again, we went back to work within half an hour, hoping it was the right thing to do. Michael Cronin had to begin that session with the death of Warwick from *Henry VI House of York*, and he never thereafter played it with more – or less – power:

> Thus yields the cedar to the axe's edge
> Whose arms gave shelter to the princely eagle;
> These eyes, that now are dimm'd with death's
>   black veil,
> Have been as piercing as the midday sun . . .

Now, so soon after, we circled round the terrible privacy of Madeleine's death, trying to be businesslike, trying not to be too businesslike, absolutely oppressed by the triviality of what we had to do. Colin was to return, delicately, to us a fortnight later in Nottingham, when the company would close quietly about him. The interim, for him, for Ann, for their son Tom and for their parents, is naturally the absent page in this book; but once he was back with us Colin's wonderful work never faltered, though the plays must have been like fields of knives for him, each move he made practised during the last eighteen months of his daughter's life, littered with circumstances and simple lines that must often have sliced into him. He played squash, he ran, and his open good humour began to build a sort of moral centre in the midst of a fellowship that instinctively looks for leaders to define its humanity. How could you complain about your dressing room anywhere near Colin? In the subsequent season we were able, with full conscience, to bring Ann Penfold into the company to play a major range of parts with him, and to watch the public recovery of two very remarkable people.

Back in Chichester, there was much to be done, trivial but alarming. It was Tuesday morning. John Dougall was scheduled to play Prince Hal/Henry V for the first time on the Wednesday and Thursday, bringing in his train a domino-like series of smaller cast changes involving many people. We had to finish rehearsing this reshuffle. We now combined this work with replacement rehearsals for all Colin's understudies in all seven plays. How watertight was the understudy system? It was early in the season; Bath and Hong Kong had poleaxed everybody; everybody had six or seven parts of

Henry VI House of Lancaster – Paul Brennen as King Henry
(LB)

Richard III: 'So now prosperity begins to mellow/And drop into the rotten mouth of death' – June Watson as Queen Margaret (LB)

Richard III: (above) Andrew Jarvis as Richard (LB);
(below) Charles Dale (Richmond) and Andrew Jarvis (Richard) (LB)

Hong Kong harbour, January 1988 (JT)

varying size to cover; and though contractually all understudies should be word-perfect by the first night, under these special circumstances it would hardly be surprising if somebody hadn't got there. Miraculously, all Colin's parts were more or less learned, except for Gloucester in *Henry VI Lancaster*, which the understudy didn't know at all. Stubbornly jibbing at the idea of someone going on with a book, a public admission of defeat tolerated too often by companies that should know better, I decided to learn the part myself in time for the play's performance on Saturday morning. It was a simple and unheroic solution: I was playing Old Mortimer in that play, a delightful role consisting entirely of a speech of historical information delivered from under rugs in a wheelchair – at the end of which the poor fellow falls back, expires from the effort, and is wheeled solemnly away. All I would then have to do would be to throw off my rugs to reveal the Edwardian morning suit of Humphrey of Gloucester and go straight back on. There would also be no domino effect, as Mortimer was the only part I was playing in the show.

So what we had to combine was principal rehearsals for Dougall and his team, replacement rehearsals (fine distinction) for Colin's covers, and a new part for me. Barely a scene in the seven plays was unaffected by the changes, not to mention people who normally moved appointed pieces of furniture now being stranded in another part of the forest and unable to do so. It is a little-known and useless fact that *Richard II* (Tuesday night) is a cinch for doubling, and therefore for understudy nights – Gaunt dies as Carlisle begins (so Carlisle can cover Gaunt); Bushy and Green are dead and available for other parts by the middle of Act III. On this occasion Michael Cronin suffered banishment as Mowbray and then returned within a moment, rolling John of Gaunt on in a wheelchair, ready to start as the Duke of York in Colin's place. He not only knew the part perfectly but had given serious thought to it, and so was able expertly to bring out the Polonius theme of the out-of-control father struggling to maintain his public life. On Wednesday I sat for the first time in an ESC audience for John Dougall's premiere, fearful of having overlooked some detail of replacement, but enjoying a very full Chichester house (how different from 1987) and the palpable presence of an excited regular audience around me, many of whom were well aware of John from his work the previous season and were intrigued by this new development. John's performance, built brick by brick, was meticulous, if at this stage lacking some of the animal drive that propels the plays from the centre, and it drew cheers at the call. I went round after the show, feeling dry and bony in the midst of corks popping, sweaty hair and eyes wild with excitement. Directors must often feel like this, subtly excluded from the party. Unable to compete with the merriment, I went home to bed with *Henry VI Lancaster*, realising soberly that it was my turn next.

In short, we honourably got through this desperate week. Another tragedy had struck, making everything else trivial; in its shadow, if one could only have seen it, there was a subtle turning of a tide in our affairs, and some of the better qualities of our profession on show. The public had been well treated. John Dougall had taken centre stage and demonstrated something about himself and what our company aspired to be, calling forth a creative flexibility in all around him. As it happened, the ESC's finances had begun to take an upward swing as well. We made as much – £40,000 – in Chichester as we had lost there a year before; although we were about to lose much of that in Nottingham, in itself it more or less wiped out the deficit brought forward from 1987 which had effectively reduced our production budget for putting on *The Wars of the Roses*. We were now able to appoint a full-time General Manager, Kirsten Oploh. From Nottingham we went on to Hull, the only theatre on the tour to refuse the full cycle and ask only for the new productions, thus making nonsense of the sequence (and of Barry Stanton's time – his big parts, Falstaff and the Chorus, not on show at all); but at least our costs were covered there.

Bogdanov: *It was here, during the course of a company meeting to talk about Tokyo and the American date beyond, that John Castle launched an attack on me for not being present enough at the performances. In vain I pointed out that I had a living to earn, that having received my fee for directing the productions, the ESC only paid me some £5,000 a year. I found every opportunity possible to catch up with the shows. It was a source of constant frustration to me that I was not able to keep them in shape. To no avail. Insisting on calling me 'Bogdin' (my real name, and the one by which John knew me from Trinity), he concluded that it must be because I had been badly brought up. Yes, that was it, I was common. I walked out. Common am I? Right. I went round the corner and had some fish and chips.*

Pennington: In Manchester and Birmingham we boomed and were reviewed by the national press, who reported 'a huge achievement ... the spectacle of the Palace filled to the rafters with an audience of all ages and all classes should convince anyone who still needs convincing that there's a real need, a real hunger for the serious arts' (*Sunday Times*); Michael Ratcliffe in *The Observer*, noting the speed with which the ESC had sprung up and confirmed its popularity 'had to pinch myself to make sure it was true. It is also time, now that the ESC is established, to ask what the company is doing, how good it really is, and where it's likely to go.' Such questions represent acceptance of a kind. Unmistakeably, we had our own audience, offering us the energetic continuity of repertory, quite deeply involved in us. We approached Easter and a financial breakeven on a ladder that looked to have only a few fragile rungs beyond. But we were also developing a history, as troubled and enhancing as three years of life itself. We had achieved the barely possible in Chichester in the immediate shadow of a tragedy that afflicted every parent in the company and bewildered everyone in their twenties. On the last night there I heard John Castle, he who had stepped into a dead man's shoes on entering the company, sobbing in the dressing room next to mine; the sound stood for what our profitable week had cost. In my own room, I had just heard that a young member of our first company who had once tried to set fire to my dressing room, run away during rehearsals, and then gatecrashed the Christmas party in Bath, finally falling asleep on my dressing room sofa there, was now lying under sedation in St Thomas's Hospital. He had been to a party, taken a swing at an actor there who had spoken disparagingly of the ESC, and then thrown himself off Blackfriars Bridge, his head and eyebrows completely shaved.

CHAPTER

7

JAPAN AND THE U.S.

April–June 1988

'It is the man who drinks the first cup of sake, then the second cup of sake drinks the first; then it is the sake that drinks the man.'
                                        Japanese proverb

'Chicago is the land of promise to all malcontents.'
            Mgr. Count Vay de Vaya and Luskod, 1908

Pennington: The ESC's nine-week visit to Tokyo, Chicago and Connecticut in April, May and early June of 1988 was our first prolonged flight from home: a round-the-world trip for which Toronto and Hong Kong had been the slimmest of preparations. It wasn't planned with any inherent logic; but having known by mid-1987 that we would need extensive overseas dates to save our financial life, we had, for this Spring, linked together various disparate organisations in a wild daisy chain. Michael's contact, Martyn Naylor, had been advising us for some time about possible promoters and venues in Japan; and the actress-producer Julie Dawn Cole had introduced us to Mr Tamura, who had dined Michael so eccentrically on his visit from Hong Kong. Meanwhile we were to be at the Chicago International Festival for the month of May; and Randall Brion and Deborah Smith of the Stamford

Center for the Arts in Connecticut hoped to present us there for a single weekend when we had finished in Chicago if American Equity could be appeased. Even after all these offers fell back-to-back into place, the whole enterprise called for a degree of lateral thinking. For example, the Japanese set was now built; the one we had played on in Hong Kong in January was on its way by sea to meet us in Chicago; and the English set, having played Glasgow the week before we left for Japan on 1st April, was going into store, to emerge for the York Festival in June and then hibernate once more before turning up in Newcastle in October. (The Hong Kong – Chicago set would by then be on its way to Australia for the autumn season there.) In general, both Japanese and Americans would have preferred to bring the show straight out to them and send it back again to England, for simplicity's sake; but since we had to move rapidly from venue to venue, they had to be persuaded to accept our circular passage and carve up the production's travelling expenses fifty-fifty, the Japanese taking the first half of the responsibility, and then so to speak abandoning their cargo over the Pacific for the Americans to pay through to Chicago and home. United only by their interest in us, the two parties regarded each other watchfully.

By April, the Tokyo Globe Project was, miraculously, on schedule, ready for us to open on Shakespeare's birthday on the 23rd. The theatre that Michael and Ted had visited had been designed by the celebrated Arata Isozaki, whose work also includes the Palladium in New York and the Sports Hall for the 1992 Barcelona Olympics. It was sitting on land formerly owned by the Tokyo Government and now released, with many caveats and conditions, to a consortium of sixty-six property developers summarised as the Shinjuku Nishitoyama Development Company, alias Tower Homes. The consortium had jumped on the offer and within twenty-two months under Mr Tamura's direction had completed, at a cost of £8 million, a complex comprising the Globe itself, an Italian-style piazza with coffee-shop and delicatessen, and the Globe Tavern (the one area which was to develop an authentic Shakespearian rowdiness thanks to Mr Tamura's exceptional hospitality to our company), as well as a small Greek amphitheatre, which he insisted – often on his way out of the Globe Tavern well beyond the witching hour – would soon be being used by the ESC for a festival of Greek tragedies. All this nestled under three high-rise apartment blocks in the Takadanobaba district, one stop north of Shinjuku on the Yamanote line; it was a typical Japanese manifestation in fact, a leisure centre springing up in a residential rather than commercial area of the city.

The theatre itself was based not on the first Elizabethan Globe Theatre but on the second, which replaced the building known to Shakespeare after it was gutted by fire in 1613. Perhaps this was an oriental deference to Sam Wanamaker, who has laboured hard and long to recreate the original in Southwark – but the difference between the two is small. Mr Tamura's policy for his first season was based on the motto 'Shakespeare and before, Beckett and after', and it was of a kind unlikely to win him many friends among the grassroots artistic community in Tokyo, as it followed the principle that big bucks were always available for classy western imports, but perhaps not for homegrown work. And big bucks were certainly needed; we were to open the theatre with our modest repertoire, and be followed in by the RSC with a series of work-shops, the National Theatre with their trilogy of Shakespeare's late plays, and Ingmar Bergman's company with *Hamlet*. A promising opening season, albeit one based on cultural borrowing. All in a theatre holding 650 only and with seat prices deflated to £20 – half the going rate in Tokyo. Recoupment was clearly out of the question; prestige and profile were all.

At first sight, as we came off the bus on a slushy April morning with snow still on the ground, the building looked startling without being promising. On the one hand, it did have the twin-gabled, cupolaed aspect passed down by Wenceslaus Hollar, sitting drawing in a nearby church tower on Bankside in 1640. On the other hand, it was salmon pink. Again, there was a large reproduction of the Droeshout portrait of Shakespeare on its front aspect; but the adjoining piazza forecourt was occupied by a demonstration model Nissan, since the area had been leased out for the time being to that company. To anyone familiar with modern Japan, such contiguities are unsurprising. What was odd, once inside, was to see the extent to which Mr Tamura and his colleagues had declined to exploit the site's commercial potential.

The operation was based on a generous sacrifice; the land under the Globe is wildly expensive and a patently uneconomical theatre sits on it. The very thought of reproducing a Shakespearian playhouse makes a theatre economist blanch: to be authentic, almost half of the whole interior needs to consist of stage and backstage, making up the Elizabethan half-moon which bisected the circular building, with no modern module stuck on for storage or dressing-room space. Accepting this and reducing their revenue still further, the Japanese developers were offering seats that were both large and prodigally dispersed: an effort to make the customer comfortable that had drastically reduced the seating capacity (the original Globe held 2,000, many standing, though the Elizabethans are thought to have been of smaller stature than us and may not have minded the equivalent of Tokyo rush-hour conditions). However, this gesture was largely confounded by the fact that all the seats, while naturally angled towards the stage, somehow faced away from its focal point; from some a spectator looked clean across the forestage into the opposite wing, from others due north upstage but way over from the centre – all in some way athwart the action; and from the upper galleries spectators had to crane and peer (rather like the Barbican) vertiginously down, getting little but our bald patches. Nor was the splendid building very user-friendly; we were going to have our work cut out. Downstage of the rather narrow proscenium opening (the equivalent of the Elizabethan pillars separating mainstage from forestage) an apron area the entire width of the auditorium fanned out. This was perhaps a subconscious echo of the Noh theatre's *hashi-gakari*, the long corridor of approach between dressing room and stage along which the audience watches the protagonists ceremonially enter; for us it presented the basic problem of re-timing every downstage entrance through seven plays – though it must be said that the distance suited well those 'Beyond the Fringe' Shakespearian entrances which are announced several lines in advance – 'I think I hear them coming . . . bloody with spurring, fiery-red with haste' – which have covered for generations of actors still hastening from their dressing rooms.

In sole charge of the productions for the time being, I now saw the sense of Michael's warnings in Hong Kong. Although there was a proscenium arch, there was no facility for flying scenery behind it, despite the height of the roof. What to do about Chris Dyer's bridge, dropping in and out of the action? There was no other means of creating an upper level to work on – or at least none with any offstage access – and I reckoned the Chichester solution of simply playing everything on the floor would not look good on this smaller stage. So we would have to use it somehow. Then, there were large assembly doors set on either side just downstage of the proscenium which seemed to promise some natty fast entrances and exits from inner sanctums; but they opened inwards onto blank walls. The window frames above these doors – the 'Juliet balconies' – could indeed now be approached by a winding catwalk from the backstage area; but it was daunting to negotiate it even in full light, let alone blackout. In the end we supported either end of the bridge on the lip of these balconies, in front of the proscenium arch. When not in use, rather than flying out of sight, it rose only to the visible level of the ceiling, and up there there was no access at all; anybody left on the bridge as it started to rise would not only have lost their route offstage but would have been remorselessly crushed against the roof when it completed its ascent.* Our twin scaffolding towers, moving swiftly around, normally created the Boar's Head Tavern, Lord Hastings' house and other locations; but here there was literally nowhere to put them: they were too tall to go to and fro under the proscenium arch, too much of an impediment behind it, and would have to be housed at the side of the apron, where they would inhibit entrances as well as blocking the beams of Mark Henderson's vivid crosslighting, on which much of the atmosphere of the shows depended. Backstage the 'tiring houses' were small but they were now adequate, and each had a pay-phone in it; but the route to the stage was up a flight of fifty-six steps, an experience which wore pretty thin towards the end of a trilogy. And even then you'd only reached the *hashi-gakari*.

Stella Bond and Sue Best and I sat in some grimness, contemplating the task of remounting the seven productions between the Wednesday morning and the Friday evening, when our first marathon weekend ever, in which all seven plays would be performed by the Sunday night, was to begin. I was reckoning without the extreme adaptability of the company, veterans of the open stage of Chichester and so quite able to dump the set and improvise, just as they were used to expanding and contracting

---

*Which could be the lesser of two evils: there is a story of a particularly obliging Japanese stage carpenter helping a foreign company into his theatre who had the misfortune to be holding on to a flying bar at the moment it was taken up during a morning technical rehearsal; only after several hours did somebody think fit to interrupt the honoured guest director and point out the dilemma of the carpenter, who was still hanging aloft like a monkey in the flytower.

their scale of playing almost at will. The fact that the shows opened two and a half days later in some style – helter-skelter one on top of another with barely a pause between each of the seven – testifies to the habit of enlightened busking that actors, staff and stage management by now had at their fingers' ends. We felt like a Shakespearian commando group, arriving relaxedly on any stage in any country, casing it quickly, tossing a couple of lines (not much more) of blank verse into the void, before buzzing off to tea and then re-emerging with more or less chutzpah as the Regency officers and lounge lizards of Richard II's lotus-eating court at half past seven. Any suggestion of a dress rehearsal in a new town, common practice in many companies, would have been howled down. It sometimes seemed that the most obviously necessary preparations were becoming superfluous.

They weren't, of course, although the gains to be had from this kind of limited virtuosity are many, particularly perhaps for young actors now rapidly becoming confident enough not to mind the size of a theatre or whether there was a set behind them at all. At a time when many designers laboriously impose their own pompous visions on the plays, there are a handful of bumptious performers knocking around who know that to have a bare stage and Shakespeare on your side is worth any amount of that. The loss of course is of a certain kind of perfectionism which, even as we were throwing the shows on in Tokyo, we tried in fits to rediscover. There are times (a Kabuki actor would understand this) when to take a single step to the left or the right will make a stage picture work where previously it was nondescript, and such a tiny choice may also suddenly clarify a character's relationship to the world around. If you move on a line rather than after it, a scene can become fluid instead of dying on its feet. So, although we were working so fast, we also invited ourselves to be a degree more precise, to spot a patch of light more accurately than we had done before. Accuracy had often been the casualty of the way we worked, and the victim production was invariably *Richard II*, which not only was the guinea pig that opened the sequence, but is in any case a highly-wrought piece – virtually every line in the play has exactly ten syllables, and there is no prose at all; it doesn't really lend itself to the rough and ready. *Henry IV Part 1* the previous year had been the equivalent guinea pig but its tone is much more rangey and demotic, the fabric much rougher. Time and again *Richard II* suffered from a faltering of tone, a residue of uncertainty about the dynamic of the house, and simply the lack of thinking time we were allowing ourselves to re-imagine the refinement of its world.

And so it was in Tokyo. The play opened jumpily to an audience that nevertheless responded to its hieratical air, its hero's fall from grace (and loss of face) and its physical restraint, although they were naturally benighted by its linguistic complications. They worried also the next morning over the smoky argot of Falstaff, but at least they could understand the story by just looking at the stage and following the action. For once the thickness of Hotspur's accent or the mystery of Glendower's Welsh was not an issue – they could both have gone twice as far. Both now and later, the Tokyo audience took the rough with the smooth; many of them had done extensive pre-reading of the plays and spurned the brief synopsis of each scene that was being offered over headphones during the scene-changes. The less well prepared just took it like men. I once watched part of *Henry V* (when John Dougall was playing Henry) from the equivalent of the Royal Box, where I lounged shoeless, only to be interrupted by Mr Tamura ushering in the Japanese Foreign Minister, who, after starting briefly at the sight of me – assassination? – settled in stoically just as a banner proclaiming 'Fuck the Frogs' was stretched across the stage and Pistol's private army took off for Harfleur in a savage parody of English football supporters abroad. He turned not a hair.

As the weekend progressed, a company that had become a bit noisy and windy in a succession of big barns settled into a congenial new intimacy of playing and a more precise attention. Paul Brennen's Henry VI was at its best – simple, affecting and deft; and the boardroom intrigues of *Richard III* had a suppleness that went with not having to present the arguments at a relentless *fortissimo*. Before the end of the weekend, fuelled by the natural excitement of being within sight of pulling off the marathon for the first time, we realised that for all its technical shortcomings, the Globe was putting us in touch with a certain magic. Many paths meet in Shakespeare's theatre, for which he wrote in a relationship much more intimate than most contemporary writers, who may know little of the space in which their work will finally see the light of day. The 'wooden O', Jaques' stage which stands for the whole world, was Shakespeare's workspace, the wood-dust he breathed in, the practical focus for his imaginings. Not only practical, either, for to contemplate the Globe takes you directly into metaphysics, the response to life of the Middle Ages and the Renaissance, their contrasted aspirations and makings. The original Globe was an exceptional architectural departure – a round building in a city that was predominantly rectangular; but it had a rectangle within it, the stage, which significantly dissected the circle at its diameter. There is a Globe Theatre in Shaftesbury Avenue, but most contemporary London theatres are named after monarchs, mythical birds and medieval forts; the Elizabethan Globe is simply a *teatrum mundi*, theatre of the world. Surviving in the building (and in Elizabethan thought) is the medieval desire to penetrate the heavens, expressed in the perpendicularly stacked galleries symmetrically prodding upwards towards the open sky. On the other hand the theatre also suggests that classical harmony of the circle which was also the circle of the outer world, which in turn, at least if you followed Ptolemy rather than Copernicus, was geocentrically circled by the sun and the rest of the spheres. So Renaissance confidence coexists with a Gothic upward push. The human figure at the centre of the stage is therefore both the centre of the world within a world and also expresses in himself the perfect human possibility of Leonardo's cartoon of man after the model of Vitruvius – man as a catherine wheel. Shakespeare himself inherited a sense of medieval superstitious magic – its physical realisation in the theatre being the heavens above, the stage as the world, and the understage (Hamlet's 'cellarage') as a possible hell. Into this (particularly in *Hamlet*) he feeds a new, post-Reformation humanism that nevertheless retains the devil and the fires beneath.

Giordano Bruno's new proposition that our world was but one of many in an illimitable system must have shaken Elizabethan confidence deeply. Shakespeare's development over twenty years of writing brought his audience face to face with the dissolution of their optimistic ideas. The globe, and therefore the Globe, was no longer the centre of the world, and the figure standing on the stage becomes at worst a gesticulating puppet, his line to God broken, spinning in a meaningless corner of an unknown universe. We are suddenly in a modern, faithless place, in which the gods kill us for their sport like flies. When Lear elsewhere begs the heavens to 'flatten the thick rotundity of the world', he is meaning the roundness of fertility, the roundness of life, the round world, the round theatre; and our History plays of course show the chronic instability of that ideal image of perfection and control, the King's round crown.

It is fearfully difficult to recapture anything of the blazing intellectual and spiritual adventure of Shakespeare's theatre. The moment a roof goes onto a playhouse – and Shakespeare himself moved indoors into the Blackfriars Theatre by the time he wrote *The Tempest* – an important connection upwards is lost. As soon as a play retreats behind a proscenium as well it becomes something simply to be looked at by spectators privately seated in the dark, no longer violently implicated. The small studio theatres and rooms from which Shakespearian production has gained such vitality in recent years are really classical rectangles in an agnostic world, and there are times when Shakespeare's towering (medieval) imaginings threaten to lift the roof off them. However they certainly connect the play to the material world. Simplistically we say that we are *there* in the room with Lady Macbeth. Indeed, the word and the body of the speaker draw on the same breath as our own and, although not open to the sky, we are closer than usual to the fierce intimacy of the Elizabethan theatre.

We who tour History plays generally stand antithetically to such an idea, pragmatically chopping and changing our dynamics week by week; but our month at the Globe, a blessedly long stay, was a relief, a refinement and an inspiration. We sometimes felt culturally remote from our audience, but we always felt very close to the author and believed we were in his true setting. As actors we could sense both the power and the futility of being at the centre of the world: a powerful harmony coming from the comedy, while at other times, 'dressed in a little brief authority', we imprecated like puppets against our enemies, tried to turn the tide of history, grieving and cursing and shaking our fists at a blind heaven.

The whole marathon event was highly Shakespearian in the end, in spite of Nissan; and I am sentimental enough to be glad that we celebrated the man's birthday there with the realisation of a dream of our own. In a general sort of way, I've always been glad to note the day; Shakespeare has given me, if not a living, a hell of a good time. Nothing could be dafter than the processing that goes on in the streets of Stratford upon Avon each 23rd April – all those delegations I imagine would have offended him – but there must be some simple and pleasant means of commemorating the day, and to be playing a non-stop septet of his plays for the first time while baptising a theatre reminiscent of his own, was a satisfaction. The issue of how to acknowledge the occasion, however, gave rise in our company to a furious debate. There were those who felt we should sing Happy Birthday after *Richard III* on the Sunday night, and those who were fucked if they would; some favoured the lighting of candles, others denounced it as naff; some felt I should make a speech, others that anybody but I should do so. In the end we did a sort of mishmash of things, and then, festooned with flowers, ceremonially broke a great wooden barrel of *sake* with the delighted Mr Tamura in the Globe Tavern, drenching ourselves, the Professor of Drama of Tokyo University and all our distinguished visitors in its aromatic flood.

This was the first great feat of hospitality of Mr Tamura, who on another occasion spent the equivalent of £140 on a bottle of Dom Perignon for me – and that was the *first* bottle. He is a most affable man, unperturbed even by being taken for a commissionaire by Paul Brennen, who once asked him to call a taxi, and he resembles a sort of well-to-do Bardolph. I remember him best sporting for several days a big white eyepatch after a particularly unruly night at his favourite pastime, which was inventing Shakespearian cocktails. Every leading character in the plays had to have an aperitif specially devised, which would in due course be enshrined in the Globe's tariff. An increasingly bleary sense of characterisation by taste led us to vodka, gin and ferocious white rum on the rocks for Coriolanus; champagne, angostura bitters and light ale for Margaret of Anjou, French Queen of England; a combination of everything in the phenomenally-stacked Globe Tavern bar for Falstaff. This menu is now firmly established, according to the RSC and NT companies that followed us in, but there are no reports from Ingmar Bergman's noble troupe, perhaps too rigorously involved in their *Hamlet* to note such frivolities. Tamura shoved everything at us – including a voluptuous business partner whose attentions I spent much of the tour ungallantly avoiding. Unsurprisingly, he combined this generosity with an ability, like Hotspur, to 'quibble on the ninth part of a hair' when it came to business. Once he called me over to his office and presented me, in the middle of the morning, with a beautifully-lacquered lunchtray loaded with *miso, sashimi,* riceballs, *sake* and green tea, and then complained bitterly that he was being diddled over the freight charges to Chicago. I said there was little I could do about it at this range – better to talk to the office in London. He shrugged his shoulders tragically, presented me with a Panasonic Walkman, and showed me to the door. An enchanting and hospitable man, a real enthusiast, even if he remains a maverick on the Tokyo theatre scene, having an undiplomatic tendency not to invite such celebrities as Ninagawa and Kurosawa to his opening nights, preferring to fill the house with cousins of the Prime Minister with whom he has a passing acquaintance, and on one occasion bringing the Emperor Hirohito's niece to see Barry Stanton and myself after *Henry IV Part 1* – a little too soon after, for Barry was still perspiring into his padding like the Michelin man, and for myself, I know no way of making the bottom half of a chain mail suit – hemp brushed with silver paint and held up with inelegantly broad white braces – into a becoming garment in which to meet the authentic 'blood royal.

Tamura is also a mildly Faustian figure, pouring his shareholders' money down the throats of rogues and vagabonds, although his bargain is at least with a god, in the form of Shakespeare. I hope we don't bring him to destruction. His generosity is tax-deductible, but on the other hand there is an account ultimately to be settled between him and Shinjuku Nishitoyama which will determine whether he and the Globe will live to fight another day.

Recovering from his hospitality, the company stumbled forth to see Tokyo in springtime. We had reached the stage when a colleague is not necessarily the person you most want to spend the day with, and most pleasures were sought in ones and twos. Chris Hunter revealed a quite uncanny gambler's instinct, and could be seen emerging with great bags of silver balls from the deafening *pachinko* parlours on his way to the redemption shop; those frustrated with their parts worked out unrealised fantasies in the *karaoke* bars, where anybody can be filmed miming with a microphone to the Tokyo Top Ten; and Ben Bazell to my knowledge swallowed whole the eye of a sea-bream while playing the *shamisen* in the private room of an old-style Japanese restaurant, while his hosts lay shoelessly (and leglessly) asleep around him. More soberly, Rosy Fowler continued her round-the-world search for araldite and sashcord for repairs to the shows, and kept them legal and furnished. She conquered the Tokyo police, who, unlike their Hong Kong counterparts, were unconcerned about firearms, but who required a virtual *curriculum vitae* of anyone who was going to handle a knife in the shows; and every week she ticked off a props shopping list that went: 10lb apples, 2lb oranges, porridge, six packs cigarettes, cigars, four bottles coke, eight bottles ginger ale, cheese, bread rolls, French sticks, coffee, milk, sugar, pencils, pens, blackcurrant juice. Not a bad haul for the Takadanobaba district. She only faltered with Fluellen's leek, having to settle for enormous spring onions instead, and with the confetti for Pistol's wedding: not to be found. Into Ueno Park she went with plastic bags to collect fallen cherry blossom, giving great amusement to the Tokyo recreationalists, who, in this one week of bloom, sit in the park all day with it floating in their *sake* and lunchboxes, ready to see the best side of things.

As were we. The boon of being there for that famous week of spring sweetens all tempers taxed by touring, and restores some balance. I don't think the company always thought well of Mr Tamura, noting that his hospitality could be rather selective, and they were as always alert to the possibility of any corners being cut in the business arrangements – especially over cooked breakfasts. Potential confrontations over these things are highly typical of life on the road, and probably more interesting than the palpable harmony onstage every night. You can hear too much about that. If our group, which was in fact full of good ambassadors, occasionally demanded as a right gigantic rates of insurance cover, measurably identical hotel rooms, free tuberculosis vaccine, or an extra breakfast sausage, it is only a symptom of the pressures of a life in the sky followed, when you do come down to earth, by jumping without a parachute for a living. The (generally) harmless target of all frustrations was either the ESC, the host manager, or what was seen as an unholy alliance between the two. Each new date and face at the airport offered a new rich potential for offence.

In this state of sulphurous wariness, the company arrived in Chicago on 30th April and glared balefully at Keith Fort, company manager for the Chicago Festival, who, with the air of a man who had just got out of bed and can't wait to get going, immediately proposed a baseball game between the ESC and the Lithuanian State Theatre, who were coming in with *Uncle Vanya*. The ESC actors then gathered up the presentation packs extended in welcome by Jane and Bernie Sahlins – bubblegum, Chicago Bears stickers, Festival balloons and city maps – and disappeared into the burrows of the Congress Hotel with them, while I went with Bernie to have a look at the Auditorium Theatre on Michigan Avenue, where, against a number of good counsels, we had decided to play.* Jetlag evaporated at once. The Auditorium is a

***Bogdanov:** *One of the deciding factors in our choice, apart from rejecting the Blackstone next door on the grounds that it had no atmosphere, was that I had seen the Auditorium on a previous occasion when visiting with*

remarkable building, its rough-hewn grey granite exterior enclosing an intricate wealth of gold and ivory ornamentation. Originally commissioned by a wealthy merchant patron of the city, it is the only important building still standing in Chicago arising from the inspired architectural partnership of Louis Sullivan and Dankmar Adler (Frank Lloyd Wright was one of the draughtsmen) that also created the Chicago Stock Exchange and Central Music Hall. Adelina Patti opened the theatre in 1890; Caruso, Bernhardt and Pavlova all looked out from the stage at the great concentric arches that soar in a single span across the width of its four thousand seat auditorium, each dotted with hundreds of miniature houselights, ornamental globes and curlicues. Marble mosaic runs through the lobbies and stairways of the building, which originally housed offices and a great hotel which was intended to offset the inevitable losses incurred by the theatre; but really it was never financially viable and would have been pulled down in the 1930s but for the fact that the cost of demolition would have been greater than the value of the land on which it stood. As it was, the Auditorium survived its lean years – in the Second World War as a Service-man's Centre it housed altogether over a million GIs and the stage was used as a bowling alley – to be purchased finally by Roosevelt University who, having restored the theatre to its original glory, now use the old hotel areas as faculty rooms and lecture theatres.

This City Landmark is thus on the face of it a real treat for a visiting company, even though Chicago's real theatrical strength lies in compact home groups such as Steppenwolf in their own buildings rather than in such grandiosities. But it has its draw-backs, as those who advised us to use the Blackstone knew, and they were exactly opposite to those of the Globe. The Auditorium's much vaunted acoustic is really a musical one, carrying the slight reverberation welcomed by singers and instrumentalists but less friendly to the speaking voice, especially when it is delivering Shakespeare at some speed to an audience divided from the actors by a common language; and the (to us) necessary act of closing its

---

Brook's A Midsummer Night's Dream *in 1971. The dominant memory was of something like eight galleries. (There were in fact four.) The actors like ants crawling around in the far distance, viewed from the wrong end of the Greenwich Telescope. The rustle, heard throughout the second half of the* Dream *was, in fact, the audience leaving in descending order. It was like emptying the sand from a three-hour egg timer.*

capacity down to two thousand by shutting off the upper galleries with angular screens paradoxically interfered with its natural acoustic values. From the outset we were cursed with an audibility problem for which audiences were uncertain whether to blame the theatre, our company or its own ears. Since they tended to declare that they could hear better as the first evening wore on and better still on the second or third night, the settling in may have been as much on the customers' side as ours.

The guinea-pig this time was *Henry IV Part 1*, which for various reasons we opened first. By the time we reached the first marathon at the end of the week, we had the hang of the place. The company was pelted with roses white and red at the call, and the front rows stood up and hammered on the stage. Truthfully, I've never heard such an explosion of sound in a theatre; and in fact have never encountered such spontaneous warmth in an audience as was shown us by Chicago in our four weeks there – even if later on in the run an element of brittle excitement was mixed in now that we were an established hit. In the May heatwave the short journey from the Auditorium stage door back to the Congress Hotel became like a *passeggiata*; even when travelling discreetly, we would continually be stopped for a lively discussion of the plays. Since much of the talk was very complimentary, I began to understand why some English actors, confronted by American success, lose all sense of proportion about themselves; but whereas in New York such headswelling stuff is linked to a certain crass definition of commercial success, there is really no Sardi's in Chicago where the worm can turn, and so the fervour can perhaps more safely be trusted.

The press was fulsome, with acid flashes. 'A Herculean theatrical triumph' announced the *Sun Times*; 'Shakespeare marathon wearies the body, strengthens the heart' felt *Overnight Chicago*; 'See one of these plays, or see them all. You miss them at your own risk' warned the *Chicago Tribune*. According to the *Shakespeare Quarterly*, a thoughtful periodical published by the Folger Library, 'the exhausted audience regaled the obviously exhausted actors with a standing ovation, with bravos, rhythmic clapping, and plain ballpark cheering . . . this achievement alone establishes [the ESC] as one of the most important and polished repertory companies in the world . . . the astonishing thing is that a company which has been together for only a couple of years . . . could have developed a repertory style so sound, so secure and well-defined, and could have brought together, playing in perfect rapport with each other, three or four actors who are absolutely splendid and many more who are very good indeed.' But the critic regretfully found 'Michael Pennington . . . a shallow actor who seems to reduce all his various roles to the same set of physical and vocal mannerisms . . . Richard II remains a very ambiguous memory.' Ah. Useless to say to myself that this man was in a minority; what if he was right? This, after all, has to be the dread shared by all actor-managers of any wit – the possibility that they are no longer really leading from the front. The thought trails in its shadow the implication of egomania found out. Even if I didn't exactly go onstage at night thinking about budgets, maybe some vital margin of concentration had been taken up by the trials of running the whole outfit, so that for all the fuss I was no longer doing properly what I was best equipped to do. The thought of leading a crack troupe round the world to the sound of ballpark cheering while delivering a dog's dinner myself made the jubilation grow faint.

However, it was for other reasons that amidst all the fun, I had developed a liking for disappearing into Room 619 at the Congress Hotel, issuing out only as far as the Art Institute to the left or to listen to Frank Morgan, a disciple and miraculous reincarnation of Charlie Parker, playing at the Blackstone Hotel to the right. (Here I would often meet Colin Farrell, a jazzman for life, whom I remember first meeting as a lad in Berlin in 1961 when we were together in the National Youth Theatre, and he would spend his evenings in the clubs listening to Sidney Bechet or Fatty George. Twenty-seven years later, looking much as he did then, he was patiently mourning a daughter.) I was taking a break, once again, from a logistical jungle. The question of re-planning for the continuation of the tour in the autumn was now assuming quite some urgency. We were to finish the season in Berlin on 3rd July and reopen in Melbourne with a marathon weekend on 2nd September. Nobody was obliged to renew their contracts after Berlin; and yet our commitments as a management to the booking theatres stretched on and on. Our attitude to this had up till now been a little Micawberish, and soon we would have to uncross our fingers. Knowing that most actors baulk at signing a contract for more than a year at a time, we had chosen to hope that everyone would enjoy themselves so much that they would want to renew and continue. How was the enjoyment going? Along the corridor at the Congress, Roger Booth had developed a vertiginous complaint which eventually turned out to be an inner ear infection, but which at this pre-diagnostic stage was causing him to spend his nights sitting propped up on the floor in a corner of his room, since without right angles behind him he lost his balance even when lying in bed. Hugh Sullivan was bent double with a back complaint. Clyde Pollitt was developing pneumonia. Another member of our company was in the grip of a distressing nervous breakdown whose symptoms were sending shockwaves through the company, but which I was gambling would be containable till we got back to England, since the sufferer's dejection at having to go home early was likely to be worse. Another year of sticking on Bardolph's red nose and being away from Ann was surely not on for Colin Farrell under the circumstances. In addition, everyone was tired and accident-prone, having been away from home for nearly two months, which I now think is the longest time a disparate group can stay away if they have any kind of homes to miss. Some, too, were chafing after playing the same parts for two years. It was the worst possible moment for cheery talks about another year of travel with not much more money in the same work. And yet this was exactly the moment that these decisions would have to be taken.

Naturally, anyone who left would need to be recast – in a minimum of seven parts; and as far as re-rehearsal went, there was barely any provision for it at all, either in time or money. Then Michael arrived from London, in time – let's show off – for us to go on the Studs Terkel show together, bringing news that was better than expected. Now audited, Chichester, Birmingham and Manchester had pushed up a small surplus over budget (or rather over the budgeted deficit). We concluded euphorically that we could after all afford three weeks of re-rehearsal in August (at about £5,000 a week) for, say, three or four replacements before we went to Melbourne, as well as making a small provision for refurbishing the productions and for costume re-design for the newcomers. Micawber rewarded. But how many people can you really put into seven plays over three weeks? We already knew of some crucial decisions. John Castle had decided to call it a day. In Tokyo I had asked Michael Cronin to take over Bolingbroke/Henry IV from him; by the time we left Japan Michael was word perfect in the part and a couple of rehearsals were enough to prove that he didn't need much of that either. Barry Stanton, to our infinite relief, had agreed to continue as Falstaff, a part we didn't relish having to cast for the third successive year, and to take over York in the *Henry VIs* from John Castle – but not before a lengthy period of uncertainty in Tokyo when, alternating my own cajolings with a more formal approach, I had sometimes found myself telephoning our office in London who would then telephone Barry's agent there, who would then call Barry back in Tokyo, where he was sitting in the hotel room next to mine: I could hear his phone ringing. Then his response would have to go through the same channels in reverse. Such are the small and expensive etiquettes of the business. But all was well in the end. However, Chris Hunter, who had been a brilliant Hotspur but was a bit under-used elsewhere, wanted to call a halt; Eluned Hawkins was frustrated by two years without new casting, and Lynette Davies was moving on as well. So though we had already had some narrow escapes, clearly the replacements were not going to be minor; in fact it was pretty obvious that if there were to be any more departures, we were sunk. And if we were sunk, we were absolutely sunk; abandoning the 1988–9 tour would not only be a bitter defeat and deprive us of a London season, it would also put us in the most serious hock; all our contracts with the theatres for the following year had been signed. The future once again seemed both impossible to achieve and impossible to abandon.

Many acting companies, seeing a management in such a hole, would have tried to exploit it, demanding difficult terms for new contracts and perhaps breaking our pay structure into pieces. It was a structure that was in any case looking a lot less satisfactory than it had two years ago. Having set various levels of salary then and offered only a 5% rise across the board for each new season, we could see inequities appearing. There were actors who had joined us to play small parts, such as Andy Jarvis and Paul Brennen, who were now carrying crucial weight and demonstrating in a deep sense what the company was all about; and yet they were pegged to low salaries set two years ago with only the standard enhancement since. Meanwhile, new actors might be coming in to play major parts – had already, in fact – commanding the higher salaries already set for that work. And *they* hadn't been flogging around for two years creating the company. It was uncomfortable, and it called into question our early, basic decisions. We projected a strong sense of ensemble and interdependence on stage, but we were all on different money. I know why, of course. Strong casting in major Shakespeare roles nowadays calls for actors used to earning a good wage, who would compare what we offered with the top at Stratford and the National; good casting in minor roles is, like it or not, cheaper. We might be an ensemble, but in that sense Shakespeare wrote for his stars. Nevertheless, many people felt keenly that our pretensions to teamwork sat uncomfortably on such an hierarchical approach to salaries. Now, if ever, was the moment, tired and homesick as many of us were, that unhappinesses would erupt. I am eternally grateful to say that as far as the money was concerned, it never happened. Nobody tried to hold us over the barrel we had ourselves constructed. There must have been a loyalty deeper than mere enthusiasm, or at least a deep wish to see the job well finished, and nobody played poker with us.

Maybe we were all just too busy. Rosy Fowler was still looking for confetti. In a country which celebrates its weddings with rice, she eventually ran it to earth in a novelty shop and bought five hundred boxes. A workshop contingent within the company were doing very successful sessions with American actors and students on Shakespeare. Paul Brennen and Stephen Jameson put on a fine version of Pinter's *The Dumb Waiter*, which they tried out on the company in a boiler-room under the stage of the Auditorium, a perfect setting; and Philip Bowen and John Castle did an elegant programme of war poetry at the legendary Second City club, meeting a well-oiled midnight audience that were expecting improvised urban Chicago comedy along the usual lines – not a comfortable evening. The Festival were writing us letters about their cash-flow difficulties, hoping we wouldn't mind not being paid on the nail; one day I refused to let the company play until the money was in our hands, which were also poised over the telephone to call the *Tribune* to explain the night's cancellation; we got the cheque at 5 pm. Audiences howled with joy at the moment in *Henry VI House of York* when Jack Cade, voicing a deep American preoccupation, leads his insurrectionists into battle with the cry 'First thing we'll do, let's kill all the lawyers!'; and the scenes in *Henry VI House of Lancaster* when the Duchess of Gloucester visits a necromancer to read her political future were gratefully received by a public that already had an inkling that Nancy Reagan might have been to an astrologer.

On the first day of June, arriving via New York in Connecticut for the final weekend marathon before coming back to England, I took a break to stay with June Havoc and Tana Sibilio in the pre-Civil War village they have created for visitors at Cannon Crossing – June and Tana live within it in a setting reminiscent of *On*

Golden Pond, and use their land as a sanctuary for all sorts of stray and straitened animals. I thought I knew about marathons until I met June Havoc. Not the least feature of her astonishing life is her survival of the marathon dances of the Depression, in one of the last of which, at the age of fourteen, she danced virtually non-stop for 2,900 hours – only to come second. I hope that the réclame of her autobiography, *Early Havoc*, and her Broadway account of the experience, *Marathon 33*, has compensated her for the disappointment, and for the slight buckling of her feet which still troubles her. June's stories put seven History plays into perspective rather, though she was generous enough to gasp with wonder at the scale of our work. I swung in her hammock for three days, feeling humanity returning as I listened to her talk about those times, about her life on the road from the age of four as Dainty June, and, later, about her own horrors in the McCarthy era, idly watching John Darrell teach his son Joby to fish in June's lake; John had to explain to him that, in this setting at least, the fish always had to go back in the water.

Neither John nor I would have taken such ample ease if we had known what lay ahead of us when we arrived in Stamford on Thursday refreshed for work. Clyde Pollitt had now gone down with full pneumonia and put himself into hospital in New York; while Ian Burford had been attacked by a mystery virus and was unable to be moved. We looked at the implications of two understudies going on multiplied by seven plays, thankful that we had survived so much of the tour without meeting an emergency like this before. It was a humdinger. *Richard II* and the two *Henry IV*s were not too much of a problem, but on Saturday night we would get to *Henry V* where Ian played Exeter and Clyde the King of France; they had an important scene together, and John Darrell, recently so content with fishing rod and rowboat, understudied them both. A number of absurd solutions suggested themselves before we settled that John should do Exeter (who carries on into *Henry VI*); but we were thus without a King of France. Chris Hunter, who was already in the French scenes as Orleans, volunteered to learn the fairly-familiar lines, while Ben Bazell went on for Orleans, a smaller part. Chris thus fell in with the grand ESC tradition of busking – daily rep – that I had begun when I went on as Gloucester in Chichester. The next morning, in *Henry VI Lancaster*, worse still, Ian understudied Clyde as the wicked Bishop of Winchester. Another black hole. Not to be outdone by Chris, I volunteered to learn that one. In this play John Darrell continued as Exeter, doubling with his own part as Sir William Lucy, a role already riddled with quick changes. *Henry VI York* was less of a problem as long as Andy Jarvis broke off in the middle of Richard Crookback to fill in as Lord Say, who is murdered by Jack Cade's mob, while I had to remember, once I had perished as Cade, to come back almost immediately and perish again as Rutland's Tutor (I died five times in all that Sunday). And so on and on. To shorten a tedious tale, there were over that weekend thirty-two understudy performances (plus the two specially learned). Our understudy system, necessarily imperfect, squeaked and strained, and we came closer than ever to real barnstorming as actors dropped scripts in the wings, rushed on in unfamiliar roles, hoping that someone would guide them off again when they'd finished, and that they could re-find their scripts and sort out their next unscheduled entrance.

And all in front of the *New York Times*.

Success at Stamford had never really entered our heads anyway. We thought we'd be lucky to get out unskinned, since the company were very tired and the theatre, though we were happy enough to play it, badly needed refurbishing and had unsafe floors; the dressing rooms were dilapidated and so small that we were jostled out of them by the costumes, which hung around like thirty or forty supernumeraries in each room, so that we tended to stand out in the corridors for air or to allow a colleague space to do a change. In this setting, the wardrobe attempted to juggle thirty-two costume adaptations (understudies are not cast primarily for physical likeness). We muttered in the corridors, and our breakdown patient climbed up and down the fire escape and beat on the dressing room ceiling with a broom. The plays inexorably went up. Surely in all these understudy permutations we would have forgotten some vital link, and at some point the action would grind to a halt for lack of someone to pick up a vital cue – he or she might already be onstage, immersed in another part. I reflected that I'd rather be on, wrestling with the problem, than to be Sue Best or Stella Bond out in the stalls, feeling their hearts plummet as they watched some hiatus looming up. Laughably, *Newsweek* was in as well as the *New York Times* – this was the closest we were coming to New York and both journals planned to drop in for a short time on Saturday before heading back to town to cover the Tony Awards. Presumably they would castigate Equity for having let us in.

So we blustered on, ranting apprehensively through *Henry IV*

Part 2. At this point I got a message that both *Newsweek* and *The Times* had cancelled their tickets for the Tonys, preferring to stay on with us through Sunday and watch the remainder of our cycle. Something told me this might not be in order to put the finishing touches to lousy reviews. Jack Kroll (*Newsweek*) rang through on Saturday afternoon and asked for an immediate interview about the company's background to accompany his notice. I did the interview in costume immediately after being crowned as Henry V, which I thought would be judicious. The light in his eyes was unmistake- able, and both reviews (which happened to come out on my birthday) stand as appeasements for the many hard times we have had since 1986. We've been quoting them to anyone who'll listen ever since.

'The complete and indispensable Shakespearian event . . . a monumental achievement . . . in New York, as in Stamford [the company] could have been its own festival' (*New York Times*); 'An awesome feat of talent and stamina . . . this amazing company achieved the seemingly impossible: they kept the complexity of the epic but made it clear as crystal . . . the rare feat of making Shakespeare sound like real interchanges between real people while keeping the power and glory of the poetry . . . wonderful actors . . . dozens of great performances . . . Bogdanov's inspired strokes . . . make it clear that Shakespeare, done with passion, power and intelligence, is still the hottest ticket in world theater' (*Newsweek*).

The road from Stamford down to Kennedy Airport was as green and mild as a spring day in Sussex. The plan had been for the company to fly home on Monday evening; but Mike Fenner, Colin Farrell, June Watson, Chris Hunter and myself had spotted a Monday morning flight and arranged with Monica McCabe that we would find our own way down to Kennedy, change our tickets and catch it. We went to the check-in desk to find we had none to change; only the husks of tickets, invalid empty envelopes with duplicate vouchers stapled inside them – 'not good for passage'. Monica, back in Stamford and presumably sleeping off the last night party, had the important bits in a stack with everybody else's; she too had thought the vouchers were all we needed. Obviously we had now regressed to an infantile state; Mummy was asleep in bed in Connecticut, we were sucking our thumbs in New York. I wondered how I'd helped create a complex three-continent company producing Shakespearian spaghetti by the yard but still couldn't get myself onto an aeroplane.

Clearly the thing to do was to spend a day of mortification in New York, join up with our mocking colleagues in the evening and fly home as per the original plan. Of course the flight we coveted was leaving in an hour, and it did have empty seats. The one way ticket cost £250. Ridiculous even to think of spending that kind of money just to get back eight hours earlier, we agreed as we drifted towards the sales counter. What a ludicrously expensive way of paying for a mistake that would be, we said as we fished for credit cards. But who would be so mean and base about such an important homecoming, we declared, buying the new tickets. Euphorically relieved, passing through an invisible veil between us and home, we went to the bar to celebrate, poorer but free. After nine weeks away, seventeen thousand miles, eleven trilogies and sixty-eight performances, one more day was one too many. We had all, absolutely, for the time being, had enough.

CHAPTER
8

YORK AND BERLIN

June – July 1988

> 'Is not their climate foggy, raw, and dull?
> On whom, as in despite, the sun looks
> pale . . .'
>
> Shakespeare, Henry V

Bogdanov: Jude Kelly had been a member of my company in Leicester for two years. From running Solent Young People's Theatre she has now taken control of the magnificent West Yorkshire Playhouse. The route has been via the York Festival where, on a number of occasions, Jude has asked me to direct the Mystery Plays. This long friendship is the background to the only occasion in England that year on which we were to play the cycle as a 'marathon' weekend, a fortnight after returning from Connecticut. 'Marathon' has unfortunate connotations. The distance is 26 miles and 385 yards, or, if you prefer, 42.2 kilometres. It conjures up pictures of wild-eyed, red-faced competitors, dehydrated and exhausted, collapsing into the arms of ministering St John's Ambulance persons: hair spiked, faces contorted with sweat, all sense of time and space distorted, all memory temporarily suspended in a blacked-out time warp. Yes, that sounds like the Theatre Royal, York, in June. It was unfortunate that the one weekend we would be there the temperature in Britain would soar into the eighties for the first and only time that year. The problem of no air conditioning in the theatre was exacerbated by the glass conservatory that had been added at the front to house foyers, café and box office. Attractive, airy and light when English temperatures were their muggy normal – an equatorial death trap when the sun gods took it into their rays to beat down relentlessly on the glass roof of York's *teatrum mundi* that flaming June weekend.

It is, of course, a beautiful theatre. From an illegal playhouse dedicated to the entertainment of the northern gentry (in between spells at the races or the card table) it has become an exemplary representative of the English repertory movement, offering widely varying entertainment to all sections of society. The little Georgian-style theatre is now an attractive mixture of Victorian bijou and modern glass and concrete. In many ways, the City of York could not have been more appropriate for the marathon. The awesome York Minster dominates the town, a symbol of the mighty power of the North. A sense of history roams the streets, and the walls and gate, which once held the decapitated head of York, so that 'York may overlook the town of York', are still standing.

It is from this town that the word 'shambles' comes, the Shambles being that collection of higgledy piggledy streets that once was the teeming underground, ricket- and lice-ridden heart of one of Britain's most beautiful cities. We were not exactly a shambles that weekend, but it was pretty tough going.

Opinions always differed wildly in the company as to the value of marathon weekends. There is no question that on the minus side the acting and technical quality of the productions suffered a great deal. Beginning on a Friday night at 7.30 pm and finishing on a Sunday at 11 pm (or frequently at 11.30 pm), the Event took its toll on mental and physical stamina. There was no moment in the weekend when somebody wasn't 'coasting', conserving energy. The problem was that individual members of the company rarely coincided on stage in what was often a subconscious rest period. The effect on the performance was odd. There would always be something strangely out of kilter, an essential spark missing, and strange rhythms would emerge. Each actor's performance being dependent on another's, if one was bashing off down a side road, another would go into overdrive up the freeway to compensate. The result was relationships that missed each other by kilometres. The problem the first year with trilogy days had been other. Then there had always been a post-prandial slump that set in both on stage and in the auditorium. For a time we believed it was because *Henry IV Part 2*, the gentler, wordier play, suffered from a lack of

concentration. However this was not true of every performance
and when, in the second year, we occasionally performed a trilogy
of *Richard II* and *Henry IV Parts 1* and *2*, it was *Henry IV Part 1*
that hit the tea-time torpor.

For Andy Jarvis, marathons were particularly cruel. After a total
of some twenty hours of acting out of forty-eight, finally he had to
come out fresh at 7.30 on a Sunday night and launch himself into
the largest and most physically demanding part of the lot –
Richard III. It is hardly surprising that his energy would sometimes
run out and the performance last four hours. Technically, too,
lapses in concentration would result in key props not being set,
lighting cues being missed, sloppy curtain work, wrong trousers
being worn . . . These were the drawbacks and most of the time
I did not like my work one bit. And yet. And yet there was
something magical in the event, seeing the story of this amazing
struggle for the English crown unfold moment by breathtaking
moment.

The audience were caught up in the excitement of what we were
fond of calling 'A Medieval Soap Opera'. And when the lights
finally dimmed on the National Anthem with Charlie Dale as
Richmond sitting behind Richard III's desk, the quick change from
armour to suit inevitably resulting in tie askew, and hair less than
sartorially sleeked back, the resulting tumultuous applause justified
the whole occasion. There were those who were somewhat more
sceptical of these standing ovations. Paul Taylor in the
Independent: '. . . you have to guard against the "long is beautiful"
syndrome . . . you have to ask whether your irritation may be just
the result of fatigue, or the theatre-seat equivalent of bedsores . . .
it would not be cynical to say that what we were partly cheering
(and what the cast were applauding as they clapped back) was our
joint stamina . . .' Not so Robin Thornber in the *Guardian*: '. . .
a robust respect for vivid, exciting theatricality rather than dusty
scholarship . . . has established a strong, graphic house style that
carries you through the seven shows with the exhilaration of a
roller coaster. There must have been dull moments, but they are
not what you remember.' There was no gainsaying the shower of
red and white flowers that regularly carpeted the stage on these
occasions.

The company had been away from home for too long, and
indeed Japan and the States were a long way away to be. Eleven
weeks. It had taken its toll. There is a psychological point that one

hits around the five- to six-week mark where a deep longing for *heimat* – homesickness – sets in no matter how welcoming or compatible the culture. I have regularly felt it myself when directing abroad and have long since made a rule that I will not take longer than that time for a production. A decision that has led to a reputation of being a very fast director (*The Wars of the Roses* may have something to do with it too . . .). There is total disbelief when I report that I am currently, in Hamburg, taking some two and a half to three months to produce one show. Only *one*?

The break between Connecticut and York had been insufficient to recharge the batteries. We were home on Tuesday 7th June, jet-lagged, and took the rest of the week off. The following Thursday we travelled to York for the weekend fit-up, having already started on replacement rehearsals for Australia (coming up soon in September, after the break). The York weekend had brought about our only formal dispute and Equity brush of the year. Sunday performances in most of the world are the norm, Monday being a day off; but not in England. In order to perform the marathon at all, it was essential to have two days off afterwards and, even so, a Wednesday performance in the week following was usually a pretty lacklustre affair. Equity wanted an extra half week's salary for the Sunday work (on top of the already incurred overtime). I negotiated with Peter Finch, Assistant Secretary, that we would pay one quarter of a week on the basis that there was time off before the weekend and a week off afterwards, prior to going to Berlin.

As with so many of our verbal agreements with Equity over the three years, this one ended in the dust and we eventually had to pay a half-week salary per person extra – a totally unreasonable demand we thought, given that the company were only being asked to give seven performances over a period of three weeks and these were all in one weekend.

The Weekend. I intended to work all day on the opening Friday in York to whip the shows into a bit better technical shape. I had a fistful of notes from Chicago and this was the only opportunity I had had to go through them. Once again the ESC jinx struck. The actor who had been in the grip of a breakdown since Tokyo but who, once home, had seemed much better, finally collapsed on the Friday afternoon. I spent the rest of the time in the company office with Michael, making frantic arrangements for sedation and transport to London. I couldn't find anyone to fetch or to accompany: not agent, not spouse. I took the actor myself by train, handing over custody at King's Cross, turning round and going straight back to York. It was midnight. And I had missed *Richard II* and the beginning of our one showing of the marathon to the national critics. In my absence, Stella and Sue and the company had performed yet another version of the three-card trick, the parts being shuffled to produce seven totally new performances from the pack. This time involving actors not only playing out of position but, on two occasions, playing a lesser part than their main role. Once again our cover system worked, but at a price. The critics didn't even notice. The weekend sweated and sweltered away. ESC fans had come from all over the country. It was here that I discovered that some followers had seen the shows upwards of thirty times. A number were from Plymouth, converted on that first Saturday of all. Jeanette Nicholls: 'What has the ESC done for me? In 1986 I was sinking into senility and middle age . . . but I peered over the top of my rut, and saw there was a whole new world out there.' At the Allied Irish Bank 'I Survived *The Wars of the Roses*' reception, three hundred weekenders were presented with a certificate. A lady from Bath presented me with a crown of the Seven Kings made in her pottery classes. Jude Kelly had cannily arranged for Brian Matthew to broadcast Radio 2's *Around Midnight* live from the foyer, and we all took part – actors coming straight off stage to the broadcast. Terry Mortimer got up a small combo to perform some exciting arrangements of his *Roses* music in the foyer: 'Funky Galliard', the Sneak's Noise number, never sounded better, I'm afraid to say. Everyone had tried their best to make it a real occasion. An exhausted, heat-drained audience duly pelted the stage with red and white roses. They were very generous. The shuffle round, coming on top of the hard road back, and the heat, had taken its toll.

Paul Taylor in the *Independent* found that 'When passion and genuine horror are called for, these productions are currently lifeless.' (He is another one, by the way, who can't tell his Barber from his Mahler.) However, Robin Thornber in the *Guardian*, headlining his critique 'Victory for the *Wars of the Roses*' found that 'The dreaded "modern dress" is in fact a liberation of the events of the plays from phoney historicism into their rightful role of universal role-play, myth . . . the strong visual style brings a brilliant clarity to an incredibly complex narrative that could easily have dissipated into an amorphous flow of lordlings.'

The year was really coming to an end. Only Berlin (West)

beckoned. John Dougall, despite the promise of sharing Hal/ Henry V fifty-fifty with Michael the following year, was miffed at not playing Suffolk – which he understudied – in *House of Lancaster* (I had asked Michael P. to take it on) and was refusing to continue for another season.

Pennington: *We had spent an eternity trying to decide what to do about Hotspur in Year Three, now that Chris Hunter was not going to continue. Should we get someone new in, or load Andy Jarvis (who understudied it) with yet more work? Andy could do it fine, of course – remember the first understudy run in Chichester? – but his very gradual emergence via smaller parts in the cycle into full light as Richard III at the end was a trick that was working well, and Hotspur early on would spoil it rather (entrepreneurial thinking, this). Eventually we decided he should do it nonetheless. I took him for a cup of tea in Pineapple's coffee bar to talk to him about it. Over his shoulder, at the precise moment I was offering him the part, I saw Mary Rutherford gesticulating wildly at me. Too late. Andy went away pleased. I asked Mary what the matter was. She had guessed what was happening and was trying to forestall it: she couldn't continue herself, she now realised, and wanted to suggest that Hilary Townley, a very good actress who happens to be married to Chris Hunter, should now play her parts, and that might be a means of persuading Chris to stay on as Hotspur. Mentally congratulating myself that we hadn't chosen to make the ESC a co-operative, I asked Mary why she suddenly couldn't come. Michael Bogdanov came up at this point.*

Bogdanov: Mary delightedly informed us that, at the age of forty, she was pregnant for the first time in her life. The father was a company member (we could have killed him). We said we were equally delighted and postponed the problem of yet another replacement. Berlin, which at one point had seemed like a highlight of the year, was feeling more like a last oxygen-defying, lung-busting gasp to the summit. The period between York and Berlin was spent doing more preparatory work for Australia and workshops for the Berlin Festival. Also one bit of re-rehearsal. Shallow's Orchard Scene had become a shambles (sic). Intentions had been lost and what was once good comic invention had become crude and brash. Worse, from the entrance of Pistol, the story went

out the window. I had argued long and hard with John Castle
about the dynamics of the scene; we all wanted to get it right. The
inevitable row ensued. This time I was ready for it. I am ashamed
to say I called him a chauvinist four-letter word and he walked out.
The current tally for this unofficial title bout for World Affronted
Dignity Champion (qualification: a walk-out) was thus Pennington
1, Castle 1, Bogdanov 1. John and I hardly spoke to each other for
the rest of the tour.

Letter from Michael Bogdanov to the Editor of the *Independent*
newspaper, November 1988:

Dear Sir,

Coincidentally I was in Berlin on Wednesday 22 November, and
bought a copy of the *Independent* and discovered therein your
Travel Special on East and West Berlin. I was there on that
particular day to see the World Premiere of *Orlando* directed by
the American, Robert Wilson, arguably one of the most important
figures on the contemporary theatre scene, and performed by Ute
Lemper, unarguably one of the great European actresses.

Imagine my amazement (and perplexity) when I discovered
that, in the theatre section, the whole output in Berlin was
confined virtually to the Opera House in the Western sector and
the Opera House in the Eastern sector, and a total of twelve lines
was given up to giving the repertoires (fairly standard) of these
houses.

Given that Berlin is one of the most important cultural cities
in Europe, and that theatre in Berlin plays a huge part in the
social and political life of the German people, it is astonishing
that no mention was made of the enormous output of theatre in
that city, outside of a few English plays on the fringe. It was as
if the Schaubühne, the Schiller Theater, the Volksbühne, the
Deutsches Theater, the Freie Volksbühne, the Maxim Gorky
Theater, did not exist. It was as if the great European
productions, the Peter Stein *Cherry Orchard*, the Luc Bondi
Botho Strauss, the Jerome Savory *D'Artagnan*, the Klaus-Michel
Gruber *Antigone* and a hundred more, did not exist. I find it a
sad reflection (once again) on the narrowness of the English
perception of European culture, that the experience of theatre-
going in Berlin can be confined to such a narrow spectrum.

Japan: (above) The Tokyo Globe (MP);
(below) John Castle and Mount Fuji (JT)

(left) Tokyo, 1988 (JT)
(below) Two asses
– Artistic Director and
friend in Stamford,
Connecticut (JT)

(left) Andrew Jarvis (JT)
(below) Paul Brennen (JT)

(above) Canberra to Perth, 1988 (JT)
(below) Ben Bazell with walk-ons (JT)

And as for not eating out after the theatre. Berlin is one of the great all-night cities of the world. Anybody who thinks that the Berliners don't go to the theatre and then sit up all night arguing about what they have seen is obviously a day tripper. Is it possible to trust the rest of the article, I ask myself?

Yours faithfully . . .

Berlin is, indeed, one of the great all-night cities of the world. There is an ease and relaxation to the conversation and drinking that would gladden an Irishman's heart. The bars have the most civilised (some would say) rules in the world. The bartender does not shut up shop until the last customer has gone. Because of the strange division forced on it by the Warsaw Pact, it is (or was) also the only city with a zoo as its central point. The ESC were staying in the Schweizer Hof, a luxury hotel opposite that zoo, with the Kurfürstendamm a step away, some twenty minutes from the Schiller Theater. The Schiller is one of the really big state theatres in Germany, unfortunately a testimony to the fact that *occasionally* too much subsidy can be stultifying. There is a total of one hundred and ten actors, many on life contracts, some twenty or so of them not having acted in years, no director being willing to cast them. The amount of state aid is DM 43.5 million, or £15 million. There are three stages. Running it, as successive Intendants have discovered, is a nightmare. Having had the opportunity to observe German theatre bureaucracy at close quarters, I find it interesting to contrast the possibility with the actuality. Technically, there is an extraordinarily high standard. The actors are skilled, physically brave and secure. They have status. Wages are such that they have no need to run off to TV and films to supplement a meagre income. The top actor's wage in my own theatre, the Deutsches Schauspielhaus, is £65,000 per annum. Even the middle actors earn about £30,000, the highest salary at the National and the RSC. The German theatre sickness is allied to the political situation. Comfort and guilt. The trauma of the aftermath of the Second World War has produced, nearly fifty years on, an artistic crisis. Nowhere is this more apparent than in the field of writing, more or less the only theme being the obsessive one of German Guilt. The scripts pile up in my office. I never want to read or see another play about Hitler in my life. The refusal to evaluate the

present and the future in any terms other than these means that
there are too few writers and even fewer new plays. The recent
titanic events in Middle Europe and East Germany could change all
that: artists may find the necessary impetus to discard the historical
shackles of the past, and propel German creativity into a new, fresh
and exciting creative era. Something *else* to write about. This
complex and continuing avoidance of their own contemporary
problems leads to an obsessive love affair with the writing of other
countries. New English plays are translated even before their
English premieres. Badly. It is a whole industry. Anyone with an
Abitur ('A' level) in English, fancies his/her chances at translation.
This act of artistic proxy-copulation means that Germany has
missed the language revolution of the English fifties. The spoken
word of the stage is High German, dialects and accents are not used
(unless Swiss, Bavarian or Austrian and therefore regarded as
national). There is no equivalent of the Liverpool or Glaswegian
play, the Lancashire, Birmingham or Yorkshire accent. All
working-class parts are performed in the rough equivalent of the
Standard English voice. Anything else is considered '*Volkstheater*'
– a condescending term for theatre that is not considered serious.
This division is catastrophic for the contemporary writer. It is hard
to understand that the gravediggers in *Hamlet* cannot have a
Hamburg accent without incurring derisive laughter.

The diet, then, is one of foreign and classical plays, and the
financially indulgent system has produced an appointment pattern
known as the 'carousel' – a group of ageing Intendants circulating
round the major theatres, eventually arriving back at the point at
which they started. I am the first outsider to break into this circuit.
All of these problems the Schiller, one of Germany's largest
theatres, has in abundance. That, however, did not concern the
ESC as we fitted up on one of the biggest stages that we had thus
far performed on, guests of the theatre festival to celebrate eight
hundred years of Berlin as a city. I am afraid we really were
winding down. The plays ran, on average, ten minutes longer than
they should have done. The audience was half full (or half empty,
depending on your mood) a lot of the time, Berlin having packed
up and gone on holiday – a marvellous time to have a theatre
festival.

I sat in the Schaubühne – a *really* rich theatre – watching one
of the greatest productions I have ever seen – Roger Planchon's
version of Molière's *Georges Dandin* – with two hundred people.

So we weren't doing too badly. The spotlight was already on me. The news of my appointment in Hamburg had spread a buzz of curiosity across the European press. (Not much in the English.) The ESC visit was the first occasion Berlin had had to assess my work. Plaudits and brickbats. The *Volksblatt Berlin*: 'The audience was completely knocked out. Sunday, at midnight, there was over ten minutes' applause for the wonderful, joyous ensemble.' However, the eighty-four-year-old Friedrich Luft in the *Berliner Morgenpost* wrote, 'The hard-working English Shakespeare Company (in no way to be confused with the glorious RSC) have finally concluded their monstrous epic . . . The question has to be asked, what on earth has it to do with the celebration of Berlin as the European capital of culture?' The easy-going, relaxed atmosphere is deceptive. Despite its prolific theatre output, Berlin is very precious about its culture. A closed, claustrophobic city (at least until recently); art often exists on a frenetic level of self-indulgence, jealously guarded and contemptuous of what happens in the outside world. (Sounds like England.) Art in Berlin is '*echte Künst*' – *real* art. None of which affects the naïve thrill I still feel on occasions like that June Saturday, when the night was talked away in a café on the Savignyplatz, in the company of Bob Wilson, Roger Planchon, Heine Muller, Ivan Nagel, and Luc Bondi. Try meeting that lot in Joe Allen's. I was the subject of many an interview about my appointment in Hamburg. I lost track of where I was supposed to be, and to whom I was talking. Sunday lunchtime I sat in a café and talked to someone I thought was a journalist, waxing lyrical about my childhood and Dublin days, before discovering he was an actor who had come to see me for a job. Berlin had also generously contributed to the ESC's now relatively booming finances. Although we were performing only one weekend, the inclusion of workshops and other fringe performances had merited two weeks' touring money, representing a welcome bonus. From starting the year in the red to the tune of £50,000 we had turned the situation right round with our policy of overseas touring, and now had a healthy surplus to take us into the third year. We had justified a lot of people's faith in us, and we found it difficult to refrain from unseemly but jubilant nose-thumbing at those who had departed in o'er seemly haste. The workshops for the British Council, devised by Sue and Stella, were particularly successful and encouraged us to think about a full-time educational programme to back up the main work. Hilary Bartlett, the British Council representative in Berlin, became an enthusiastic supporter and has paved the way for a return visit with smaller offerings. A joint workshop between actors of the English Shakespeare Company and the Schiller Theater has established strong Anglo-Germanic relationships. Individual projects also began to emerge. John Castle and Philip Bowen revived their programme of German and English war poetry, now entitled 'Front Lines', John displaying a remarkable mastery of the teutonic 'glottal-stop'. The audience was somewhat bewildered by the project, irony not being a strong point in German comic awareness. Stephen Jameson and Paul Brennen performed *The Dumb Waiter* again, later to be repeated at the Young Vic in our London season, directed by Stella; and Roger Booth, always surprising, gave his one-person rendition of Kafka's 'Letter to the Academy'.

Considering the fatigue level of the company, this development of ESC extras in the dying days of the tour was warming. We had also used the occasion for a Works Outing. Prue, Sue Evans and Janet Morrow had all come for the weekend, so the entire staff of the ESC was, at one and the same time, in Berlin. We all limped home for a well-earned rest. It had been a traumatic year. Deaths, illness, injuries, breakdowns – and yet we were still there, with an extraordinary spirit of collective togetherness and an awareness of the unique adventure we had all been on. Two months later, all but five of the company were to come out again for a third dose of ESCitis.

PART THREE

AT LAST DESIST

PART
THREE

CHAPTER
9

THE THIRD TOUR: AUSTRALIA

August – October 1988

'You have no idea of the ignorance
prevailing in this Colony. The writer of
the principal paper, The Herald, in
remarking on the production of Richard
2nd stated that their King was grandson of
Richard 1st! That the Duke of Lancaster
was banished!! and then said that my
delivery of the speech from the walls of
Flint Castle to Norfolk was very finely
delivered, Norfolk being banished,
Northumberland was the person I
addressed.'
Charles Kean, on playing in Australia,
1864

'For physical beauty and nobility of
bearing [the Anzacs] surpassed any men I
have ever seen . . . and reminded me of a
line in Shakespeare:
"Baited like eagles having lately bathed"
(Henry IV Part 1).'
John Masefield

'Often I hate [Australia] like poison, then
again it fascinates me, and the spell of its
indifference gets me.'
D.H. Lawrence

Pennington:

> Ay, Edward will use women honourably!
> Would he were wasted, marrow, bones and all ...

The character of Richard Duke of Gloucester pushes out of the two-dimensional patchwork of the *Henry VI* plays and insinuates into the inner ear. This sound, the voice of our most malevolent desires, is one we haven't heard before in these works of Shakespeare's apprenticeship, in which the hands of Kyd, Greene, Nashe and others – the summit of their achievement being Shakespeare's starting-point – are usually assumed to be present. From speech to speech it sometimes feels as if the pen has changed hands; nevertheless the overall effect remains uniform, the corporate style energetically telling an eventful story in which we can often grasp a man's or woman's complete and unchanging character from the helpful announcements that go ahead of them:

> Is this the Lord Talbot, uncle Gloucester,
> That hath so long been resident in France? ...
> When I was young, as yet I am not old,
> I do remember how my father said
> A stouter champion never handled sword.

What more do we need to know? Henry VI, the speaker, is too young to rule; his father, Henry V, was a shrewd judge of a soldier; and John Talbot is everything the English bulldog should be – whether he is in practice handling broadsword or, as in Michael Fenner's eye-patched sweat for us, a combination of sabre and pistol. It is all clear, momentous, unequivocally hurrying forward without inner contradiction. An actor can see that the sense is contained strictly within each blank verse line, and the clinching word will invariably be at the end:

> But if your title to the crown be weak,
> As may appear by Edward's good success,
> Then 'tis but reason that I be released
> From giving aid which late I promised.

If, idiosyncratically, you were to accentuate any but the obvious words, the text, unable to sustain secondary meaning, would buckle and the sense become difficult to catch. It is a very long way from *Troilus and Cressida* or *The Winter's Tale*, where, like a jazz improvisation, the argument contracts and expands under emotional pressure across a metrical structure whose pinions you can hardly sense. *Henry VI* is, shall we say, strictly pre-bebop.

So the actors in these plays get used to serving a rather confining brief, that of simply moving the story along – especially when subtleties of character have been further ironed out by ruthless cutting; the audience becomes hypnotised by a rhythm dynamic enough to hold the interest but not to trouble the imagination over much. Until the Duke of Gloucester's normal, spiteful voice breaks in.

He has in a way sidled into the play. In the second scene of *Henry VI Part 3* (the transposed opening of our *House of York*), a momentous family is quietly introduced. The father, Richard of York, we already know; his three sons, who are not at first identified, seem to represent three sides of him: Edward, the eldest, is a golden boy, a charismatic family leader but with a special weakness of judgment when sexually attracted; Clarence is unreliable, witty and soft-centred; and Richard, who suffers from some physical deformity, is ... what ? The first real smell we get is his disconcerting reaction to the news of his father's death in battle:

> I cannot weep; for all my body's moisture
> Scarce serves to quench my furnace-burning heart ...
> Tears then for babes; blows and revenge for me!

This brother's character seems to lack a certain human sympathy, and for a play and a half we watch this lack turned into a horrible strength of purpose.

So now Andy Jarvis, well played into the part by the time of the opening of our third season at the Victoria Arts Centre in Melbourne, in a svelte dinner jacket which quite flatters his humped back and club foot, comes easing with his champagne glass towards us out of the party his brother is giving to celebrate his marriage. He looks like a friend, and rakes the audience with a conniving grin:

> Then, since this earth affords no joy to me,
> But to command, to check, to o'erbear such
> As are of better person than myself,
> I'll make my heaven to dream upon the crown ...

Irving Wardle of *The Times* was later to see in Andy's 'beaked profile and gleaming bald head . . . the likeness of a hyper-active vulture. Within that controlling image he has an inexhaustible reservoir of false identities, and the psychopathic ability to steamroll horror into commonsense practicality.' Andy also has a most unusual gift for directness; he can skim the language down to a colloquial common denominator without losing its scale. Later on his acting tended to broaden and coarsen – as did mine and virtually everybody else's – as we approached the end of our journey through cavernous spaces; but at this point, rested and at his best, he flicked and cajoled his audience into collusion with his merry, unthinkable schemes, using language that swayed and strained with Richard's own restlessness:

> And yet I know not how to get the crown
> For many lives stand between me and home;
> And I – like one lost in a thorny wood,
> That rends the thorns and is rent by the thorns
> Seeking a way and straying from the way;
> Not knowing how to find the open air
> But toiling desperately to find it out,
> Torment myself to catch the English crown;
> And from that torment I will free myself
> Or hew my way out with a bloody axe.

Early on Andy and I had discussed Richard's thwarted sexuality, like that of a crippled twin bonded to his successful, womanising brother; Michael Bogdanov had aimed him at the joker and vaudevillian implicating us in his own guiltiness; Andy had added his own form of deadly casualness: flicking his butterfly knife airily, his foot up on the bed of the murdered Henry – 'I am myself, alone . . .', pouring a bucket of slops over the corpse on his way out as if he were tossing cold tea down a sink. It was unnerving in the extreme, and, by the end of *Richard III*, nightmarish. Here, with all that ahead of him, he coaxed us into complicity, swung himself away, checked, and returned with an afterthought:

> Can I do this, and cannot get a crown?
> Tut, were it farther off, I'd pluck it down.

The Melbourne audience, like many before and since, broke into unbegged applause. At four o'clock on Sunday afternoon, nearly forty-eight hours into the marathon premiere, they were re-engaged and apprehensive, possessed by Richard (as they had earlier been by that other dream of the subconscious, Falstaff) and sensing that it was he who would now carry them through to the end. Andy had confirmed his claim on a famous part; and the ESC had re-cycled itself once again.

And of course, we had almost not made it. In the short summer recess we had rustled up two new recruits to the stage management team, Niki Lawrence and Joanna Reid; and made a promotion to Wardrobe Supervisor, Annette Heron, to be armed with two new assistants, Joanne Pearce and Donna Eagles. In the acting company, the shuffling about was so extensive that it has to be abbreviated here: but in two weeks' rehearsal Jenifer Konko had stepped into the Welsh role of Lady Mortimer and a bewildering string of other supporting parts; Ann Penfold (aka Mrs Colin Farrell) had gone into Lady Percy, Alice, Queen Elizabeth, a Duchess of York and a Duchess of Gloucester; Robert Hands, whose first professional job it was, was fitting in all over the place and standing by to play John of Lancaster whenever John Dougall vacated that part to play Prince Hal; Jack Carr was the new Mowbray, Burgundy and Tyrrel; while Francesca Ryan was going into no fewer than five major roles: Queens Isabel and Katherine, Doll Tearsheet, Joan of Arc and Lady Anne. The swordfights alone should have taken a month to prepare. Inside the existing company, apart from Andy Jarvis as Hotspur and Michael Cronin as Bolingbroke, Paul Brennen was Pistol, Ben Bazell Westmoreland, Barry Stanton York, I was Suffolk, and Charlie Dale and Stephen Jameson all had sizeable new work to do. Our combined brain-strain was certainly as great as the frustration of the rest of the company who were still playing the same old parts. None of it should have been possible. Jack Carr didn't believe it was: 'The ESC exploded into my life one day in Bath, when a giggling boy of a middle-aged man suggested that a trip to Australia might lift my "Soap"-jaded aspirations onto a fresher, not to say crazier, level. So I joined. I almost quit many times; probably the reason I didn't is because I had no time to. These guys didn't so much rehearse as swashbuckle. Their attitude was "fuck it – we've done the impossible, now we'll consolidate it." I was convinced some of them thought they could get to Australia without a plane.'

In fact, the word in those days was that there *was* always The

Plane; a twenty-four hour flight to Australia, with a sizeable wait
at Delhi, was a significant opportunity for rehearsal. Cheap for us,
too. I was told by the new members that the only comforting aspect
of the hasty preparation for them had been that, whatever happened, they could definitely not have been sacked; now, on the
plane, the comfort to us was that they definitely could not escape.
As we headed for the inevitable, the company disappeared behind
switched-off British Airways headphones to check through not only
seven parts apiece but labyrinthine lists of exits, entrances, costume
changes and a host of menial tasks; or else, scripts in hand,
promenaded the aisles with a preoccupied air, seeking out the
cherished colleague, stage manager or director who would be able
to remind them of something or help them read their own writing.
The unwitting sponsors of these *répétitions*, Anthony Steel and
Marguerite Pepper, who were presenting us as part of Giancarlo
Menotti's itinerant Spoleto Festival in Melbourne, were
presumably sitting comfortably at the other end, looking forward
to greeting the fluent and self-confident operation they had so much
admired in Toronto eighteen months previously.

Bogdanov: *What re-rehearsals there were had taken place at
Sadler's Wells, which in October 1989 was to become our new
home. ('The ESC changes offices more often than a tart changes her
drawers' was the bitchy remark of a rival company.) We had had
little more than two weeks. The younger members, after two years
of being fêted, were now pretty cocky; où sont les neiges d'antan,
when they had listened in 1986 with wide-eyed wonder in a
restaurant in Plymouth as their wrinkly elders groaned their way
through Guy Mitchell and Rosemary Clooney, setting a standard
of late-night revelry they, in their youthfulness, could only marvel
at? John Dougall arrived back two days late, tanned, and
sartorially Milan. Where were the tartan trenchcoat and Tweedie
Trousie of yesteryear? Paul Brennen, with Henry VI behind him,
now tackled Pistol with the same resistance to the concept as John
Castle. He fell right into the trap of over-melodramatising the
rhetoric. Mind you, he appears to be in the same company as Kean,
Macready and Colley Cibber. I am convinced that a plain theatrical
ham is boring. John Price had demonstrated that if the language
could be absorbed as a natural means of communication with no
self-awareness of the speech mannerisms affected, the role is a
study on many levels, not merely comic. Ann Penfold, with much*

text to absorb, had possibly the hardest task of all, including the recurring problem of that ancient ritual known as 'The Throwing of the Water'. It was about to defeat the third challenger for the title. In the Hotspur/Lady Percy scene in Henry IV Part 1 *(the famous shaving one, remember?), Lady Percy is so incensed by her spouse that she picks up a large jug of water and hurls the contents in Hotspur's face. Splash! Right into the front row of the audience, insurance claims for damaged minks. The problem is a simple one. If you hold a tall jug by the bottom in one hand and the handle in the other (try it) and then attempt to throw the contents straight, the arms come round in a curve and the water goes either sideways (in the case of Ann), backwards (in the case of Mary Rutherford), or everywhere (in the case of Jennie Stoller). The trick is to sort of jerk the jug straight in a very artificial movement so that the water shoots out in a forward trajectory. (Rehearsals of this and the resulting frustration have been known to make strong men weep and the ladies stamp their feet.) The final rehearsal to solve the problem was to take place by the swimming pool of a Melbourne hotel at 3 am one morning, when a well known director of the ESC, attired first as a Sumo wrestler and then somewhat less sartorially, took a dose of his own medicine, or water, full-frontal from Ann Penfold.*

Pennington: In-flight rehearsals were more peaceful than that. One makes the most of such respites; you never know what's going to greet you. First there's the welcoming committee, then the bus, then the hotel. In this case Anthony Steel and Marguerite Pepper were indeed delighted to see us, but our bus was nowhere to be seen, and there was an anxious ten minutes while we felt the company beginning to seethe behind us – with twenty-four hours of jetlag accumulating, the slightest hitch in the arrangements could be read as a wilful slight, and our necessary good cheer while chatting with our hosts perhaps seemed like collusion. Of course the transport turned up in the end. Kirsten Oploh, our General Manager, who had fortunately been in Australia a week ahead of us, sat next to me and whispered – further collusion? – the bad news about the hotel. Our contract had specified a minimum of three-star accommodation, which in England of course implies breakfast, at least a continental one. Perhaps Australia's star system was different; the mouldy-smelling, lightless Lodge on the edge of Chinatown into which we had been bundled would not have furnished a boiled egg. Marguerite had refused either to change this accommodation or to accept the extra cost of whatever Kirsten found, which, after a long trudge round the city with a map, was an eccentric family-run motel towards St Kilda's Beach which would do its best to meet our needs. In the end the proprietors' willingness made up for their air of chaos, and was in its turn thoroughly abused by a relentless all-night carousal by ourselves which involved (apart from water-throwing rehearsals) a certain amount of bar-raiding, a few unsettled bills and some boisterous skinny-dipping in the tiny kidney of a pool that perhaps flabbily emulated the great Australian traditions. The ESC, transformed for the moment into Aussie Hemingways and Scott-and-Zeldas, were not at their ambassadorial best in Melbourne; and the hotel staff retaliated in style at breakfast time each morning by sending out from the kitchens a succession of flaming orange-headed waiters who exemplified a certain kind of ear-splitting macho gayness rather typical of the city. They quite terrified our own left-handed brethren.

Hoping that they had heard nothing of this carrying-on, we went to settle accounts with Anthony and Marguerite, keeping as usual in our back pocket that well-thumbed old Won't Play card, which looked as if it might be needed even more than in Chicago. We pointed out that comparable companies at the Festival seemed to be in the city's best hotels and we had been down-graded; and that although this thorn had been plucked by Kirsten's tireless footslogging, something told us that we weren't being treated like the – erm – major international company we were. They hastened to reassure, and did pick up the increased tab for the hotel including cooked breakfasts – for Melbourne only; but it was the first of several *oeillades* between us. For example, on leaving Melbourne a fortnight later, we very nearly didn't get to Brisbane at all; instead of the three closed containers of precise dimensions that had been agreed for transporting the shows, we were presented after getting out on the Saturday night – when the drivers eventually arrived – with two open wagons in which our set and equipment, open to the elements, had to rattle the eight hundred miles to Queensland. The prognosis for the later, longer trips – for we were to go on to Adelaide, Canberra and across the continent to Perth – was not good. Our confidence as well as the set was shaken, I was sadly to declare on that occasion to Anthony outside the Queensland Art Gallery in Brisbane – I was trying to look like one of the iron-headed Sidney Nolan Ned Kellys I'd just seen, but felt more like the alarmed aboriginal *mimi* spirits who live in the interstices of the desert rocks. Anthony had to acknowledge there had been a slip about the wagons; it wouldn't happen again. While he was on the back foot, I then demanded free cooked breakfasts for the company for the rest of the tour, with rather less contractual justification, hoping that he would accept that this would be automatic in England and so implicit in our contract with him. He agreed, and then came down the pitch at me, declaring that Kirsten Oploh had over the weeks taken advantage of her own not quite perfect command of English (she is from Düsseldorf in Germany) to obfuscate the terms of our deal with him, that in general we were the most difficult company he had ever done business with, and he certainly wouldn't touch us again. I felt rather flattered. I also felt I could afford to give away his towering stroke for six if it meant I won the match. I could after all, knowing my company, hear a certain familiar snapping sound at my heels, even as I looked into his angry face.

Back in Melbourne in week one, the matchwinner we were relying on as we argued about details was the quality of the shows we were about to hit him with. But the company was still locked into hotel rooms, muttering over pieces of paper, wrestling with jetlag. After three free days, we then assembled at the Victoria Arts Centre on the Thursday and immediately imploded. Loretta Bircham, Deputy Stage Manager for all seven shows, had been taken ill that morning. Within an hour it emerged that she was pregnant and might be miscarrying. Loretta had joined us at the beginning of *The Henrys* as a junior ASM, but in the second year she had become a DSM – that is to say, in charge of the prompt copy and cueing of several of the plays. By the third year, she was passionately keen to run all seven – didn't really want to stay with the company if she couldn't. We had agreed to this with some reluctance, not because we doubted her ability, but because we knew that until there was time for an ASM to understudy Loretta's job by herself learning the books, we would be in mortal trouble throughout the cycle if Loretta were ever to be ill. The knowledge of the book of any show is a complex and personal business, depending as much on instinct and a feeling for performance rhythms as on literally following the notes, and the sheer complexity of the Histories can be imagined. The job took a good bit of doing, even with a lot of practice.

Now Loretta was pregnant and in trouble. Getting rather used to this by now, Michael and I simultaneously rejoiced, worried for her and hit the roof. Why had nobody told us of her condition before we left England? There were, it transpired, a number of people who knew, including Monica McCabe, the Company Manager; and clearly someone had decided not to tell. The news would not have affected Loretta; we couldn't and wouldn't have left her in England; but we would have been more alert to the urgent need for a deputy. Most of all, we wondered whether we were losing control of our own outfit. Two years ago we had started with a hands-on policy, by which we and Fleur knew about and controlled every detail; now the company had expanded and we had learned to delegate, and this was the result. Was there a new kind of middle management blooming among us that was exercising discretion as to what the President should be told?

It may be remembered that Stella Bond, now an Assistant Director, had stage-managed *The Henrys* in 1986. Stella had always been one of the best. She didn't know any of the new productions from a cueing point of view, and her technical memory of *The Henrys* could be faulty. Still, she would probably be all right with those three on Saturday if she took over, but what about Friday and Sunday? In the event, though not well herself at the time, Stella took us through the lot faultlessly; Loretta got better, stayed till Christmas and now has a baby boy; and we played in Melbourne, to our biggest audience yet – 2,004 for *Richard III* on Sunday night – with a miraculously assured new cast. Did I say miraculously assured? Francesca Ryan: 'I was off for the St Alban's scene as Margery Jourdain, but was condemned to be burned anyway. I would have been off again as Lady Anne after hearing I was to be Queen of England had not Michael Cronin spotted me dazedly wandering towards the dressing rooms. In silence, his hands gently on my shoulders, he turned me round and guided me on again immediately for my Coronation.' Jack Carr walked on for a scene and walked straight off again, recognising nobody on the stage. But he was wrong. He was expecting to see John Dougall, with whom he had last rehearsed, as Henry V and Robert Hands as Lancaster; instead he had seen the current cast, myself as Henry and Dougall as Lancaster. The alternating cast for the Dougall/Pennington solution of Prince Hal was an exquisite refinement of Jack's torture.

We stayed in Melbourne for two weeks.

Bogdanov: *The Victoria Arts Centre is one of the best designed of all the modern theatres we visited. The facilities radiate off from the broad deep stage, ensuring that contact can be made with all the essentials needed for the smooth running and controlling of a production: dressing rooms, wardrobe, laundry, etc., all placed no more than a few seconds' step from the stage – well equipped, light and set along broad corridors.*

A long way from Bath. The front of house too, had five or six catering points and bars, with a variety of snacks and meals available all day, from bowls of soup to champagne and oysters. A model of theatre management. Considering the speed with which the shows had been remounted (I had to re-light yet again), jetlag, and the strange shuffling around of parts that had taken place, I do not think I have ever seen the shows in better shape than the performances given in Melbourne. Some strange chemistry was at work in this new combination of roles which had felt something like shuffling a deck with half the pack missing and the court cards reversed. The plays and performances emerged explosive and shining, new minted and gold. I felt prouder of our achievement than at any point and marvelled (not for the first time) on what it is that makes a performance click in such circumstances. Theatre only happens at the point it happens. There can only be a subjective appraisal of that one moment. One night half the cast are ill, a loved one has died, someone has broken a leg, it is pouring with rain, the house is half full and the audience all have got colds. The show is appalling. The next day the sun is shining, someone has won the pools, got laid, had a birthday, the audience is packed with merrymaking, pissed holiday-makers and the performance is wild and wonderful. One group says it is the worst show they have ever seen, the other – the best. Both are right.

Critically, there is no defence of the one performance, apart from the old comment (and I sometimes hear myself saying it) – 'A pity you didn't see the show last Thursday.' Well, my old mates, you should have seen them in Melbourne. I was to think back longingly to this Golden Age, where we drank the hotel clean out of wine (it was so good), when we reached the ranting and raving stage of the following year. Meanwhile, September was pushing winter out of the way, and I took a trip upstate to try my hand at shearing merinos on a Victorian sheep farm, before leaving with the Mobil Golden Pegasus Award for the Best Contribution to the Spoleto Festival. This gilded statuette is a monument of awfulness and

stands on my mantelpiece with 'Mobil' turned to the wall.
Nonetheless, a much loved symbol of my pride at our achievement.

Pennington: The Victorian Government is committed to backing
the Spoleto Festival at the rate of $2 million a year, so it is a well-
cushioned event that understandably attracts the hostility of local
theatre and dance companies still struggling for a crust of
subsidised bread, and we did hear from some of them. We went on
to Brisbane as the main stage attraction of Expo 88, and then to
Canberra under the rather vague umbrella of Floriade 88, the city's
spring flower festival ('a million blooming bulbs'), to Adelaide, and
finally to His Majesty's at Perth, a beautiful Edwardian house, each
for a week. The plays were received with the usual balance: violent
enthusiasm and a minority of violent objection, best expressed by
the lady in the front row at Canberra, who leaped up early in *Henry
V*, and yelled out that we were 'prostituting Shakespeare'. She then
turned to her companion and told him (I quote) 'Edward! Take me
home. I don't care what you do to me, but take me home.' But she
was no match for the presumably much-barracked Will
Shakespeare, since the Chorus' next line, leaped on with delight by
the wily Barry Stanton, runs:

> for if we may
> We'll not offend one stomach with our play.

The ovation that greeted her departing back told us we'd won the
match again. The press was generally ecstatic: 'an achievement
which overwhelms even the *Mahabharata*'; 'magnificent . . .
nothing has matched it, nothing ever will' (*The Australian*); it
resonated also with some Australian preoccupations: watching me
was 'like watching a batsman on succeeding days of a Test' (*The
Adelaide Review*); but 'Why bring them out here at Festival time?
. . . We could successfully take on the same challenge . . . we have
artists in this country who have done and will continue to do as
much' (*New Theatre*). There was also an interesting perspective on
us as an English troupe: 'For this company, York, Lancaster, Wales
and Ireland are not merely princely titles or foreign locales . . . they
are the venues and communities the ESC was set up to serve. And
the relationship between these communities and the seat of power
in England's south . . . remains much as it was in Shakespeare's
day: antagonistic. That a soldier wears a mixture of chain mail and

commando gear, then, is no affectation of design but a gesture towards acknowledging historical persistence. What makes the ESC both valued and unique is the sheer Englishness of its vision. This quality should not be confused with the culture of London and the dominant southern counties. They are served well enough by the Royal Shakespeare Company, the National Theatre and the Government of Margaret Thatcher. England, as the historical plays consistently demonstrate, is a bigger phenomenon than London ... This is no updated staging of a series of antique texts, but a reaching into the past in search of images of the present ... The great struggle between the forces of national unity and cultural autonomy that has characterised English history continues still, and is consistently and specifically touched on ... an insight into the heart of Britain today, responding variously and violently as it does to the continuing urge to dominate in the South ... in this respect the ESC comes to us as an accessible but essentially foreign company, and it is for this reason that its visit is so important' (*The Melbourne Herald*). In Canberra, 'Every politician in that nice, new, clean Parliament House across the river ought to be forced here to see every one of the seven plays. But the pollies are too busy reliving history to heed healthy advice' (*New Theatre*).

Bogdanov: *You can't ask no fairer than that, Guv. The critics were not just fulsome in their praise, they were also gratifyingly accurate in their assessment of the ideas. Why is it one had to go to Australia, Canada, provincial America, to get some coherent views (good and bad) of what we were attempting? The reputation that these countries – the Mid West, the far-flung remnants of the Empire – have for conservatism is completely belied by the quality of the writing and the minds at work in journals such as the* Toronto Globe and Mail, *the* Sun Times *and the* Chicago Tribune *to name but three. It merely confirms one's impression that London is the real provincial, bourgeois capital of the world. Any attempt to get a genuine reaction to something challenging is like diving down to the bottom of a barrel of treacle. In a way, it is lucky for London that America exists. The euphoria with which British shows are greeted on Broadway serves to sustain the English belief – much quoted and flaunted – that English theatre is the best in the world. One gets the feeling that if America weren't there and we had to look to Central Europe for our laurels, we would get very short shrift. One quickly discovers that much of the rest of*

Europe is not aware of what is happening in English theatre,
although the reverse is true of English politics. Yet there is a
massive continental interchange of shows from countries, East and
West, that we are not part of. England is looked on as the home
of 'Voice' theatre and not much else. The real artistic and political
movements in theatre this century have all stemmed from elsewhere
– Russia, France, Germany, Ireland – although England is much
admired for its wordsmith playwrights. And lest any should think
that this sour-griping is simply a desire for critically vacuous praise,
the Herald *also observed: 'In some cases [the approach] failed to*
bear so much rich fruit. The 'necklacing' of Joan of Arc in Henry
VI House of Lancaster and the summary shootings of Richard III
obliterate the plays' truths rather than drawing them out.' Dead on
the ball.

Pennington: We had certainly come a long way for our work to be
seen in the context of English society. And as the incident of
Loretta had shown us, our enterprise was changing shape all the
time, and we needed now to check mentally on what we were doing
and whether to continue. Michael and I took advantage of a few
days together in Melbourne, sat down and tried to be serious. The
ESC was a good thing and should have a future; there was life
beating in it that shouldn't, on the whole, be stopped. Our acting
companies had had a sniff of an exceptional exhilaration and self-
belief and it would be a shame to let them drift back into the
industry's well-worn old paths of dependent tail-wagging with
nothing to show for it all but a string of anecdotes. As we repeated
to each other the very good reasons for continuing, we became
bored, abstracted and rather bad-tempered. A dread responsibility
seemed to be settling on us, taking the sparkle out of our talk; and
if we lost the sparkle, what was the point? I felt subtly angry with
Michael for not rekindling me, and he felt the same. Fuck it,
perhaps. He had a good job to go to in Hamburg, and a mightily
absorbing one; I was thinking fondly about parking the
responsibility of management and becoming a hired hand again.
Even if we managed to rebuild our finances, if we were still going
to be this dulled we would surely become the sort of half-hearted
institution the ESC had been set up to rebuke. Nobody had forced
us to start, nobody could expect us to continue. With what,
anyway? We had naturally thought of three Roman plays – *Julius*
Caesar, Antony and Cleopatra, Coriolanus – but quickly seen that

they would invite the wrong sort of comparison with the Histories, since they are in no real sense a cycle, but three pillars standing close but distinct. As to other 'cycles': the *Oedipus* Trilogy, which Stephen Spender had asked me to do in his translation and which we'd thought of taking round the Mediterranean, would be rotten box office in the UK, as would a Golden Age Trilogy of Calderón plays. I imagined the faces of certain theatre managers as they received such a suggestion. There was indeed a difficulty in aligning UK touring with what was attractive overseas: Calderón was too rich for the former, popular Shakespeare perhaps too bland for the latter, who could do *Hamlet* for themselves. It seemed that by instinct and chance we had hit in the Histories on an unrepeatable formula, English enough to export well, half-popular and therefore intriguing at home. The whole problem was making us bored and hungry. We cobbled together a four-point plan - a Landrover Tour for the Outback, an English touring group (which would do a Chekhov Festival), a separate overseas touring group, and a university workshop tour, and took Philip Bowen out to a fish dinner and asked him to run the Landrover Tour. We sent a fax back to Prue in London outlining the Plan, making up in bullishness what it lacked in detail. Its self-righteous tone nearly caused her to resign. We were in all sorts of ways a long way from home.

The cherry blossom was out in Queen Victoria Gardens, making it our third spring of the year: the blossom had been down when we left Tokyo and in full blaze when we arrived in Chicago, and here it was again. The company emerged from its moiling and sniffed the air: the schedule offered a commodious invitation to have a good look round. We travelled on Sundays, and between then and each Wednesday opening we could explore the continent's 'tyranny of distance' - though Ayers Rock and the Great Barrier Reef did lie too far off - and get some sense of this extraordinary land, in which the sybaritism of sand and surf and those depressingly English names - Camberwell, Croydon, Torquay - sit in uneasy truce with a threatening environment. Bushfires, to take an obvious example, can travel at a mile a minute, as they did in 1983, turning the beaches to glass, cracking the wattles open like sticks and stifling the atmosphere with the intoxicating flavour of gumleaves on fire. People have jumped into their water tanks for coolness and been boiled in them; koalas have become welded into the molten eucalypts or burst into pieces as their oil-stuffed tummies expanded and exploded. On the other hand, there are the blandishments of temperate weather, a relaxed style and the joys of the barbie. Our company was rather short on frontiersmen — except for John Tramper, one of this book's photographers and an actor of ever-increasing confidence. John was in the grip of a programme of worldwide exploration which made the rest of us gape. Seemingly impervious to jetlag, he usually had in hand an immediate getaway from each airport, so that we might not see him at the hotel until the day of the opening night. By the time the rest of us had reconciled our bodyclocks, John might have got as far from Hong Kong as mainland China, as far from Chicago as the Rockies, or as far from Tokyo as a *ryokan* at the foot of Mount Fuji. Now he lurked with his camera under a bush in the outback, his eye trained on a fan-tailed lizard or echidna, his attention riveted by a desert wildflower, sleeping three nights under the southern skies before trudging home to play Francis the drawer. It is a wonderful ability in him, this rapid assimilation; and the birthday present that we once as a company gave him, a massive illustrated book of the World's Birds, though it reduced him to tears of pleasure, was a thin enough acknowledgement of his passionately curious spirit.

Most of the company settled for easier and more earthbound pleasures. Some got no further than the *Neighbours* studio next to the theatre in Melbourne, hoping to meet Kylie Minogue. The rest of us fanned out to Healesville Sanctuary for the koalas or the Dandenong Hills for the lyrebirds; or, in Philip Bowen's case, accepted the warm welcome Australian cities extend to the gambling man, starting on a rake's progress that led him to temporary bankruptcy in Adelaide. Here he could be found taking ultimate advantage of the hardwon company breakfast – steaks, chops, liver, sides of bacon – to build up a daily hump he could live on, so that he was obliged to spend not a cent for the rest of the day. In Queensland, homosexuality is still against the law, so there were early nights in Brisbane for some of our nighthunters, with compensatory daytrips up the Sunshine Coast to Noosa for Australia's best beachlife. In Adelaide, we fled from Pennington Terrace, where the theatre stood, down the Barossa Valley for the wineries or to the half-timbered cakeshops of Hahndorf to sample the mellower fruits of Lutheran settlement.

High above the Nullabor Plain on the flight to Perth I looked around a tanned and weatherbeaten company, taking a mental photograph which is still vivid. We were swapping seats, kneeling on our own to talk to the row behind, patrolling the aisles, inoffensively fizzed up on Australian champagne. The faces were without exception happy and delighted. The company had been fêted and adventured and we appreciated each other. We would soon be going home, so some of the negatives of touring – homesickness, separation, anxiety – would shortly be eased. I rarely saw a group of people for a moment so content, blinking and beaming and climbing into each other's chairs. It had been an adventure rare in these days. And if I hadn't had a silly quarrel with the National Theatre and if simultaneously Michael's *Mutiny* hadn't been such a pig to put on, absolutely none of it would have happened, none of the applause, fewer friendships, fewer reminiscences for life. Knowing that I must be sparing about such moments (and never let on about them), I wallowed in satisfaction.

No doubt the euphoria was partly due to having just left Canberra, a contrived city like Milton Keynes that can fill you with a deadly fear. London Circuit, National Circuit, McCoy Circuit lie like concentric quoits round a city centre where nobody lives. Ahead of us was the prospect of Perth, the flower of Australia's West Coast, which in its imagined splendour loomed like Samarkand. The city is famously beautiful, its gardens protected by the ocean on one side and the desert on the other, so that the floral variety is enormous; its liberalisation is evident in the surprising number of accredited aboriginal outlets where you can be reasonably sure that your money will mostly go to whoever actually *made* the *dijeridu* or barkpainting you long to see on your wall; and the sanctuary of Rottnest Island, where the quokkas – indigenously unique little charmers like squirrels with ratty tails – live, lies only a few miles offshore from the city centre. But it was in this temperate setting that nature's red tooth and claw threatened us most. On arriving, Ben Bazell, Stella Bond and Simon Elliott hired a Suzuki jeep and headed out for the Pinnacles, a fossilised forest a hundred miles north of Perth. Stella remembers me warning her as she left not to make the mistake of wandering away from the jeep if it broke down. When they weren't back by Wednesday, long after the jeep should have been turned in, we called out the police, who were immediately tailed by ABC Television in helicopters. What they eventually saw, in the middle of nowhere, was the jeep immobilised in a bog and the three adventurers huddled in its shadow for protection from the sun. They had been waiting with only biscuits, dangerously lost for two days. Rescued, they became instant media celebs, tanned and sandy faces peering out from the six o'clock news and the pages of *West Australian*, imperturbably telling their story, from which they emerged as unflappable heroes. But the truth is, the outback had nearly got them. A few months later, when the summer takes hold, incautious travellers have been known to roast in their cars out there, or been reduced to drinking the antifreeze in their radiators, preferring a death from Glycol poisoning to final dehydration, choking on their huge tongues.

It was the last and most dramatic in a series of indiscretions that had caused the company to look on occasion a little less stream-lined than usual. Once or twice in the tour I had climbed wearily onto a highish horse to preach about being late for the half-hour call (or in one of our cases missing the beginning of the show altogether), the not learning of understudy parts, and various other subterranean etiquettes of theatre life. It was an intensely boring feeling. After all, on a trip to Australia you must have fun. Was I about to pontificate at these incautious desert rats, who had missed the first night in Perth? Of course not: I was too relieved. The old fart in me stayed silent, and I remember only the Cheshire Cat smile on the face of John Tramper, who had viewed the antics of his bushwhacking colleagues rather with the air of Ranulph Fiennes hearing about a scrape in the playground.

The Earl of Richmond having ushered in the Tudor dynasty to the strains of the National Anthem in the Edwardian graciousness of His Majesty's Perth, Richard II next reopened his sybaritic court, where all the trouble started, on the banks of the Tyne ten thousand miles away – though really Newcastle (17th–22nd October) was a whistle stop en route to Utrecht. Three weeks under grey Netherland skies lay ahead of us, followed by the continuation of earnest business – Leeds, Cardiff, Liverpool and Plymouth before Christmas, with Germany (West and East) to open the New Year. Australia was thus the last really glamorous date, if you discount Amsterdam, and the company set its face to the rest of the winter knowing that this was really what it was all about, but certainly with a twinge of regret at the passing of tourism, together with the unplanned felicity that had allowed us to avoid so much North European weather in 1988. Still more improbabilities lay ahead: after Germany in January we would achieve a certain kind of consummation by playing the Old Vic for the first time in two years, this time with the complete cycle, and this would have seemed the right moment to stop; but we would still be four short of our quota of ten UK dates for the year on which our Arts Council grant was hung, and would have to play out time somehow, despite the fact that one way or another most of the safe dates on the circuit had now seen us at least once. Feeling the wedge thinning, we had accordingly scheduled Eastbourne, Norwich, Southampton and Swansea for March and April. Even the most dedicated ideologues among us, pioneers of hell-or-high-water touring, could be allowed to feel that if not exactly a whimper, it certainly didn't feel like going out with a bang; and if ever an Eastbourne house weren't to rise joyfully to us, or a Southampton critic were to question our qualities, a certain amount of huffing and puffing might be expected in the corridors as our international stars gathered their skirts about them.

This compromised vision was exactly paralleled in the ESC treasury. The newly-reopened Swansea Grand would guarantee us our costs; but Norwich are an unyielding management, despite a huge catchment area and a previous visit with *The Henrys*; and neither Eastbourne nor Southampton were used to Shakespeare and were offering nervous terms. On coming back from Australia we found that bookings for these final four dates were so far minimal; cruelly, we stood to lose perhaps £60,000 on them – and that after two years' determined efforts to pull ourselves back into the black from the £46,000 deficit of 1987. So we could easily fall at the very last jump, a jump that perhaps as a company we had less than complete enthusiasm for taking. Well, we were saying to the Arts Council, you are in effect forcing us to play these dates to earn our grant and now you'll stand by and watch us drown – how about an element of additional underwriting on them so that your favoured clients may live to fight another day? Not a chance . . . You have our moral support; good luck.

In poorish humour therefore, but at the same time not wishing to seem ungracious to the good people who were looking forward to our visit and certainly deserved our best endeavours, we dropped in on the newly refurbished Theatre Royal in Newcastle. At least we were guaranteed. £9.3 million had been spent on doing up this fine old theatre and making its notorious stage – impossible alcoves and inconvenient brick buttresses – more practicable, and also on bringing its dressing rooms into the twentieth century. Very much into the twentieth century, because, bewilderingly but familiarly, each dressing room contains a television – not a good idea – a pointlessly large bathroom and a cramped dressing area with about enough hanging space for two lounge suits; you would think the Theatre Royal specialised in William Douglas Home, not the epic Shakespeare they take in from the RSC, Renaissance, the Actors' Touring Company and ourselves. A sense of Shakespearian glut slightly affected our audiences too, and for the first time in England we encountered faintly jaded palates – my dresser expressed the hope that I would soon be rejoining the RSC. We played with a will; I banged off a rudish letter about the refurbishments to the theatre management and caught the plane to Holland, feeling that we had done better by our audience in the north-east in 1987 by going down the road to Sunderland, where our like had certainly not been looked upon for a long time by customers paying half as much. Grumpily puritanical, we advanced on the fleshpots of Amsterdam.

CHAPTER
10

HOLLAND, U.K. AND GERMANY

November 1988 – January 1989

'From side to side I wander
And wonder where I am;
And can you be in England
And I at Rotterdam!'
Thomas Hood, 'To *****'

Pennington: When Wim Visser from Wim Visser Impresariat of Amsterdam, round-spectacled, enthusiastic and looking about sixteen, had come to see me at the Old Vic in 1987, wanting the promised seven-play sequence for a Dutch tour, I confess I had doubted his capacity to transport such a burden. But since our meeting took place on the afternoon after the PTC Hearing on the Ninth Performance, perhaps my jaundiced view that his guilders might never take the place of his mouth could be forgiven. In fact Wim then went back to Holland, scooped up the entire British Council (Netherlands) drama budget for the year as well as some local sponsorship, exacted some fierce guarantees for himself from the Dutch theatres, and then made us a confident offer which we now proceeded to honour. The visit was very much adapted to local conditions. For one thing, we were (apart from a straight week at the Stadsschouwburg in Amsterdam) to play split weeks for the first time, and would thus have to bisect the repertoire. We opened in Utrecht – a pleasant university city where James Boswell, studying the law, used to be distracted by 'many beautiful and amiable ladies' – playing *Richard II* and the two *Henry IV*s over two days, before moving on to Eindhoven to complete the cycle; and similarly the following week we straddled Rotterdam and Gröningen, capital of an interesting northern province where there survive circular villages originally built on little tummocks to lift them above the surrounding marshes. From here we took the Afsluitdijk road south, a severe straight causeway with the Zuyder Zee as far as the eye can see to the left and the Waddenzee (Mud Sea) to the right, to arrive with pleasure in Amsterdam; where, quite apart from wildly enthusiastic audiences and the city's broader attractions, any time spent in front of Rembrandt's *Jewish Bride* or the four miraculous Vermeers in the Rijksmuseum makes one feel that the touring life is a good and renewing one after all.

In fact we did well only in Amsterdam, where we sold out effortlessly; everywhere else we would have to acknowledge a box office failure, which hurt Wim more than us and the theatres more than Wim. The argument underlying the tour contradicted itself in a rather circular way: on the one hand it was noble and right to go into the regions, but, on the other, outside of Amsterdam only the diehards came; and those were the people who were in any case quite prepared to travel the forty miles from town to town themselves to see the whole cycle. We could have stayed in Amsterdam for the full three weeks, and they would probably have come to us there. The strain on our technical team, getting in and out of two theatres a week, was worse than on the long hauls; and the acting company, perhaps sensing the paradox underlying the tour and feeling they were undertaking the equivalent of split weeks in Watford, Croydon and Stratford East, found almost everything to their vague distaste. The hotels in particular were thought ill-appointed; one cast member went to the trouble of establishing that Dutch three-star rating is arguably the equivalent of English two-star, proceeding to the argument that Wim Visser was in breach of his agreement to provide three-star accommodation; and since he had spotted it, why hadn't the ESC? Actors were naturally incensed to come off buses to find front-of-house photographs of their 1986 predecessors in various roles; and a large and incongruous row broke out over the extent of the insurance cover we had taken out for the company, which was in fact rather generous and certainly well in advance of Equity minimum requirements. It all proved that people were vaguely unhappy and needed to find a reason. Fatigued, the English Shakespeare Company management of one retired to his room and read Ian McEwan for two days, coming out only to perform at night and appreciating why actor-managers went out of business for so long.

Perhaps in the end we did the most good for the rather cowed Dutch theatre community. Dutch is such a little-spoken language, lacking also the glamour of Russian or Japanese, that its theatre (as opposed to dance) companies rarely travel abroad; and though we could do nothing about that, they seemed to draw some energy from our visit. For ourselves, it seemed we might be embarking on a winter of discontent, presaged by our first overall failure to connect, and to be confirmed by the ominous dates ahead.

We opened our week in Liverpool on 29th November with *Richard II* to two thousand schoolkids, alarmingly unchaperoned, who drank, farted, nipped out for a smoke and picked pockets in the best Elizabethan traditions. We even managed to hold them, but the take for the remaining seven performances of the week barely matched that of the first night alone. We thus added £6,000 to the notional loss predicted for the New Year dates. At this point we were offered a week, or rather a marathon weekend, at the Singapore Festival in April, immediately after the last contracted week of the tour: a chance to make some foreign money. The company turned down the offer by a small majority; they had had enough, and our financial problems were not theirs.* Feeling a bit surly about this, I spent most of my time in the weeks before Christmas – for *Henry IV* and *Henry V* at least – in the back of various stalls, making picky notes about audibility and line endings and, more cheerfully, watching the Dougall Solution consolidating itself. We had settled with John that he should play Hal/Henry at all the UK dates (apart from London, which we split) so that he would get the exposure he would most benefit from, while I did the 'ambassadorial' overseas ones. Stephen Jameson now played Nym, Simon Elliott the Drawer, and Robert Hands continued his professional baptism of fire (understudy emergencies always seemed to devolve on him; I had also made him be diplomatic front man in the Netherlands, Dutch being his second language) by playing John of Lancaster. This team was now playing a continuous run of weekly performances rather than odd, infrequent

---

*__Bogdanov__: *I was against it too. It would be hard. The final deal was not all that great and there seemed little point in slogging all the way back out East to finish a long way from home. Much better to whoop it up in Swansea. Let's forget it.*

ones, and John's Hal was becoming a completely confident
alternative to mine – closer to the right age. I sat and watched,
feeling what I suppose was the warm glow of patronage, but also
a proper pleasure that the whole machine was propelling itself
forward without my doing anything to stoke the boiler myself. But
lest all should turn to sentiment, I was also bothered by elements
of John's work, particularly his handling of Henry V's wooing of
Katherine, which I thought sentimentally out of key with the
production, which was at pains to underline the political
expediency of the scene. According to Bogdanov and Pennington,
the defeated French are desperate to make terms and offer Kate as
an expedient means of political union, and Henry then brutally and
carelessly claims her as 'our capital demand'. The 'wooing' that
follows, we always felt, has an uneasy edge to it, the latent cruelty
that deepens and darkens all good comedy. Historically, Kate and
Henry's bargain turned out to be a lovematch, and so in the end
it is in Shakespeare; but initially there is nothing to suggest that the
conquering Henry is in love or that Kate is at all happy about being
a political trophy. John's line on the scene was altogether more
romantic. He was on his knees, fumbling for his French, getting his
girl. I looked crossly at my watch, feeling the play had finished its
useful life. John's divergence, apart from proving that when it
comes to Shakespeare there are many ways of skinning a rabbit,
illuminates what the whole experience of the role-share was like for
him.

John Dougall: The Dauphin's description of Hal as 'a vain, giddy,
shallow, humorous youth' always struck me as very interesting.
Shallow he certainly isn't, but he is vain and egocentric, he has a
dark wit laced with cruelty, and in the depths and heights of his
behaviour there is a recklessness, a danger, a need to push
situations to extremes and test himself and those around him. But
I hoped also to have a sense of adolescent vulnerability, to show he
was not simply a manipulator but is himself manipulated, by
Falstaff his surrogate father, and by the ambivalent nature of
kingship, which both attracts and repels him. When it came to
Henry V, I felt it was essential for me to retain the vulnerability I
had found in the prince, and carry it into the king. Bogdanov's
production of this play was the most overtly political of *The
Henrys*, and consequently gave me less room to manoeuvre.
However, some things I was determined to change. Michael

Pennington and I had a longstanding disagreement about how the Wooing Scene at the end should be played. And 'Once More Unto the Breach' had been delivered astride an ingenious if distinctly unstable plywood tank in a welter of smoke and gunfire, with the battered English cowering downstage, mouthing obscenities. I knew I had to get in among them and relate to them directly, trying to stop the all too easy rhetoric of the speech. I only ever got near to what I wanted once or twice, but it was an innovation that stuck, Michael started doing it as well, and the tank got trundled off into early retirement.

Michael P.'s commitment and energy was always going to be a hard act to follow. He gave me immense encouragement and sound advice, comparing *Henry V* to a steeplechase, fences coming at you in quick succession, each with the potential to knock you out of the saddle. I sensed he was more than a little pleased to see the back of Hal, and that the real excitement only started for him as the fully-fledged monarch. But I also knew, when I was on, that it was very hard for him not to perform, as his instinct told him to lead from the front. My own problem was different. I was never able to have a run at the part – I think four consecutive weeks was my record. So the gaps, sometimes of months, meant living with the fear of forgetting great chunks of text. It certainly made for spontaneity. But it also caused the excitement of the opening performances to trail off for me into frustration. In Australia I went into a spiral of discontent. I revelled with a vengeance, and one morning failed to appear for the opening of the show. Michael P., at his most managerial, read me the Riot Act, and I responded with a rather pathetic tantrum. Relations between us reached a very low ebb. But when we came back to England for the final stretch and I began to perform consistently, the rift between us started to heal; our disagreement over the Wooing Scene was resolved with Bogdanov's assistance in a compromise between my instincts and the needs of the production. At the Old Vic I played Hal and Henry for the previews and press nights, and later in the run for a Saturday trilogy, a feat which at the outset had looked like a mountain I would never climb. But there I was on the summit, the stage of the Vic, somewhat breathless and short of oxygen, but there.

Bogdanov: *'Sam's oil paintings crowd the walls around the chintz sofa and chairs . . . the bedrooms are tiny and neat. Sam entered* *the dining room to a chorus of "Good morning", a greeting from his guests. His inquiries as to the weather, their breakfast and their plans for the day were all in English – for Sam speaks only a few words of German. As Ann cares for their guests, Sam entertains them with reminiscences of his career in the Royal Air Force and laments the lack of interest in his favourite game – cricket.'*

No, this is not Surbiton, it is a guidebook description of a bed and breakfast guest house in *Schleswig Holstein* – a short distance from Hamburg. There are those who regularly boast that Hamburgers are more English than the English. Certainly there is much truth in the belief that it is possible to live there without even having to speak more than a few words of German. Accents here – when speaking English – have none of the Americanised influences of further south. (Easy to tell whether someone comes from Hamburg or not by their English accent. The 'O' here is sometimes so rounded that it makes 'Orchsford' sound common.) It is not surprisingly the most open and liberal of German cities and its links with England are industrial and historic. It is a mighty trading port on the banks of the Elbe, a shuttling lifeline for river traffic into the heart of Europe and out into the North Sea and the Baltic. Understandably Hamburg was a target for much bombing during the Second World War and by the end the centre was little more than a pile of rubble. But the miracle of inner city planning has meant that the surviving buildings have been blended in with their modern counterparts to create a skyline of green-capped spires and the mellow feel of an older age. (Pace Birmingham, Plymouth, Newcastle ...) I suspect that if people know anything about Hamburg at all, it is that it has a port, a red light district of renown called the **Reeperbahn**, and that the Beatles once played there. (Sie liebt dich, ja ja ja ...) It is something of a surprise to find that the city is spread out round a lake, the Alster, and has a network of canals running through it that beats Venice out of sight. There are two thousand four hundred bridges in Hamburg and the majority of the capacious residential areas escaped the bombing. The result is an impression of lofty old houses, eighteenth- and nineteenth-century architecture, set in broad leafy roads and parks, with a glimpse of water and sailing boats never very far away.

It is possible to live and work in Hamburg and never see the port at all. A pity, for it contains the Speicherhauser, one of the largest free trade ports in the world. You need a passport to get in to view the mounds and mounds of oriental carpets, stacked in their

*John Dougall: (left) as
Prince Hal (JT);
(below) 'Hold, Wart, traverse:
thus, thus, thus . . .'
– as Wart (with Philip Bowen
as Silence and Colin
Farrell as Bardolph) (LB)*

(above) 'France and England . . . may cease their hatred' – Philip Rees, Andrew Jarvis, Siôn Probert (JT); (below) The flight to Tokyo – Petra Bradley (Wardrobe), Rosy Fowler (Props) (JT)

The Quickest Change – Charles Dale (Richmond) with Jimmy McCarthy (Wardrobe) (JT)

(above) 'The Crummleses with class' – Colin Farrell and Ann Penfold in East Berlin (JT);
(below) The Scheibebühnenfeld, Frankfurt – Barry Stanton (JT)

thousands. On a warm summer evening, seated in a fish restaurant in Blankanesee, out along the Elbe, the power and size of the port is evident as gigantic container ships from all parts of the world pass by every five minutes on the evening tide. A magnificent sight.

There is, of course, the usual European café life on the pavements, and, on picking up a book entitled The Hundred Best Restaurants in Hamburg, *I was devastated to find my favourites not even mentioned. There is obviously a culinary life to be experienced elsewhere at some point. (Not at the counter of the Deutsches Schauspielhaus, however, which, although cheap and wholesome, offers up to the public the not very entertaining proposition of limp lettuce, fatty stews, and an assortment of sausages. Catering is not high on the list of theatre priorities in Germany.) Hamburg is proud of its culture. There are forty theatres (including two English-speaking ones) some two hundred art galleries and museums, and the city has just renovated two magnificent glass and brick warehouses – the Deichtorhalle – by the harbour, for use as exhibiting centres, to the tune of £7 million.*

Hansestadt Hamburg is one of the eleven federated states in the Bundesrepublik, with its own government of a hundred and twenty seats, its Bürgermeister (Mayor, but politically carrying the weight of a Prime Minister) and its own Kulturbehörde (Ministry of Culture). The importance of the arts is emphasised by the fact that the position of the Minister for Culture is also that of Zweitebürgermeister – Deputy Prime Minister. Hamburg is the city of Lessing, where the German National Theatre was born some two hundred and forty years ago. The Deutsches Schauspielhaus is ninety years old and is a magnificent white rococo building with a plush red auditorium that seats one thousand four hundred in one of the most perfect audience/stage relationships I have ever encountered. It is no wonder that all German actors long to perform on what is known as the erste deutsche Sprachbühne *('the leading stage of the German-speaking world'). The audiences, a catholic mixture of young and old, paying prices set by the Ministry of Culture at a standard level of DM10–DM40 (£3.20–£14) are nothing if not enthusiastic. On our first visit with* The Henrys, *we had been cheered for twenty minutes, still our record. During the lunch interval on that election Saturday (as the politicians looked at themselves on the stage), I had been invited to dine with the then Bürgermeister Dr Dohnanyi, the brother of the conductor. Over the fillets of* scholle *– local plaice – he casually asked if I would be* *interested in taking over the Schauspielhaus on the departure of Peter Zadek.*

You could have knocked me down with a blutwürst. *The thought had never occurred to me, but the idea of being in charge of some £13 million of state subsidy sent the artistic blood somersaulting. I really didn't think it was a serious approach. The then Minister for Culture, Frau Schuchart, chased me to Paris, to our awful hotel in Clichy, to talk further. Everything went quiet and I forgot about it. Eighteen months later, following a campaign in the local paper, a poll, and a petition from the actors and the technical staff, the position of Intendant was finally offered me. I thought long and hard. I was going through a strange mid-life crisis that had made me, after getting* The Wars of the Roses *on, want to work much less and leave London. (We moved to Bath.) My body said no, my head said yes. When was I ever likely to get such an opportunity again, to run one of the major European theatres with these kinds of resources at the heart of European culture? And status. No more defending one's position in life. 'Can you actually make a living at that?' Michael and I discussed the implications and decided that we could keep the ESC going as well. My German contract allowed me to do one production a year elsewhere. I would use my summer break and part of the beginning of the Hamburg season to direct the major ESC shows and, anyway, communication was only a phone and a fax away. (Fax machines – the greatest invention of the last fifty years and our salvation.) We were used to this method of operation, one or other of us always being somewhere else, rarely coinciding in the office as we had in the early days, Michael out on tour, or me on a crust-earning exercise somewhere else. (This inability to get us all in the office at the same time drove Prue mad. Prue, who also lived in Bath, would book an official meeting with me up and down to London on the train.) Michael and I both knew that the situation would create difficulties, but we both recognised the potential advantage of my having such a magnificent building under my control. By the time of the ESC's second visit in 1989, I was already setting up my first season as Intendant, and although not starting officially until the following August, I was visiting Hamburg on a fairly regular basis to facilitate the preparations. It was a working weekend. In between running up and down to see how* The Wars *were going, I was holding a series of planning meetings in the offices upstairs. Schizophrenia.*

There is a curious pattern to theatre-going in Hamburg. The same thing happened on our second visit as on our first. Bookings looked paltry on paper. Then suddenly, half an hour before the performance began, a chaotic rush swamped the box office and left not a seat empty. Unfortunately, as with our visit to Berlin, the shows were not good. The three-week lay-off at Christmas and then the scramble to perform a marathon as the first set of performances after the break had meant that there was no time to build up the concentration needed. Technically, too, the shows were sloppy from our point of view. The staff and stage crew at the Schauspielhaus theatre had, as usual, offered all the help they could. They are a wonderful team, dedicated to their work and passionately proud of their theatre.

Our team slipped back only slowly into the ritual and routine needed to run the shows efficiently. The lighting was all over the place, the curtain work disgraceful and the prop setting disastrous. I kicked myself for not having had the foresight to schedule some performances elsewhere before attempting a 'weekend' in Hamburg. However, not for the first time, the Schauspielhaus had plugged the difficult January hole, the necessity for European dates being the consequence of the English Panto season. Though the applause was the usual warm, Hanseatic reception with cheers ringing out, this time it lasted for only twelve minutes and on my appearance on stage at the end (a European tradition) there were one or two isolated boos. I laughed. But the thought crossed my mind that maybe the honeymoon was over before the wedding. There had already been a surfeit of Bogdanov: in the space of two and a half years – Julius Caesar, The Henrys, Reineke Fuchs, The Mayor of Zalamea *and now* The Wars of the Roses. The Mayor of Zalamea *was as big a flop as* Julius Caesar *and* Reineke Fuchs had been successes, giving cause for alarm in some circles that maybe I was the wrong man after all. This feeling hardened through the forthcoming summer, and the situation was not retrieved from the hysteria that surrounded the beginning of my Intendantship until my first production, Hamlet, opened in late October with astounding success. Till this moment the Hamburg press were less than begeistert – knocked out. I thought back to a conversation with John Price in my local theatre kneipe (pub) – the Dorf. Somehow John, with his extraordinary capacity for making friends everywhere, had picked up the rumour that I was a hot favourite for the job. I thought he was joking. As I stood on

stage two years later, the joke was now on me. Maybe the odd
'Boo' or two was only the start. It was in this frame of mind that
I followed the company on to East Berlin.

Pennington: The young wolves of the ESC, who had sold a
hundred flirtatious lines to a hundred credulous campfollowers
across four continents by now, looked sheepishly up into the eyes
of the East German border guard as she shuffled through their
papers at Lauenburg, the crossing point by road from the
Bundesrepublik, where we had sat queasily for nearly two hours.
Their unusual shyness' in the face of this attractive Communist
coincided with an anger they were beginning to feel at their own
boss class at the back of the bus. Why are we on a bus at all, trailing
across Central Europe to East Berlin? The heat, the fumes, the lack
of toilets. The fact was that the only flights out of Western Europe
into East Germany were from Amsterdam and Brussels,and we
were coming from Hamburg; the train from there, which would
have left at eight that morning (a marathon having ended the
previous night), had notorious border formalities and an equally
notorious lack of refreshment; so we had settled for the coach,
thinking it more comfortable and probably faster. What we hadn't
expected was this hiatus; any more than we had expected, in
calculating the timings, that, once in the East, drivers would be
confined to an eighty-kilometre speed limit on main routes which
they wouldn't be inclined to infringe. It was a maddening
restriction; we nibbled at miles of straight and empty road ahead
that could have been taken in gulps, and our journey in the end
took seven hours rather than four, so that Kirsten, Michael and I
had to keep our heads down for several days.

   This all feels like history now, many details rendered obsolete by
the sensational events in Eastern Europe of the subsequent six
months. In January 1989 we were one of the last groups to come
face to face with the more obvious divisions of Germany; the less
obvious ones linger on. Had we gone later in the year, we could
have walked from our engagement at the Volksbühne in the East
through the Brandenburg Gate to the Schiller in the West, taking
our audience with us; we might not have had the same trouble
getting the ESC's fee out either, though it probably wouldn't have
been worth very much.

   Meanwhile, in these last moments of old time, we sat at the
border, our boys assimilating the unexpected glamour of – for

many of them – their very first *apparatchik*, proud Socialist woman dressed in a little brief authority, hoping to detect the signs of a different system, a sinister education or a common biology. They were understandably vexed, for the crossing of borders is forever strange, and this one specially so; and any contemplation of the divided island of Berlin inevitably awakened a mournful sense of history. To have to pass beneath these fortified motorway bridges – a full mile of them – to go from one identical terrain to another was one thing; to know that once through them you were not really in the other country at all, but in an edgeless but rigid corridor that snaked past Wittenberg and Ludwigslust and close to the Polish border before entering East Berlin as it were from the back, was to become deeply pessimistic about human nature.

Pessimism would have been a superficial reaction to arriving in East Berlin, however, even in the greyest of grey January dusks under low voltage sodium streetlights; there had at least to be a melancholy quickening of attention. The huge empty avenue of Karl Marx Allee, and its great blind apartment blocks on either side, punctuated by the Moskva Dancehall and a single travel agency sarcastically advertising worldwide travel, were very much like those of a Soviet city, and it is tritely true to say that one felt much closer to Moscow than to Frankfurt, and very much closer to it than to the Kurfürstendamm only two miles away, where we had cavorted on our climactic trip to West Berlin the previous July. Less close than usual though, at that moment, vibrant as Moscow was with *glasnost* and its various consequences. As Soviet thinking was becoming, from the East German point of view, dangerously progressive, more and more inclined to tolerate the old shibboleths of the west, the ailing Honecker regime was withdrawing self-destructively into itself, with the results that everybody knows.

In reality East Berlin is, in its showpieces at least, a stunningly beautiful city. The Unter den Linden is dotted with fine buildings: a carefully reconstructed eighteenth-century opera house, the baroque St Hedwig's Cathedral, and the Humboldt University, the second largest in East Germany. In the Pergamon Museum there is a marvellous display of Western Asian architecture (as well as the Pergamon Altar itself) – the Ishtar Gate and part of Nebuchadnezzar's throne room particularly awesome. It all reminds you of how much the East gained architecturally from the division of the city; the old city centre, the Lustgarten, ended up in

the East as Marx-Engelsplatz. Many beautiful places are very
unhappy; Berlin's painful division was blatant of course and dotted
with melancholy ikons – the Reconciliation Church on the western
side completely surrounded by the Wall, and Hitler's bunker
marked by a small gloomy mound. In the nearby city of Potsdam,
from the great rooms where Churchill, Truman and Stalin carved
up the vanquished nation, we looked out at the brick and barbed
wire marking the south-western border of Berlin that was the direct
consequence of their deliberations – they had looked out at open
landscape.

For the moment our company's horizons were rather narrower
than the ample perspectives of Alexanderplatz. We had checked
into the Berolina Hotel – all the usual Eastern bleaknesses in the
form of unfriendly staff, a postage-stamp-sized bar and brown
bathwater – to find that an important trade delegation had
suddenly been billeted upon it and we were to be summarily moved
across the city to the Hotel Unter den Linden. Useless to complain.
We also arrived to find that the Künstler Agentur, our official
bookers, were proposing to send us back west to Frankfurt the
following weekend on another coach (cheaper for them as it could
be paid for in East German marks) rather than by train (payable
in western currency) as we wished. We now wished it even more,
since the coach to Frankfurt would clearly take twelve to fourteen
hours, and after this particular day we didn't fancy our chances of
convincing the company, who would break their hearts and
possibly our necks. The Agentur's preference was a neat example
of the currency tangles created by visiting the eastern bloc, but it
was not the first. It has never been easy for a western company to
extract its fee in hard currency from such dates, since there is a limit
to the amount of western capital available to the host presenters,
who are regulated by their government as to how much of the
precious gold is to be exported at a given time. Between the time
of booking the week in East Berlin and our arrival there, these
restrictions had dramatically tightened; and it was now apparent
that Künstler Agentur was not going to be able to foot our agreed
fee of £35,000 – indeed could only meet it halfway. Rather than
cancel the date and take a loss at such short notice, we had decided
to go anyway, somewhat encouraged by the assurances of various
British agencies there that they would make arrangements to get the
money flowing out to us when the time came. As time goes by,
these assurances are beginning to look a little pallid, and, in spite

of all sorts of wheedling, we have had to accept a loss of £8,000.

These managerial difficulties formed a neat counterpoint to the personal predicament of our members who, having had a generous daily subsistence paid to them in East German marks, were throughout the week haunted by the fear of not being able to spend it before we left the country, whereupon it would become useless once again. I never knew a group of actors so bewildered; trained for life to save against the rainy days of which our profession is so prodigal, we now found ourselves forced to deliquefy at every turn; mmming and ahing at every overpriced meal we ate, disappointed at the low cost of taxis, thwarted by the sheer shoddiness of the goods that were becoming our assets. Never were so many international phone calls made at the expensive end of the day, partners in England overwhelmed by suddenly talkative consorts calling from East Berlin. I myself bought a huge chocolate cake for the company (arousing suspicion – is it a bribe?) and a fruitbowl the colour of a haemorrhage that I couldn't even *give* away in the west. Colin Farrell and Ann Penfold, meanwhile, paid as much as they could for an Estonian cookbook that detailed every variety of blood pudding, going to peruse it in the Ganymede Restaurant, where Adolf Hitler used to meet Eva Braun; sitting there self-sufficiently, sipping on brandies and soda and chuckling rudely to each other, they struck me as the archetypal touring couple – the Keans, perhaps, without the snobbery, or Crummleses with class. The Madeleine Farrell Fund, which they had set up to endow a place at the Bristol Old Vic School for a student who might not otherwise be able to afford the fees, was now standing at £10,000; her parents' closeness was a beautiful thing to see.

As the ESC actors thus behaved like demented millionaires, the ESC management contemplated a large hole in its income, breaking off every day or two to go on raids into the Western sector to capture the soda water and fresh vegetables required by the show, in pitiably short supply in the East, and stealing rolls of lavatory paper from the British Embassy (softer). Meanwhile our week of performances was completely sold out: had indeed been so for weeks on minimal publicity. We were to play the Volksbühne Theater, which, though its fame has receded now, was in the 1920s the base of Erwin Piscator, whose epic techniques deeply influenced Brecht, who for a time was in his company. Piscator's methods, which included film projections and, sometimes, no scripts, were linked to the Freie Volksbühne Movement, which was committed to providing good plays to ordinary people at prices they could afford – like Lilian Baylis, but with more sophisticated methods, and a more specific *realpolitik*. Piscator eventually got sacked after using provocative film of the Russian Revolution in a production; the company moved its centre of operation to West Berlin, and the old theatre in Bulowplatz has never really recovered its former energy – any more really than has Brecht's Berliner Ensemble, who now give off rather a musty air. The Ensemble welcomed us warmly one afternoon there, the Intendant declaring that there were three great theatre companies in the world – themselves, the Comédie Française; and us. I didn't know we'd come quite so far so soon. Only when his subsequent *spiel*, despite his interpreter's' embarrassed circumnavigation of the phrase, unmistakably kept referring to the *Royal* Shakespeare Company, did the euphoria wear off.

The audience response to our week of English history, so unfamiliar as drama and, one might have thought, so politically remote, unexpectedly brought us the reward of an audience engagement such as Piscator worked his life for. I don't know if it was deserved; but it was of a kind completely impossible to forget, going far beyond simple praise for a job well done to a tangible will to take hands across a divide as extreme as the abysmal wall that spliced the city. The company was rushed at from the auditorium as well as pelted with the familiar roses, and then besieged backstage by professionals needing to talk. Most nights, the backstage lights didn't go out till the very small hours.

There is no better thing an entertainer can do than take part in this public bargain; that it can be done shows quite simply the iniquity but also the idiocy of political divisions; it gives the members of a notoriously beleaguered profession, at last, a sense of value. Along with this validation comes an invitation to do better. There is a scene in *Richard III* in which Richard of Gloucester, within sight at last of the crown he craves, rigs up with the aid of Buckingham, his political fixer, an elaborate display of public piety. He dresses as a monk and demurely confronts a gathering of citizens while Buckingham speciously refutes the claims of all other contenders to the crown and urges Richard to take it on himself in the absence of a legitimate heir. However, the citizens are not the mob of *Julius Caesar* or *Coriolanus*, gullible and divided within themselves, but rather the Lord Mayor of London and his aldermen, envisaged in our modern context as captains of industry who, one has to believe, are worth Richard's while to seduce – not least because they know that all the legitimate claimants to the crown have been eliminated by Richard himself. In other words, these men are indispensable to Richard's final step to power. At the end of the scene in our production they were all cajoled to their knees as Richard accepted his destiny 'at their vehement importunity', and a journalist arrived to photograph this evidence of his public esteem.

The scene had been troublesome since the beginning, as I suspect it always is. We were uncertain how 'comic' it should be. Richard's preposterous disguise and moral breast-beating could fool nobody, ran one argument, and he can treat the citizens with contempt, knowing that they are really his catspaws; and so the scene is a black burlesque characteristic of this play, and the actors playing Richard and Buckingham are free to play over the heads of the citizens to the theatre's gallery, signalling their insincerity a mile high. The contrary view denounced this approach as crude and unpolitical and altogether unworthy of the ESC. If the scene was to have any purpose at all, there must be the tense possibility that Richard will be turned down at the last moment of his headlong career. Therefore Richard and Buckingham must work harder, much harder, to be plausible and to convince their audience onstage (and by association the theatre audience) that Richard is the man for the job. If they are political conmen, then let them be seen to be good at it.

The debate had simmered away for a season and a half. The argument for plausibility was convincing, but Shakespeare himself often seemed to be coming down on the side of burlesque. How could anyone with half a brain believe in Richard of Gloucester as a *holy man*? Perhaps for once we had come across a real problem in the modern-dress approach to the play which was serving us so well elsewhere. A Plantagenet prince might be able to stress his relationship with the church in this way – perhaps would have had to; but could we picture Neil Kinnock or Michael Heseltine doing a constituency walkabout in a surplice? So how should the citizens react? As if they were credulous fools, prepared to believe in the sham? As if they were intelligent men who were not using their intelligence – the reason being that they were afraid, in thrall to the two most powerful men in the land who had already demonstrated their methods of dealing with dissent and were now eyeing them up with beady amiability? What kind of society in any case

were we imagining, and how significant would the City's vote be
in this decidedly post-democratic world?

Meanwhile the performance was still going off half-cock, on a
wave of humdrum comedy, and in the continuing uncertainty the
actors' enthusiasm for playing the scene was coming adrift. The
response of the Volksbühne audience put us to shame. They took
the sequence in appalled silence. It was as if a communal breath
was being held. Immediately we could feel that we were playing to
people for whom the idea of extreme political coercion – the most
threadbare velvet glove covering the iron fist – was not an
intellectual conceit but a daily reality, and not in the least bit funny.
East Germany was at that moment so far to the right, so little
convinced of *glasnost*, that the Russian satirical magazine *Sputnik*
was banned, and the *Moscow News* reproduced only selectively. In
such a climate no ordinary person could fail to recognise Richard
and Buckingham, or to identify with the citizen who opens his
mouth to protest and then closes it again.

Taking a fast cue from the startling quality of the silence, we
played with the most serious intent both this scene and the rest of
the one performance of the play, and, obscurely chastened, climbed
onto the train to Frankfurt (we had banished the bus) the next
morning, bound for the 'freedom' of the west. I wish I could say
that the new seriousness of purpose was to last; but the smug
western sentimentality that we are different and morally superior
to the Communist world – that such things could never happen
here – was soon to reassert itself. In general, London customers
were treated to a performance of the Citizens Scene that had taken
one step back after taking two forwards, and a well-upholstered
audience guffawed once again at the *cheek* of Richard and
Buckingham; but perhaps some trace remained. If an Eastern
European audience instinctively confers on performers the dignity
of apologists and spiritual sensors they rarely feel in the west, so
it demands an integrity to match. It occurred to me, as to many of
us during that week, that we ought to take a sharp look at
ourselves.

Bogdanov: *In East Berlin, I took part in a seminar on* The Wars of
the Roses *chaired by the critic Ernst Schumacher in the company
of lecturers and Shakespeare authorities from all over East
Germany, bussed in from Weimar, Dresden and Leipzig. If Michael
Billington thinks my productions are Marxist he should try being*

grilled by this lot. They gave me the most thorough political going-over I have ever had in my life. They took the productions ruthlessly apart and found them wanting on almost every ideological point. They were not fanatics, Stasi or party brainwashers. They knew their texts, they knew their stage. No amount of ducking, bobbing, weaving, diving, blagging and bluffing could get me off the hook. 'Gotcha!' I felt wrung through a mangle and limped off brain-damaged into the night to reconsider my position in theatre. The 'Boo' Factor. If anything was going to come out of Hamburg it had to be a new challenge to myself. A reassessing of my work methods, and my centre. Maybe I had settled too easily for the 'enfant terrible' status of what passes for radicalism in Britain – little more than the soft titillating underbelly of compromise. Hmmmmm.

Pennington: Frankfurt lay at the dizzying end of a train journey that started in the fortified compound of Friedrichsstrasse Station, then the only rail link with West Berlin. Here boyish guards with Dobermans explored the undercarriages of the trains for stowaways before letting them roll away to the west, without presumably imagining the desperation that would lead to such an attempt. We quickly jolted into the high-rise technology and neon of West Berlin, reversed the juxtaposition by moving westwards into East Germany again, before arriving in the Bundesrepublik at last. It is a fascinating ride; but our destination was to offer a prospect bleaker in some minds than anything Eastern Europe could offer. This was the Scheibebühnenfeld – literally 'turning-space field' – the new playing space found for us in Frankfurt by the Theater am Turm, a new management which was turning its back on conventional theatres – particularly now that the Schauspielhaus had been damaged by fire – and was offering us the opportunity of opening a disused railway depot: or rather the part of it where the rolling stock used to trundle in to be washed automatically and rolled out to work again. They had recently put Peter Brook's *Mahabharata* into a similar space and were confident of their policy.

As were we. The prospect of opening such a venue, a departure for us, seemed to me an exhilarating prospect; but I was having a job convincing the company, who were by now tired and inclined to rattiness. There had already been a loud company meeting in Liverpool, when the subject of the Scheibebühnenfeld had provoked a row; many of the company felt that not enough information had in decency been given them about the place, particularly about its temperature and its physical amenities; and quite possibly this information was being withheld by me for fear that they would revolt. In fact, the problem was that the theatre was being built specially for us, supposedly to our specifications; but it wasn't ready. I was offering all the information I had at the time; but maybe I just looked creepy.

Michael Cronin recalls: We had been asking the same question for weeks: where are we performing in Frankfurt? What had appeared in the schedule as 'a possible third week in Germany' had become 'Frankfurt', which had become 'a wonderful challenge', which begat 'an exciting space'. But the Sunday before the meeting I had phoned a friend working there to find that the 'turning-space-field' was just that: a sprawl of derelict, cathedral-like sheds where until recently trains had been repaired; it was vast and glass-roofed; it was strewn with inspection-pits and abandoned machines; and it was bitterly cold even in November, leave alone January. Surely the plays could only suffer? And us, too. Hadn't we the right to be concerned? The ESC was not a co-operative, we knew that from the outset. But we also felt that its achievement was a shared one; we were an ensemble. Yet it seemed we had no voice in the company's affairs; the policy seemed to exclude us from the achievement. It was this that created the rolling debt of bitterness which was so often present during these clashes. But why, asked Roger Booth finally, does it always have to come to this? Why is there never enough information? The Germans have assured us it will be ready in time, countered Michael P.: they are working very hard. But why are we never allowed the full picture? Are you suggesting that we're holding out on you? said Michael P.; because if so, then we all knew exactly what we could do. And he promptly did.

Pennington: I'm afraid it's true. I had stormed out into Lime Street, feeling unjustly accused: a weak but unpremeditated gesture that brought the final tally of managerial huffs to Bogdanov 1, Pennington 2 (not counting the Special Award to John Castle for having variously caused both ESC directors to walk out of their own company). In truth, the upsets were becoming wearisome, and were perhaps making all of us long, momentarily, for the end.

Roger Booth

From my point of view, I felt that we had developed a home breed of prima donnas, looking for four-star featherbeds where once they had been kept warm by a spirit of adventure. On the other hand, many in the company felt that this spirit of adventure was being carefully stage-managed throughout to reflect glory only on Michael and myself, while they patiently stoked the boiler-room. The fact that this new boss class was represented much of the time by a fellow-actor, who had somehow become a guild traitor and might at any point try to sell them a managerial pup, lent particular edge to their anger.

Thus at odds, the company jumpy and I confused, Kirsten Oploh and I went to fight more obvious battles with Theater am Turm. Not for the first time, we felt rancidly hostile to fundamentally friendly hosts who in extending their welcome had merely over-looked one or two details. Or three. Our technical plans had been wrongly read, so that the set didn't really fit onto the stage. A determination to sell out the capacity of the house had led to a bold marketing initiative we had never had the courage to try ourselves: prospective customers had to buy all seven plays, and bookings for single shows or groups of shows were not being accepted. It says as much for German theatre-going habits as for our reputation that the house had been sold out on this basis for all seven, completing a Royal Flush for us; a three-week, three-city German tour without an empty seat. But such was the demand that there were literally too many (moveable) seats in the auditorium, some of them with a very imperfect view of the stage: a bad practice for which I guessed the ESC would be blamed. Our sound desk and lighting board, which should logically have occupied the spaces unrequired for human purchase, had consequently been banished to a most precarious platform high up at the back of the improvised auditorium that looked untested and unsafe. The acoustic, also untried, was a brute; it was indeed freezing in the cavernous backstage area, where lines of rolling stock stood in eerie ranks beneath the washing equipment that serviced them; everything was stony and filthy with oil, and there was a three hundred yard walk among the locomotives from the ad hoc dressing rooms to a stage unnaturally heated by its lamps. Perhaps the company had been right in Liverpool; we seemed to be doomed, after two years on the road perfecting our act, to finish the tour and open to the London press the following week with ensemble pneumonia.

Kirsten and I won what concessions we could and bit the bullet on the rest. We insisted on thermal underwear for every member of cast, stage management and technicians – forty sets of them. In these we all then nestled under our Regency frock coats, chain mail and combat fatigues, dreading the moment when a bare chest or legs would have to be brazened. The actors were lucky, being allowed to run around for a living; others shared the fate of Jo Reid, confined to the book, sitting huddled over her personal blow-heater, wrapped in scarves and coats, blue fingers on the buttons.

Huge plastic caterpillars attached to industrial heaters bellowed forth warm air to service the backstage area before and after the show and during the intervals, hardly impinging on the cold at all but causing the scaffolding and piping to expand, so that it clattered and banged throughout the performance, suggesting that more was at stake than the fall of kings. We walked in red Coronation cloaks on ironic red carpets between rows of railway carriages. We were having to evaluate the shows for the last time before opening in London, and nobody had much heart for the exercise. We yelled our way through the plays, achieving by the crudest of means a nightly success that delighted an audience enduring almost as much as ourselves. On the last night, the British Council, overjoyed, brought us champagne and went on about the verse speaking. The company's natural sense of the humour of all this was tinged with fury, especially when – unkindest cut – Theater am Turm wanted the thermals back after the last night. When, at the end of the week, we posted a rehearsal call for the following Tuesday before the Old Vic opening (we were to fly home on the Sunday) the very idea was so unpopular that a senior member of the company scrawled CANCELLED across the notice.

Our return home was on Pan Am 103, the flight that had exploded over Lockerbie a month previously. While we were waiting to board, a bomb threat came through and the flight was cancelled. The actor who had objected to the rehearsal call now turned on the airline, arguing that we were surely entitled to a number of free meals and telephone calls. We most nervously boarded a new flight five hours later. Everyone went home and quarrelled with whatever unfortunate was to hand. We had in a sense reached the climax of our whole enterprise at this moment – seventy-one weeks down, forty-seven cities played and London to come – but once again a climax coincided with an exhausted decline.

Forty-eight hours later we met in the auditorium of the Old Vic in London in the highest good humour, watered and scrubbed and keen to have another go.

CHAPTER
11

THE OLD VIC AND TELEVISION

February–April 1989

> 'Everything hath an end and a pudding
> hath two.'
>
> Proverb

Bogdanov: One way or another all roads (and trains) over the past twelve years of my life have led to Waterloo and the Cut. The Young Vic for two years, the National for six and two seasons at the Old Vic Theatre. I know the Cut, where the Old Vic sits, pretty well. The rump of my old company from the Young Vic still meet on Friday night in the Windmill pub to pay homage to our time next door; the Greek family at the Acropolis Restaurant with its unchanging menu of English breakfasts and aubergine; Bob's Barrow, cheerfully manned in all weathers by carbuncular Bob himself, is still the place on Saturday afternoon where, when in London, I buy the weekend vegetables. The chip shop has furnished me with many a bolted means of sustenance, and although the old Stage Door pub has disappeared, to be replaced by a series of bistros and wine bars, the cafés and stalls spreading westwards from the Welfare Centre and *Ristorante La Barca* produce a nostalgic 'bacon butty' whiff of earlier times when Lambeth was the heartland of villainy. Eddie the Eel is gone, his wide frame no longer propping up the bar, checking the dogs, but his eels are still there, somewhere underneath the pavements, a slithering pipeline to the Eel and Pie shop next door to a gallery. I did a certain member of a certain stage crew a favour, in return for which he said that if I ever wanted 'The Biz doin' down the Cut, if they was ever givin' me grief, bovver, know what I mean, in the fee-ett-er like, just let 'im know. 'Arf 'is family was there. His uncle was back from doin' life, lived over the 'bacconists. Give us a bell, and we'll be right there.' The canal (hence the Cut) had long since been filled in, before Lilian Baylis's time, but the area and the Old Vic still have something of the old Globe and Swan feeling, standing outside the city walls across the river, where the hooligans and thugs, pimps and prostitutes of the 'stews' gather to gamble and revel away from the reaches of the Lord Chief Justice. The clientèle and fare of the Old Vic are somewhat more upmarket than those good old days around 1600; but the odd bag lady and bag man sometimes find their way into those pink and grey bars, the line-up for the soup kitchen opposite the stage door stretching even longer as Thatchermania bites deep into the pockets of those with little enough in them.

Michael and I had decided that John Dougall should open as Prince Hal in London. We had some debate as to Henry V itself, a part which Michael, rightly, was unwilling to relinquish quite so easily; on its day, it was probably the best performance of the cycle.

Logic prevailed. There was no point in splitting the role of Hal/Henry V between two actors. John should have the individual performances for the critics, Michael would take the marathon. The decision to expose the shows to the Press one by one, their openings spread over the first three weeks of the season, was, in retrospect, not such a good one.* I think we were influenced by the 'sauna scenario' in York where the work (unlike in other cities) had often received press coverage of barely one column to analyse twenty-four hours of Shakespeare. Take away half the inches (half-inched?) for the customary prejudice and it left precious little space to analyse the performances. We felt that many of the company had had a raw deal and had not received the attention their work merited. In what was a surge of naïve optimism we had visions of John Peter *et al.* seeing each performance and gradually compiling an in-depth analysis of work that had scarred some three years of our lives. What a joke. When critics came at all it was selectively, many seeing mainly only the new work, and relying on memories

---

**Pennington: *I'm not so sure about this. At least, opening one by one, each show had a chance to settle. But we certainly overrated most critics' attention span.*

of *The Henrys* from 1986. They thus missed John Dougall, Michael Cronin as Bolingbroke, Barry's Falstaff (a comparison surely merited) and, of course, all the new women. Second stringers were the norm, sometimes third; different critics from the same newspapers, seeing separate performances, tried to assess the whole cycle by guessing what the rest were like. Milton Shulman of the *Evening Standard* lasted the course until *House of York* but, not having liked *Lancaster*, skipped the afternoon and thereby missed Andy's marvellous build to Richard III. (The first season, he had gone to sleep, snored loudly, been woken by a lady telling him he ought to be ashamed of himself, left *Henry IV Part 2* at the interval, gave us rave reviews, recommended me for .an Evening Standard Award.)

It was ghastly. We had inadvertently dug an elephant trap for ourselves and fallen leadenly in. Imagine our anger and frustration on reading a one-off analysis from someone unknown on the style of *Richard II* in which the writer was assuming that the rest of the cycle was the same. Or another, dipping into *Henry IV Part 2*, saying that she couldn't imagine what *Richard II* had been like. No wonder. The problem with seeing only one performance in a considered cycle of seven meant there was no context. Faith in the London critics, never very strong at the best of times, was finally abandoned in favour of artistic atheism. 'Bunter' Billington (the recipient of many letters of protest on the occasion of his first review – three printed, many more written) had modified his opinion: 'I have some doubts about Bogdanovisation of the Bard but at least I feel I am watching a company show ... Two years ago I suggested Mr Bogdanov was offering a Marxist view of these plays. I take that back.'

Why? Even if they were, so what? It may be unfashionable to embrace Marxism in these heady days of unification and independence, but the least the productions should merit is a serious analysis from England's leading left-wing critic. (*What* did you say?) *Pace* all others.

The Melbourne memory was somewhat dim. As with two years previously, the problem was the shouting. The company had arrived tired and hoarse from the Frankfurt Railway Shed, and two days was not long enough to turn the clock back. The grip on the simplicity of our story-telling technique was very tenuous and before long had been let go. We fared much better with those critics who covered the marathon. Christopher Edwards's review for the

Spectator was headed 'Magnificent Seven' and contained such phrases as '. . . magnificent venture . . . deserves high praise . . . a riveting story . . . brilliantly sustained . . .'.

I had an interesting debate with Nicholas de Jongh. He wrote, in the *Guardian*: '. . . Although it looks as if Bogdanov has done something radical with *Henry V*, the production is, in truth, conservative, traditional and not that consistent.' Amongst all the silly things that had been written about our work, here was something that was perceptive at last. It was the problem of two actors (Dougall and Pennington) sharing the central part. I rang him up, unusually, to talk about his review. I think he was astonished when I told him that I thought his assessment was accurate. (I knew from the silence at the end of the phone when I said my name that he thought he was going to be metaphorically or literally punched on the nose.) I invited him to see a performance of *Henry V* with Michael playing the part (he had seen John the first time) and then to see if he still felt the same. If he did, I admitted, then we had got something (or something had gone) radically wrong. I had a genuine desire to know his opinion. I invited him to a note session on *House of York* to show him how things were still changing. He arrived and must have been fairly – what? – impressed at the degree of genuine democratic debate. The nature of the work and the company had led people to be completely open about each other's work. On this particular afternoon, among many other things, he witnessed Charlie Dale relinquish a part and a speech to Ben Bazell on the arrival of the Duke of York from Ireland in order to clarify the story. We lost an anonymous soldier from that scene in order to build up the character of Norfolk (Ben). It would happen that night. It is at moments like this, when theatre is fluid, changing, continually being reassessed, that I feel the true power it exerts over me. The challenge of the times. Unfortunately Nicholas never did see Michael P. in *Henry V*, so I shall never know whether there was an inherent imbalance in the production or not. I shall send him a video.

Not until Irving Wardle (*The Times*) did Andy Jarvis receive the kind of praise that we, and audiences all over the world, believed he deserved. 'I was expecting the English Shakespeare Company's cycle to end with a bang but was still unprepared for this tremendous production [*Richard III*], which comes over not only with the accumulated weight of the rest of the cycle, but with the force of modern history and the modern stage's re-workings of the Richard fable . . . Jarvis is an actor who starts with his feet. In this case, he adopts a wide-legged stance to reduce the weight on one bad leg, from which he develops a wild swinging run, slack right arm flapping over his head . . . His zest and hypnotic power are tremendous; and he adds not only to Richard's comedy but also to his last nightmare hours, stabbed, shot and spat upon by the Bosworth ghosts before awakening with childish sobs.'

For someone who had originally agreed to play two small roles for us, Andy had turned himself into one of our major attributes, exuding a charisma that people identify with the company wherever we are talked of. (It is said that the Lyubimov *Hamlet* was enthusiastically booked in Australia on the basis that Andy was playing Claudius. There was intense disappointment when he withdrew.)

The Old Vic saw several performances almost saved by the bell. Stephanie Howard came back in after two years to look at the state of the costumes, and was horrified to see the deterioration. Many of the original ideas had been compromised as costumes had been torn, lost, changed through expediency, and no money had been available for replacements. Also, wilful alteration – 'improvements' – had done nothing for the balance of the shows. We completely re-did Francesca Ryan's Doll Tearsheet, returning to the original idea. All Fran's outfits were completely overhauled, costumes having been adapted for her out of expediency from those worn by Mary Rutherford – another actress, another time. June's wig for Margaret in *Lancs* and *Yorks*, a constant source of worry, was teased and tousled right until the final moment. There were tears in her eyes as I assured her, prior to her entrance, that she looked magnificent. What a devastating flowering into Margaret in *Richard III*. Her dotty, vengeful figure, military cap askew, medals pinned to tatty uniform, the little legs dangling from the throne, is one of the great memories.

Ann Penfold, at last, had a new Lady Percy outfit and numerous boots, hats and gloves were restored. (For some unknown reason Roger Booth, as Williams in the trenches in *Henry V*, insisted on retaining the white knotted gloves he had picked up from somewhere en route on the disappearance of the originals. The theory was that it made them easier to identify. On a soldier they just looked daft.) Much to my regret, Chris Dyer did not come anywhere near the re-run and had even questioned whether his name should be on the programme at all. I refused to take it off but felt great sadness that, having travelled such a long Shakespeare path with him, at the point where we really should have been riding it out together we had drifted apart. Chris felt alienated from the project, I suspect because his earlier involvement had not been total. (Normally he would do costumes as well.)*

We launched, for the first time, a Supporters Club. Through our own quarterly newsletter, we gathered a series of volunteers to help sell our merchandise, T-Shirts, photos, badges – *'I Survived The Wars of the Roses'* – on a rota basis. The Old Vic, too, saw the inception of an ESC Appeal Fund (it's still going, folks). We decided on a system of self-help to raise funds for capital equipment. Audiences were invited to contribute either by dipping into their pockets there and then, or by covenanting. In our short season we received nearly £10,000 and our supporters were indefatigable in their efforts.

We were parting company with the Allied Irish, after three warm, friendly years. The personnel had changed in the last season. Responsibility had been devolved to the branch managers. Niall, Joyce, Declan and Martha no longer travelled the road with us and were virtually unknown to the new members. The send-off at the Old Vic was nostalgic rather than euphoric. Niall and I tried to recreate the mood for 'Seven Drunken Nights' but the times they had a-changed. We were trying desperately for a Grand Slam finish to the whole venture. The one major city we hadn't been to was Dublin. It was crazy. Here we were, sponsored by an Irish bank, and we had never played the city of origin. The problem was the cost. Dublin is abroad, Ireland is a foreign country. All the requisite hotel costs and *per diems* pertain. Prohibitive. Joe Dowling, at the Gaiety Theatre, tried to move the Rathmines and Rathgar Operatic Society to a week later; the Abbey was losing money and frightened of the scale; the Olympia Theatre was free, but there was one snag. They had done a crazy deal with Radio Telefis Eireann for them to use Saturday as a 'get-in' for a series of Sunday programmes. It meant that the playing week finished on a Friday. We couldn't do a trilogy. We would lose a fortune. I was once, after all, a

---

*Ironically – and rightly – in April 1990 he received a nomination for a Laurence Olivier Award from the Society of West End Theatres as Designer of the Year for his work on *The Wars of the Roses*.

Producer/Director with RTE. I rang old friends to see if we could shift the 'get-in' to all-night Saturday after our own 'get-out'. They agreed, indeed were very accommodating. The problem was the cost. Regretfully, we turned Gerry Sinott at the Olympia down. I rang Michael 'Fixer' Colgan at the Gate Theatre. He had for many years run the Dublin Theatre Festival and had now turned the Gate into the hottest date in town. The Gate was too small, but did he know of anywhere else? He investigated the Royal Dublin Society in Ballsbridge. We could certainly take the venue, but there was nothing there. We would have to hire seats, heating, lights . . . Dublin bit the dust. In any event, we were now quickly overtaken by extraordinary developments.

For two years, Michael and I had attempted to raise the necessary finance to televise the cycle. At various times we had put together a package that included Central TV, a local station in Chicago and an unidentified flying video unit in the Australian outback. (I suspect Ben, Simon and Stella were trying to find it the night their disappearance alerted the whole of Western Australia.)

The difficulty of marrying these disparate elements is self evident. To all intents and purposes we had failed. And then suddenly there was Tim Milsom, an independent television producer. We didn't believe him, of course. It was eight weeks to the end of the tour, we were in the middle of the Old Vic and here was someone saying he could raise a million in a month! Impossible! (We were right. In the event, it was two months.) Michael and I were sceptical. After two years of trying to raise the cash, we had given up. We were not about to be taken in by any old blagger who came round to the stage door. Actors' agents started receiving phone calls from the Jane L'Epine Smith Agency, doing deals. Naturally, to the actors, this was a case of the ESC management going behind their backs. 'What,' they demanded, 'the hell is going on?' We didn't know. It quickly transpired that it was on Jane's advice that Tim had taken up the trail. We said 'Cool it, do nothing until something is firm.' We thought it would go away. It didn't.

Tim Milsom: Having just attempted to finance a TV version of the Young Vic's *Romeo and Juliet*, I knew this project would be fraught with difficulty.

Quite apart from everything else, the BBC had recently produced the entire Shakespeare canon for TV and had sold it to virtually every broadcaster in the world, thus reducing the potential market for our series. But there were other serious factors to consider. How were we going to film it? Live (exciting and cheap) or studio? What was the budget? £1 million? What to do about Equity – big problem. Equity are not keen on filming live theatre 'because it puts other actors out of work.' (Pardon?!) Actors' and stage staff's salaries? The obvious solution was to pay everyone exactly the same rate. Very socialist, and difficult for a company to object to.

It was mid February. I spent a week on the phone calling every TV company from Tyne Tees to NHK, Japan. The first positive response came from the Arts Channel, which went out on the Sky satellite. They agreed to come in with £100,000 for UK satellite rights and £150,000's worth of post-production facilities, a total investment of £250,000.

Central Television offered £250,000 against a UK sale and Victor Glynn of Portman Films put up £400,000 against the 'rest of the world', i.e. for the world rights excluding the UK. We were almost there. Unfortunately the original Central offer proved to be a non-starter, so I contacted John Gau of BSB – a new satellite company – who had already expressed interest in the project. We struck a deal. BSB were to come in for UK satellite rights for a ten-year period at £740,000. With the Arts Channel's £250,000 we were there and had no need of Portman.

Then disaster struck. BSB, loaded with its own problems, delayed its start-up date by a year. Consequently all deals were off. Where did that leave me? I had a budget of around £1 million to raise and only £250,000 in place. Mercifully, Jim Reeve of Contracts International called me. Contracts International specialise in marketing independent productions and would invest £400,000 against UK Terrestrial TV rights. I now approached Victor Glynn again to see if his original offer still stood. Victor had reservations, but he did want in. Once more it appeared I had the budget.

Then disaster struck . . . again! The Board of Portman Films would not agree to commit the money. I spent that afternoon with John Paul Chapple of Portman (the eventual producer) drawing up lists of sales agents who might invest.

It was the middle of March. The phone was glued to my ear again. Finally, a week later, Angus Fletcher, Sales Organiser of ITEL (International Television Enterprises Ltd), expressed enthusiasm and within a few days of our first meeting with them, ITEL were in.

We then became ensnared in legal technicalities. The lawyer commissioned by ITEL to draw up the agreement inadvertently added the £100,000 of the Arts Channel sale (which I needed to make the series) to the sum that Contracts International had to recoup, effectively making Contracts International £100,000 short. At this time, Jim Reeve was travelling abroad and almost impossible to contact. What's more, his UK office would not accept that the lawyer, by his own admission, had made a mistake.

By this time, we had started setting up the production and were liable for some sizeable bills. My only way out was to find another £100,000 so, for a third time, I went back to Victor and Portman Films. That was not the easiest of meetings ... but after much animated discussion Portman put up the missing £100,000. For the third time, I had raised the budget. I kept my fingers firmly crossed that it was 'third time lucky'. It was April 1st.

Bogdanov: We left the Vic in mid March, not yet convinced but at least a bit more optimistic that, at the last gasp, we would pull the TV off. It was really out of our hands. I had mixed feelings about it all. On the one hand it was gratifying to think there would be a permanent record of the work, however fast it would be shot. On the other, so many moments from the original productions had been lost, so many performances had been changed, the acting was three years old, and I was mentally unprepared for it. I was trying to get my head round Hamburg and huge structural changes there. I would have to take at least two to three weeks out from my planning.

The first thing was to get a record of the shows as they stood, in order to brief the technical crews. We videoed the shows on one camera in the Norwich week in late March (which turned out this time to be highly successful, our reputation in the intervening years having grown). Briefings would be the next week in the Southampton Park Hotel during the day, followed by viewing of the plays in the evening at the Mayflower Theatre. (What a place to see them! A renovated cinema seating two thousand – here comes the shouting ...)

The organisation had now been taken over by John Paul Chapple who, as the project progressed into the editing stage through the winter of 1989, was to do more than anyone to pull the project together. He now engaged Andy Ward as Production Manager, who put together a brilliant team. It was a skeleton version of this team that met in our specially hired room in the Southampton hotel to listen to me try to explain what the fruits of three years had been. We were Louise Lee – Assistant Producer, Simon Fone – Number One Cameraman, Howard Bagder ('Badger') – Number Two, Bob Mackenzie – Sound, and John Treays – Lighting. It was pretty hard going with our one-camera version from Norwich, distant, out of focus, the dialogue sounding as if it had been strained through a congealed mound of old coffee grounds, and me talking all the time.

The fact that they weren't totally confused by all this testifies to their patience and their professionalism. (I had intended for them to see the shows first and the videos second. It would have made more sense. For reasons of time, this was not possible.) It was one more example of the 'anything is better than nothing' approach which we had always adopted. We got through the week covering most of the shows in one form or another. *The House of York* and *Richard III*, the final two performances on Saturday, were unbriefed, though at least seen on stage. On the Sunday we headed for Swansea.

A Day in the Life of the Joint Artistic Director.
Pennington: Antica Trattoria, Southampton, Thursday 30th March, 11.30 pm. To supper with John Paul Chapple to talk about the Back End.

The last leg of the tour, which the company (who are on their own last legs) have nobly tried not to see as an inglorious coda, is in hand. We have sat in the Seafront Café in Eastbourne drinking Nescafé dressed up as cappuccino and watching the March wind howl along the front, reflecting that this homelessness is our charter, rather than the jubilant warm plush of the Old Vic we have just left. We are true once again to the self-parodying traditions of show business: all roads lead to Eastbourne, even if they first circle Mount Fuji and Ayers Rock. Later at night, serving our audience, we count the gaps in the house by the dim light of the auditorium lamps, which in the Congress Theatre cannot finally be extinguished. Final loss on the week of 13th March: £1,776.

The grey uniformity of all this has been shot through, for the company, with bright hints of the Television, in whose seductive vocabulary concepts like the Back End, the Buy Out and the Capitalisation Cost twinkle. For them, the high spot in Eastbourne was to have been the visit of Tim Milsom and Victor Glynn to talk

to us about how exactly and at what price twenty-four hours of live
Shakespeare is to be recorded for posterity in Swansea in the very
final week. But as it turns out Tim and Victor aren't quite ready
for that meeting, and it is cancelled, feeding the suspicion lurking
in many breasts that the whole dangling carrot has been just
another fantasy of the Michaels, devised to keep everybody in some
obscure form of thrall.

And quite a bulging carrot it is: a flat fee of £7,000 for every
man, woman and child of us (ensemble at last!), from the King all
the way through to Cassie Meyer, who joined as a replacement
dresser only three weeks ago, and is rather surprised. That detail
was firmly settled first (even before the overall budget was finally
confirmed), since to enter the labyrinth of free bargaining at this
stage was just too horrifying a thought. £7,000 is possibly not so
very much for the unlimited commercial exploitation in perpetuity
of your Falstaff or Richard III; but on the other hand virtually no
extra work is to be involved, since we will be doing in Swansea
what we are there to do anyway, giving seven theatre performances, on which seven cameras will be trained. So really seven
grand feels like a fairly refulgent handshake after three years of
slog; homes are already being reinvented, and a dreamy poolside
look is appearing on many faces. Even without a signed contract,
it is clear that in many pockets the money is already as good as
spent.

In Norwich the week of 20th March (final loss: £780), a new
meeting with Victor and Tim has been set up, for which they are
very late; whatever their entrepreneurial skills, they neither of them
seem able to catch a train. But eventually they turn up and confirm
the company's potential crock of gold, offering everything except
contracts – they are promised for next week. So one last breath
has still to be held. On now to Southampton, where a potentially
disastrous week at the box office has been averted by the expedient
of my giving a Press Conference arm in arm with Postman Pat and
Jess, who are following us in next week; this has done wonders for
our advance bookings (final loss: only £5,382!). Now, while
Michael Bogdanov takes the camera crew through the rough
videotapes, giving them some idea of what they have let themselves
in for, it falls to me, with Prue Skene as witness, to sit across a
restaurant table from John Paul Chapple, Executive Producer, to
pick the bones out of a very big fish indeed – the question of a
facility fee for the English Shakespeare Company itself.

This is a point that, in all the negotiations, has been skated over: rather imprudently, for why, apart from the glory, are we doing the television at all, if not to underwrite some part of our future – especially now we are losing money again? And there is the office staff to consider: Sue Evans, Jane Morgan and Prue Skene are not included in Portman's £7,000 handout, yet the company's success is, in many important particulars, theirs. (Jane especially has of late, by inspired marketing, rescued our box office on these much-feared last dates.) We need to look after them and ourselves as an entity by securing a comprehensive fee; and now, with other salaries and equipment committed, the £1 million budget looks to be stretched tight as a drumskin. So it is urgent.

This is where, from John Paul's point of view, the Back End comes in: that is, the notional point at which the programme will have been made and sold, and the accruing profit can be dipped into by any number of investors and participants who have kindly waived their fees: the moment of claiming, in other words, an agreed deferment. It is naturally his job now to persuade me on behalf of the ESC to accept virtually nothing up front and an untold wealth of percentage at the Back End. John Paul is the new, relaxed, post-Puttnam producer; he may be carrying the thousands I'm after in his pockets, but they are of torn denim, and the sneakers in which he does his skilled footwork are old. But beneath the Florentine gipsy look – he looks as if he might have stepped out of Guido Reni's *Strage degli Innocenti* – the old values are firmly in place: mercifully, for the manipulation of large capital sums for television films is not for dreamers. Now, flicking his hair out of his *minestrone*, John Paul is telling me that there really isn't any more in the kitty for us and that he is under blunt instructions from his partners finally to 'get the ESC to sign'. Overlooking this, I now suggest hopefully that we seek out some fat in the budget and skim it in our direction. For example, there is 'Costume Renovation: £20,000'. Could we take £5,000 out of that? But the crowns we are wearing, the letters and weapons we are handling, will, without some tarting up, certainly embarrass the searching eye of the camera. The theatrical mutation by an audience's imaginary forces of poor sticks and cloths into the great talismans of kingship and power won't really wash with the viewers at home who can't be expected to know that these items have done three years' punishing service on the road. So we can't save on that. 'Music royalties: £20,000'? The untangling of copyright for screen purposes of our mélange of performers and composers, alive and dead, is unquantifiable and already giving John Paul a headache. In short, you might as well get fat off a skeleton; and as further emaciation, I can't help noticing (but not pointing out) that there is hardly any overtime provision at all, and not even much in the way of a contingency figure, that essential 10% hedge against overspending in any budget that three years in management have taught me to respect most deeply.

In other words, John Paul is up against the wall as well, and means it when he says that £25,000 upfront and £25,000 when the show goes into sales profit is the best that can be done for the ESC, though he acknowledges that that is about half what a producing company in these circumstances might normally expect.

I stab at my liver (*veneziana*, that is) and try not to think of the £7,000s already pocketed. The Back End looks pretty remote to me. We are about to try something very difficult. Shooting the shows in the very last week of their life, once and once only, even with a rapid-reflexed camera crew that have earned their spurs covering sport (and indeed they might as well be unrehearsed at Highbury as trying to spot the difference between the Duke of Gloucester and the Earl of Oxford – who may anyway have been playing Lord Dorset in the previous scene), is the most dangerous way it could be done as well as the only way. If the gremlins are out, we won't have a hope. For all the talent involved, we may end up with an unsellable banana, and that will be that. And we badly need the money. Stab stab. I can't quite bring myself to say yes.

The fact that Friday is about to dawn along the Channel and we are due to start on Sunday, with a technical crew of sixty contracted and the Grand Swansea bought out for the week, is a weapon in John Paul's hands, but also in mine. I plunge, taking Prue into the icy water with me, making an ill-humoured return to first principles. I am sorry, I say (thinking of Michael Fenner's pregnant wife), but in the absence of an adequate fee upfront for the ESC I don't see how we can proceed. It really isn't (thinking of Stephen Jameson's new sitting-room) worth our while. And while I'm at it (thinking of John Tramper's new camera), the structure of the new production company that we are together planning for future television work is all wrong: the ESC should have a 33.3% share, not 25%.

And so we parted on a rancid and unresolved note, in a swirling peasouper about two in the morning, John Paul with a sad look in his eye as he foresaw the collapse of his fragile package caused by the intractable Joint Artistic Director. Sometimes, though, it's good that there are two directors of the ESC, especially if our telepathy is working. I went to bed with a headache, got up with one, and went to see my widowed aunt in Winchester, pausing only to confirm what I had hoped would happen: at breakfast Prue and Michael Bogdanov (refreshed by an all-night viewing of the videos) had cheerfully picked up the cue and further pressed John Paul to a new offer. £35,000 upfront for the ESC, plus £10,000 of any unspent budget on programme completion, and another £25,000 at the moment of sale. And the 33.3% as well. Everyone had slapped each other on the back, and John Paul has been invited onto the Board of the ESC.

The tonic of my aunt's magnolia trees having washed away the squalid fumes of the previous night's binge, I then got back to Southampton at teatime on Friday to find that Barry Stanton was stranded on the Isle of Wight, where last night's peasouper had now moved in and strangled the ferries, and was unlikely to be back in time to play the Chorus in *Henry V* that night. He might arrive by the interval.

No matter. Our understudy system was our pride and joy, an interlocking machine bedded down in Connecticut, Adelaide and Amsterdam. But then a whisper began to filter through. The actor understudying the Chorus (had been for two years) knew not a word of it – was indeed improbably claiming that he had been promised he could go on with the book in his hand if push were to come to shove. Not much point in our getting pompous about this, though it rankled that for two years an £11 per week understudy payment had been pocketed for nothing – not to mention a certain point of professional honour. I still hated the idea of anybody going on with a book, and was beginning to feel an ancient and unwelcome call to arms. John Dougall would be playing Henry V that night and so I would be dutifully sitting in my room as his token understudy, standing by for the unlikely event; I was thus horribly available for this still unlikelier one. Could I put on a lounge suit and play the Chorus myself? I didn't really know the part, though I'd heard it often enough; but was not I supposed to be this Shakespeare machine, blank verse oozing from my finger tips, and did I not have my hastily-learned Humphrey of Gloucester and Cardinal of Winchester behind me? I could be fairly sure of Act I ('O for a Muse of Fire') because of its fame, and of Act IV ('Now Entertain Conjecture of a Time') not so much because of the last two years but because Laurence Olivier's version of it used to spin endlessly at 78 rpm on my turntable when I was twelve, I entranced by the picture of the night before Agincourt which he conjured in a voice that was like diamond under velvet.

But the rest was a hotchpotch of subordinate clauses and apostrophising about England: 'For now suppose . . . oh now behold . . . oh do but think . . . oh England' (did the man never learn to cut?), together with occasional prime pitfalls like the 'huge bottoms drawn though the furrowed sea'. I might do worse without the book than the understudy would with it, and for that I wouldn't be easily forgiven. But I was pissed off by the alternative, and assumed the audience would be as well. And I did have the course of each Act (twenty minutes?) in which to try and learn the next choric speech. OK. I breezed on, hurtled through the part (in order not to have time to think of the folly), word perfect but manic, getting a delirious image of myself from afar as a tiny Pulcinello gesticulating wildly, rushing headlong away to stuff more words in, and rushing back into the circle of light: every moment hoping for Barry's titupping step along the corridor to relieve me. When he did arrive at the interval, the salt sea still on him, he was astonished to be embraced passionately by the very colleague he had come to grovel to. He then took over for the second half before an audience that may have wondered why the Chorus had grown stouter and lost (a little) more hair, while I was routinely made much of by a company who had witnessed the proceedings with a certain chilly neutrality. It had been just what I *would* do under the circumstances, and perhaps they detected a certain folly and conceit in it, a pernickety dream of perfectibility that made me feel remote to them once more. In any case, none of it was news; saving the day had become an affectation.

And that was my day. Russians had been shooting at Armenians, and like a blind mole I had been casting up little hills of quite meaningless virtuosity. But to each his own capacity. My aunt's magnolias were the best part of it.

Bogdanov: April in Swansea. It could so easily have been Singapore. (Not to mention Paris, but who wants to spend April in Paris . . . ?) That it wasn't either of these was a question of finance. The final week of all. Our Grand Slam finish. Dublin? A week in the West End? A fast plane to Bangkok and a slow boat back?

No. Swansea – a town much dear to me, Dylan Thomas's grey hill tumbling into the sea, in the environs of which dwell a veritable choir of Reeses, all one hundred and fifty-seven of them cousins of mine. A newly refurbished Grand Theatre and grand indeed to play. A stone's throw from the Gower (peninsula that is, but no less golden). After three long, weary years, a quiet conclusion. Quiet? We recorded all seven plays, twenty-four hours' worth, a Rose a day, in that one week. In a way that the Fates have of arranging things for us (despite my existential belief that you make your own choices, change your own luck), things were not really in our hands any more. Six weeks earlier we had not even considered the possibility that we would be filming the shows in the final week of the tour. There has been a theatre on the site of the Grand for over two hundred years. It is a sobering thought to realise that one of the more technically advanced and aesthetically delightful theatres in the UK only escaped being a bingo hall in 1969 by the skin of the Council. There is also a history of live and recorded performances from its stage, mainly for HTV, but also for BBC Wales. The previous October, I myself had hosted six one-hour-long programmes interviewing Welsh personalities. In the middle of Victor Spinetti's 'Sergeant Major' sketch, on asking for volunteers to come on stage, I had found myself face to face with Charlie Dale's father ... The Dales come from Tenby, Pembrokeshire.

Of all the modern conversions, Swansea Grand is one of the best. A new fly-tower, scene dock, space out the back; outside – good access to the stage for sets; and, as with Victoria Arts Centre in Melbourne, dressing rooms off the corridors alongside the stage. A big car park immediately by the dock doors allowed ample space for the pantechnicons to set up, and the scene dock had space enough to set up a second camera unit.

This would house Assistant Director Chris Short (Andy Ward's choice) who would be doing a second 'cut' (i.e. selecting the camera shots) from the cameras I wasn't using for my main cut. When I came to view the tapes back later, I was eternally grateful for Chris's experience. He got me out of trouble time and again, whenever I failed to get proper coverage of certain moments. The one big snag was the schedule of performances. The whole week had to be changed to accommodate the shooting schedule. Instead of beginning on Tuesday, with a trilogy on Saturday, we would be starting on Monday and finishing with *Richard III* on Sunday, one show a day. Many people had already booked tickets to see shows on the original dates, some were travelling long distances to be in at the final kill. The new performances would be free, and they could get their money back. But how would they know before they arrived that the show they wanted to see was not being performed that night? 'Don't worry,' said Sean Kier, Acting General Manager of the Grand, 'we're used to this, we know how to handle it.' The first I knew that something was wrong was when a worried friend rang me in Southampton to say that he had tried to book tickets only to be told that the performance was cancelled.

Then a friend from Wales also rang to say that he had been thinking of going but that an advertisement had appeared in the *Western Mail* to say that all performances had been cancelled. '*Ring the box office for information.*' I tried it out. Yes, they were cancelled, they wouldn't give me any more information. It was *possible* that there would be a performance. Would I ring back later? I rang Sean Kier. 'We know what we're doing.' 'How can you, if people think the whole thing has been cancelled?' 'Look, we have to find a way of letting people know that the performances have changed. This is our first duty, to announce the cancellation. When we've traced them, then we can issue them with other tickets.' 'Yes, but why on earth not do it positively? Take an advertisement that says *Wars of the Roses – Performances Changed Due to TV Presentation*. Create some excitement in the project?' '*Cancelled* catches the eye more.' 'Yes, but . . .' 'We know what we are doing . . .' The result was some houses half full, rows on the phone and at the box office. I spent quarter of an hour before the start of *Henry V* placating a lovely lady supporter, Margaret Berwyn Jones, who had gathered eleven people from all over the country to celebrate her birthday with a performance of *Henry IV Part 1*, only to find it was to be *Henry IV Part 2*. Not only that – her seats had been front row, and the choice she was now being offered was back row of the upper circle or money back and she could lump it. No wonder she was in tears. We prided ourselves that in the three years we had built up a reputation for friendliness, approachability and a consideration for our audiences. Through the insensitivity of an element of the Swansea management we were blowing that reputation in the dying days.

Not that our relations with the theatre in general were bad; on the contrary. The staff were infinitely helpful, the crew professional

*Clyde Pollitt: (right)
'We knew where the
bona robas were' –
as Justice Shallow,
with Philip Bowen
(Silence) (LB);
(below) In Southampton,
March 1989 (JT)*

Three Bolingbrokes:
(above) Patrick O'Connell
(1986) (LB);
(right) John Castle (1987)
(LB);
(below) Michael Cronin
(1988) (LB)

Two Falstaffs: (above) John Woodvine (1986) (LB);
(below) Barry Stanton (1987 and 1988) (LB)

The last night in Swansea: (above) The Company (LB);
(below) Michael Bogdanov (LB)

and first class. (Unlike our surly experiences at the Cardiff New – possibly the most unfriendly crew on the tour.)*

Four hours' sleep on Sunday, up next morning for a fresh briefing of five new members of the crew joining, for whom the whole experience was completely novel: Floor Manager Brookie, cameramen Dave Rose, Glen Williamson, Joe Petrowski, Dave Oakley. I had seven cameras and a crane. Number 7 camera was locked off permanently on a wide shot in the circle so that, if we ever got into trouble (which I did, often), there was always something covering the action. Number 6 was beside it on a long zoom. I would have been better following my original idea of a platform in the middle of the stalls for this one. Camera 3 was stationed in the well of the orchestra pit, thus giving me close-ups on 6 or 3 that offered the choice of a bald patch or a double chin. Cameras 2 and 4 were at stage level left and right and cameras 1 and 5 were hand-held, able to be mobile up and down stage and available for tower and bridge work.

We were recording four separate versions simultaneously – my cut, taken from cameras 2, 4 and 6; Chris's from 1 and 5 plus anything from my cameras that I had missed; camera 3; and camera 7. Simon Fone, on 3, anchored the shows, following the action mostly on a medium shot, going in close and out again on my instructions.

In the years between 1966 and 1969 I had trained as a producer with BBC TV and then, in the space of two years, had as Producer/Director done over a hundred programmes with Radio Telefis Eireann. Everything from Gaelic Football to religion, Outside Broadcast dramas up mountains to live Rock shows. I had also (for Victor) filmed *Hiawatha* and *Shakespeare Lives* for Channel Four and, for ZDF in Germany, *Julius Caesar*. I wasn't exactly out of practice, but the technique was pretty rusty.

The first harrowing experience of *Richard II* left me limp. I had reason to thank my Vision Mixer, Pam Hinckley, for getting me endlessly out of trouble, and my PA Anthea Dudley for phlegmatically briefing the crew about future developments. During *Henry IV Part 1*, Anthea immortalised herself with a directive to cameraman Dave Oakley of – 'Tart on 4'. (The tart

---

*As we finished, so we are to begin again. September 1990 sees the launch of our next major tour, of *Coriolanus* and *The Winter's Tale,* from the Grand.

in question being Francesca Ryan as Doll Tearsheet.)

It should have been simple to stick to the rules, but I would get excited when a great shot came up on Simon or Howard and Glen and cut to them needlessly. This was particularly the case when I had tied my own cameramen up in knots and was seeking a way out. It was hard to keep remembering that it didn't matter if there was a mess on my cut at certain moments; if the shot was there on Simon, it was being automatically recorded. I pride myself on being able to react and think fast, but what these hardbitten, freelance professionals thought of this bungling amateur, I do not know. They remained cool in the face of all hysteria, contenting themselves with a phlegmatic 'Are you sure you mean that, Mike?' In the face of nineteen countermands. Even allowing for a couple of hours' fast forward briefing, their task was pretty Herculean. When has anybody recorded twenty-four hours of live drama in seven days?

It was maniacal. Despite familiarity with the shows (mine, not anyone else's) the moments came at me so fast, I was always one camera or one line behind. Or simply behind. Some famous close-ups missed: 'Once more unto the breach . . .'; 'I know thee not, old man . . .'; 'Thy bedchamber . . .' And, of course, that most famous of all lines which didn't appear on any camera in any form: 'My Lord, there's letters for thee . . .' (Who said that?) An eighteen-hour day, briefing in the morning, pick-ups in the afternoon, paralysis setting in at 7.30 pm, depression at roughly 10.45 pm.

Shouting like a fool, swearing like a tro**per . . . 'Close up of Michael on 2 . . . missed it! Give me the 2 shot. Go wide! Go wide! On 6! Close-up of Andy on 4 – I mean 2 – I mean 3! ****! Missed it again! Take 6!' Take anything! Take me home, country roads! Saved by a wonderful crew, a wonderful Production Assistant, a wonderful Vision Mixer.

Each performance was preceded by myself apologising to the audience for any change of schedule and an exhortation to them to treat the evening as a normal performance and enjoy themselves. Easier said than done. The cameras were obviously a barrier and many of the comic sequences, by now a well worn groove of Pavlovian laughter, were played to an eerie silence. We nearly didn't start at all. I went in for the first briefing of the actors to find a rumour flying about that nobody was going to get paid. The production company had run out of money, it was said. A motion was put not to allow *Richard II* to be recorded unless the money was in the bank. In a heated altercation (reminiscent of the old days) it transpired that John Paul Chapple had unwisely told Colin Farrell (now Equity Deputy) that he had run out of cheques and had sent to London for a new cheque book. Hence the panic.

Plus ça doesn't change. The brief to the actors was as follows: no looking for cameras, just play it as you normally do. It was the only way I could anticipate what was to follow. Terrific. Directed for stage and not for TV, the plays are restless and the action moves everywhere. If some of the scenes look static from a distance, try following them in close-up. Andy Jarvis and Siôn Probert gave particular trouble – head movements back and forward – long-lensing the cameras time and again. In one sequence in the Elizabeth scene in *Richard III*, I succeeded in getting the back of Andy's head five times in succession. I gave up and held him in mid shot. The same thing applied to Siôn in *Henry V*. Siôn, playing Fluellen on his home ground, blossomed in Swansea and gave some of his best performances of the tour. The wily birds with TV experience scaled down their performances for the camera, others kept up our high decibel tradition. It was hard.

In the afternoons, we taped the pieces that I thought needed some special attention. All the fights were done on hand-held cameras, Badger here doing most of the work. I had a number of scenes set down for high shots from the crane – the Conspirators in *Henry IV Part 2*, the Dinner Table Scenes in *Richard II* and *House of York*. I sent the crane home after two days. There was not enough room to operate it on stage and it was expensive. The Southampton scene in *Henry V* was a candidate for a special shot from the bridge as was the commando raid on the sleeping camp in *York*. During the editing we could not find this last – frustrating, as it was shot particularly well. A couple of scenes were re-recorded out of expediency, John Dougall's Nym make-up was so heavy in close-up that we had to re-do the Pistol/Nym/Bardolph fight. And in the Mortimer death in *House of Lancaster*, Stephen Jameson had his face buried in Barry Stanton's shoulder, and was invisible. I could not get a shot of him at all. We did not overrun once. I even managed to turn round at speed and re-do the end of *Henry IV Part 2*, as time ran out. At the point where Falstaff was being banished, I only seemed to have shots of the punks up the towers. The crew were the real heroes of this crazy exercise. The final quality of the lighting, sound, camera work, given the circumstances, was extraordinary. Lest anyone remark on the roughness of some of the sequences, remember that all were doing it virtually sight unseen. Heroes all.

I have spent some crazy weeks in my life but only my battle with the boat in *Mutiny* rivals that week in Swansea. On the final night, as we were pelted with roses, I couldn't even raise a smile. We were through, we were finished. The three years had climaxed in an extraordinary fashion. It felt like a great, wet flannel.

John Paul Chapple: The Saturday after shooting finished, I was at home when Andy Ward rang up. He had noticed a small report in the *Guardian* which stated that the Arts Channel had gone into liquidation. If true, this meant that the series could not be edited – the Arts Channel's investment being in facilities and time rather than money. What was worse, the entire show – video tapes and audio multi-tracks and all – was sitting in the Channel's premises in the bleak Rassau Industrial Estate in Ebbw Vale, Wales. When the receivers came in, they would doubtless regard them as assets of the company. We could lose the entire thing.

We decided that the only thing to do was to mount a commando raid. We guessed – correctly as it turned out – that, as the notice of receivership had been made on the Friday, nothing would happen until the Monday. Andy and I met at Heathrow Airport, hired a Toyota Space Cruiser and headed for Wales. When we arrived, the place was utterly deserted and, having considered and rejected the idea of breaking in, we rang around a few of the Channel's staff who had been in Swansea, and eventually gained entry. About an hour later, we had loaded the van and were on the way back to London. We stored the mound of tapes in Portman's small London office and went home to think about what to do next. Legal advice the following day confirmed that in all probability the receivers would have considered the tapes as an asset of the Arts Channel, if only for their value as blank stock. It had been a close shave.

Bogdanov: The editing was necessarily postponed. We finally clinched a deal with Windmill Lane Studios, Dublin, but by then it was August and I was in Hamburg. We initiated a system whereby I viewed a rough-cut prepared in London, dictated notes onto a dictaphone, couriered them, rang to explain, waited for the re-edited version to return, then more of the same. The third version would go to Dublin for the 'on-line' (the final edit).

John Paul Chapple: As a TV programme is both pictures and sound, editing involves both vision and audio processes. When both parts are done, they are combined on a master tape which is the finished programme. The vision part is usually also divided. This is done for the simple reason that editing one-inch tape (on which the *Wars of the Roses* was recorded) is extremely expensive (about £300 an hour).

The common practice is to transfer the master material onto cheaper tape (U-matic) and edit on that using cheaper machines (this is the 'off-line' edit). This way you can experiment, look at different versions of the same scene and generally work under less pressure, as it is not costing an arm and a leg.

Printed onto every frame of the material is a time code which is exactly the same on the master material as on the transfer. Once you have a completed programme, you simply collate the codings on the U-matic edit with those on the master tapes and (with a bit of fine tuning here and there) you should have a programme. (This is the 'on-line' edit.) And herein lay yet another problem.

The deal with Windmill Lane did not include the off-line process, as this would not be done in Dublin. We therefore had to find a way of off-lining elsewhere and, as London was the place where most of us worked, lived and, above all, knew the sort of people who would get involved in a scheme like this, London seemed the obvious place to do it (except, of course, that the director was in Hamburg). What was being proposed, then, was that an off-line editor would work in London, an on-line editor in Dublin and that the director would oversee them in . . . Hamburg.

Michael Pennington says that Michael Bogdanov believes it is possible to be in two places at the same time . . . literally. And often he is!

Bogdanov: My living room is littered with about a hundred rough-cuts and edits. Throughout the autumn, by a combination of fax, courier, phone, plus a trip to Dublin at the beginning to establish the style, we managed to get through. I lived on with the *Roses* from 5 am till 8 am every morning until December 1989. I have reason to remember them. John Paul Chapple supervised the Dublin end. Indefatigably, and kept the momentum going. He was my eyes and ears. It was unsatisfactory. It was editing by proxy, but it was the only way.

John Paul: The stage production contained a large number of music cues, many of which were recorded by well known (and very expensive) artists. Had we re-licensed the music precisely we would have ended up with an astronomical bill. So a composer, Mark Fishlock, was employed to re-score many of the cues and, in some cases, to re-record the existing ones. Some of the original music had to stay; 'My Way' in *Henry V*, for example, and Barber's *Adagio for Strings* in *Richard III* were so integral a part of the scenes in which they featured that they simply could not be replaced or a whole part of the scene's meaning would be lost. We argued about one particular piece, at length, the incidental music behind the battle scenes in *Henry IV Part 1* (and elsewhere) entitled 'Maniac Subway Killer'; it ran for almost nine minutes and cost something like £400 per 30 seconds to use. Michael was loathe to drop it but, in the end, we simply could not afford it.

By October, *Henry V, Henry IV Part 1*, and *Richard III* were almost finished, on time for the big sales market in Cannes. Everyone sweated blood over the title sequence. Hubert Montag and Philip Owens, Windmill's graphic designers, generated hundreds of ideas and faxed them to Michael P. in London and Michael B. in Hamburg. An original logo design commissioned for marketing purposes by ITEL, the distributors, from de Wynters, turned out to be pretty uninspired and we hoped to get something better.

Philip Owens came up with a waving flag concept, and spent a weekend filming images from the plays projected onto a moving sheet. Brian McCue finally cut the sequence together a week before the market. We then, of course, realised we had a mute sequence, but Windmill Lane, who seem to have the resources to rise to any occasion, pulled one of their resident composers, Dennis Woods, out of the hat.

Two days later we had title music, though by this time Michael had to be satisfied with hearing it down the phone ('. . . Sounds a bit like a brass band . . . I think.') And the first three plays went off to Market.

Bogdanov: Without John Paul, I do not believe we would have succeeded. Some crucial decisions had to be taken. Apart from cutting for time, I was also faced with a peculiar and difficult situation. Where an actor was doing him/herself a disservice, should I leave in, or take out? At the end of this book, Michael P.

talks of a wonderful moment of actor magic, as he describes Michael Cronin's reflections on the onerous duties of kingship. Michael C. on form was mesmerising. Not so on the one crucial occasion in Swansea. After agonising long and hard, I removed the speech. I preferred the memory of it and the quality of his acting to which this book pays tribute.

CHAPTER

12

CONCLUSION

'What! We have seen the seven stars ...'
Shakespeare, Henry IV Part 2

Pennington: Only 6% of people go to the theatre in the UK – many more, even so, than visit opera or ballet. Since the Second World War and the Council for the Encouragement of Music and the Arts, the body that has had public charge of this minority interest (remarkable nonetheless for its tendency to survive) is the Arts Council of Great Britain, a politically independent organisation, financially dependent on the Office of Arts and Libraries. The extent to which the Council has remained free from political influence is a measure of the success of individual chairmen as much as of any governmental neutrality, but of course it depends, beyond the detail of Treasury budgets, on implicit government approval of the arts as a public service. Sometimes its very validity is questioned: when Mrs Thatcher recently declared that if the arts were as important to the country as people told her they were, then surely the public would be prepared to dig deeper into their own pockets for them, she seemed to be denying the principle of state subsidy altogether; however, since later the same week an unexpected 19% rise in grant aid to the Arts Council was announced, one must assume she was instinctively indulging a small political tendency – to depress the expectations, and then offer a nice surprise.

This form of brinkmanship was nicely echoed within the Arts Council itself when we applied to the Touring Department for our first grant in 1985. In matters great and small the Council has begun to take a stylistic cue from its paymasters, even mimicking their language when, not long ago, the pharisaic new concepts of 'feasibility', 'cost-effectiveness' and 'viability' subtly entered the vocabulary at 105 Piccadilly. Plunging further into the undergrowth, one might have heard admiring talk of 'shakers and rollers', 'big players down at the cutting edge'. The Touring Department even went so far as to set up its own internal commercial management, Upstart, committing £250,000 of its own to launch it and soliciting investment from the City to put on a national touring production of *The Hobbit*, in the fond hope of seeing a return. As recently as the summer of 1989, the Conservative and Labour Party Conferences were treated to two separate Arts Council manifestoes trimmed to their perceived political stances, the Tory one pleading the case in terms of the arts' earning potential, marketing skills and attractiveness to sponsors, and the Labour one in terms of how many 'ordinary' people go to arts events in the year, comparing the RSC's attendance figures with those at Wembley Stadium. There are times, it seems to the Council's old friends, that the monkey prances rather too readily on the barrel organ.

Nevertheless, a £20 million increase has been achieved, largely due to the determined efforts of Richard Luce, Minister for the Arts, to beat down the doors of the Treasury, the sympathy he found there in Norman Lamont, the Chief Secretary, and to the efforts of Peter Palumbo, Arts Council Chairman, in forcing the debate into the public eye. For a moment it almost seemed like a political issue. Euphoria would be out of place, however. The figure is really only a straw offered to the dam after many years of effluence; and the Council, ground between two impossible wheels – government meanness on the one hand and deserving clients on the other – is still forced to make invidious decisions on which organisations to cut back on, which to axe altogether, and which to cast increasingly on the mercy of local councils. At the time of writing, this unpleasant task is to be taken from the Council, and the Minister is proposing an almost complete devolution of funding decisions to those councils – a move the arts world views with the most serious reservations.

The English Shakespeare Company is a typical Arts Council client, hoping to offer an unfashionable cultural service, falling in precisely with the Council's policy of devolution from London, and with just enough of an air of enterprise to fit the entrepreneurial style of the late 1980s. (It is also, by the way, by its nature a very

bad candidate for local government control.) And sure enough we
have been rewarded. But it is interesting to note the real extent of
the state support we have received since 1986. With the Histories,
we did thirty-three weeks of UK touring for an Arts Council input
of £325,000: that is, £9,864 per week; and in 1990 we have played
fourteen UK dates with *The Comedy of Errors* for £100,000: that's
£7,143 a week. Exactly ten years ago, Prospect Theatre Company
were going out for sixteen weeks with £18,750 a week. To put it
another way, over our first three years the Council contributed
38% of our production costs (and nothing to our running costs).
The balance of 62% was drawn from commercial sources. In its
deliberations, the Council operates a 'pound for pound' approach
(Incentive Funding), by which £1 of commercial money is
theoretically matched by £1 of subsidy, and every £1 of subsidy is
dependent on the same sum being raised from the private sector. If,
instead of £1, clients manage to raise only 75p in sponsorship, then
they are symbolically penalised by seeing the Council's contribution
go down to 75p also. In other words, the beleaguered state subsidy
body is acting as a watchdog of our skills at the *bourse*.

In practice, this means that in hunting for sponsorship one may
find oneself across the table from some beady-eyed banker or
corporation spokesman, reassuring him that the Arts Council is on
one's side, knowing that it isn't strictly true until the gentleman
opposite is convinced that it may be so and coughs up accordingly.
It is not very good for the nerves. We enjoyed an unique
relationship with the Allied Irish Bank which we hope some day to
repeat. They certainly didn't allow their guests to get drunk on a
first night of *Hamlet*. But the search for sponsorship is time-
consuming, and itself calls for a new breed of sponsorship
consultants who must charge arts organisations for their services;
and even if it is secured, the tendency of commercial sponsors to
pull out at the last minute without explanation and certainly
without liability is well-known in the trade. It is interesting to
remember that, on its formation, one of the first offers the Arts
Council made was to Anthony Quayle at Stratford; he turned it
down, fearing to become dependent on state subsidy, and instead
took his company on a highly successful Australian tour that saved
the finances of the Stratford-upon-Avon theatre. When he came to
set up a tour for his Compass company thirty-five years later – a
tour that was to be based extensively on sponsorship by Thermalite
– a sudden takeover of the sponsor by Marley Tiles led to the

money being withdrawn at the last minute; he might have been safer (though poorer) with the Arts Council. When this happens, all the disappointed sponsoree can do is smile graciously and wonder where to find a new partner in a hurry or else how to extract himself from signed contracts and mop up what is already spent. Perhaps the most dismaying aspect of it all is the speed – five years – with which the whole dodgy pursuit has become accepted not as our option but as our bounden duty. We who live to please must please to live indeed; but one wonders whether this kind of bed-hopping is quite what an artistic community should be up to.

The ESC's plans for 1990–92 are logically aimed ('targeted' I should perhaps say); they involve two large companies offering four Shakespeares – *Coriolanus, The Winter's Tale, The Merchant of Venice* and *Timon of Athens*; a Ben Jonson – *The Alchemist*; a musical classic – *The Beggar's Opera*; and a new musical – *The Hunting of the Snark*, as well as educational and outback groups. We are thus bringing up baby, which is a lot more difficult than conceiving him, and the search for sponsorship is tougher in some ways than when we had no name in 1986. Times may have changed too. The Arts Council grant is once again conditional on sponsorship; Glen Walford's highly successful production of *The Comedy of Errors* (Spring 1990) has been made possible by an extraordinary private donation by a Leicestershire businessman, Mike Edwards, who out of enthusiasm for the company has made a gift of £50,000 which underwrites the one third of the production budget which the Council felt unable to afford. All that Mike seeks in return is appropriate public identification and to be allowed to attend rehearsals as an observer. The gift has no strings attached and is not an investment. An investor, of course, does require a return; and no face in late 1989 beamed more broadly at me than that of David Mirvish, to whom I reported an overall ESC surplus of £50,000, of which, under the terms of our initial agreement, he was entitled to 40%. His amazement was as great as his delight, and he immediately put the money back into the company, astonished that his *enfants terribles* had made a profit. Yes, a profit. The television deal for *The Wars of the Roses* had been a bonus; but even without it, we had a small margin to show.

And it was done entirely out of touring Shakespeare.

*

To have managed this would suggest that we might have to justify ourselves no longer; except that the theatre always has to justify itself. Some people view it as completely unnecessary. In fact, it is a thing that grows stubbornly in the dark like rhubarb, and is related to a manichean balance between spiritual need and material prosperity. When it bathes in affluent northern sunlight, as I recently found it does in Iceland, it may not flourish. There the standard of living is high and, according to the disgruntled dramaturge of the National Theatre in Reykjavik (he looks startlingly like Henrik Ibsen), the most worrying theme a playwright can find to write about is the marital difficulties of two professional breadwinners who never see each other. In East Berlin, we found that an audience whose tongue was to some degree tied thirsted with its eyes and ears for the sustenance of theatre. In what seems like a dream still in Czechoslovakia, the nation has found its public tongue in a playwright, whose cogent language blows like a breeze through the world's Press. You can actually understand what he's saying. The malaise of Britain is more subtle, the cultural siege more insidious. Advance in the technology of communications has not been particularly good for communication. If you have a fax machine, wondrous convenience, you can spend the day making unanswerable statements through it and not have to talk at all. We half-talk on the telephone from everywhere, even from the steering wheels of cars (why isn't this dangerous practice illegal?) and, as I happened to notice last 5th November, fathers are able to continue their business on the phone from the fringe of their children's bonfire parties. Might we soon have to ban Vodafones from theatre auditoria?

Not really. For even as we look set to become cellular barbarians, audiences may be turning to the theatre again to feel the yeast of argument, the bulby paste of real emotion, or simply, as the language itself shrinks and contracts, to participate (like Don Armado in Love's Labour's Lost) in 'A great feast of language' – even if, like him, we end up having merely 'stolen the scraps'. It remains one of the few places where minds can quietly be heard to change. In Henry IV Part 2, as the old king lies dying, he and his son struggle to become reconciled to each other and, in the process, secure the succession. When it was well played in our production, the hush that attended it was the one actors wait and wait for. Many fathers were thinking of their children, many children of their parents. This great scene ritually exorcises private fears and frustrations: some fifteen hundred strangers placed shoulder to shoulder in the dark colluding in the possibility of improvement. Such is the gift of a great storyteller (and the burden of his interpreters); and we are still flocking in to listen together to him. In fact we need him more than ever. A certain kind of social decline leads to bad acting in the streets and paradoxically gives the theatre a chance. For all its absurd failures and follies, the theatre now has an opportunity to recall its audience. And so, among other things, companies like ours must go out and find it, considering as we do that if there were once again a healthy local repertory system in the country, touring would be a degree less necessary, and our fan mail would not need to strike its occasionally plaintive note of '*please* come back *soon*'.

I've dwelt in this account not only on my own painful efforts to learn how to wear two hats at once, but on some of the 'down' sides of this arduous search: the irritations of the road, the feistiness and deadlocks. The noble cause of touring can quickly degenerate into petty squabbles. 'Are you calling my wife a drunkard?' I once heard one of our company bellow at another, relieved for once it wasn't me getting the blast. This sort of thing is no surprise; certainly no blame is attached, and I hope for absolution myself. The touring life is in fact a hell of a strain, and calls forth all sorts of exceptional and excessive behaviour, some of it magnificent, some of it not. The memories of an actor who tours are of a passing acquaintance with many cultures, privileged and remote. Sustained by a network of small support systems he will have drifted towards successive deadlines, conditioned to checking in and out, able to recall different theatre interiors but hesitating over which countries they were in; he may have felt personal competence under threat, and have longed on occasion to boil water in a pan, cook some potatoes and eat them. Touring can aggravate personal problems to a sometimes tragic degree; it makes you long for small sanities; it is damnably disorientating. No wonder it attracts eccentrics and claims its victims. Very few people can do it indefinitely. It can also form an exceptional bond between people, especially if the work has a sense of path-finding built into it. It is quite difficult to re-adjust to 'normal' work again. I went straight from *The Wars of the Roses* tour to spend three months in Tuscany, filming John Mortimer's *Summer's Lease*. The job was a dream, but of course it was simply a job which started and ended. If we hadn't been available, other actors would have been chosen. I then went on to the RSC to do a new play by Stephen Poliakoff. RSC-bashing is an ignoble sport – the company has been the crucible for much great achievement – but they don't half ask for it. Suffice it to say that the Barbican is as bad to work in as you've always heard, unsanitary, untheatrical and confusing; and during my six-month stay no member of the Artistic Directorate, apart from the director of the show itself, came to see this world premiere or even waved in greeting, until, in the final fortnight, I made such a fuss that two or three of them came forth. Bureaucratisation has entered the bloodstream of this great company, and nothing could have better revitalised my enthusiasm for the ESC. I longed to get back on the road, to real theatres with clean dirt, with a group with a sense of mission. The ESC did have that, in spades, and for a moment the hellish humiliation of many actors' lives was masked by a sense of indispensability, of being an absolutely necessary part of the machine. It is good, of course, that such a group should be disbanded, if only temporarily. Self-confidence can become complacency, the sense of being needed turn into the fallacy of being an élite. But if our companies got anything from their time on the road, apart from a sea of used air tickets and a rather chancy knowledge of medieval history, it could have been a rare and barely definable sense of pride.

Such pride would be difficult to sustain were it not that we were handling daily the richest imagination that has ever been applied to the theatre. The language, in the end, is the sustaining miracle.

Bogdanov: My love of language is a passion inherited from my father. A genius of a linguist and a librarian, born in the Ukraine, married to a wild Welsh woman from the valleys. He loved language. And books. Books were the key to learning, knowledge. They were to be treated with reverence, with care. In pre-revolutionary Russia before the turn of the century even, in the world in which my father grew up, the word was the power. The balladeers, the pamphleteers, the poets, the novelists, the playwrights – those who could read and write held the key to the future. In a world of such devastating illiteracy, they were the truth. They were the word. There is an episode in Maxim Gorky's autobiographical trilogy when, as a child in the dye sweatshop, he witnesses a pamphleteer standing on a table to deliver an oration to those gathered round in awe to listen to this spellbinding wordsmith. My father spoke English with devastating grammatical perfection, as only someone for whom it is not a native language can. And he had the vocabulary to match. Which brings me to the centre of my thesis. Were my father alive today he would be shocked to realise how many of the words that he used in everyday speech are already under threat. With every new edition of the *Concise Oxford Dictionary*, words are removed as no longer in common usage. They are replaced by words like hassle, drag, cool but these hardly compensate. Language must evolve of course. The battle for the survival of English in America is already on. An inexorable wave of Spanish is slowly flooding its way up the North American continent as the Mexicans take back from the Americans by stealth what was taken from them by force. Los Angeles is already 75% Spanish speaking. What will the map look like in a hundred years' time? Already there is legislation against Spanish in some states, the first sign of a beleaguered minority about to dig in and fight a reactive battle against the force of time. What price Shakespeare in fifty to a hundred years? With words dropping yearly out of use, what will be left of our understanding of his plays in centuries to come?

Once upon a time theatre practitioners outnumbered the theorists by a thousand to one. Now it is the other way round. In the future, only a privileged few will have access to the language; an educated élite, treating the plays as literature and not theatre, will hold the secret, mystifying us with their cross-referenced analyses and theories. E'en now, somewhere in Athens, Ohio, or Paris, Texas, someone is publishing a new thesis on an obscure aspect of *Cymbeline*. E'en now the keepers of the nation's culture are closing ranks, binding their ropes round a man whose work, once upon a time, was so completely in the public domain that he did not even bother to collect the plays together and write them down for posterity. That was left to others after his death. The *ad hoc*, improvisatory nature of some of the pieces and passages has spawned a whole industry. An ever-expanding area of argument and controversy as to where the comma 'really' should be. Where in all this is the theatre? How do we stop the plays being swamped by the gelatinous blancmange of academia?

My fear that the language will be lost to all but a fortunate few within the span of my own children's lifetime has led to a desire to give contemporary audiences some kind of folk memory as to what the stories are about. The effect of live performance on the mind is always more deeply etched than any amount of reading of the plays. On the page they are not drama, they are literature. Not until live performance do they become theatre. One of my seminal experiences with Shakespeare (my one memory from my school days that made me think that maybe the old fart had something) was the Burton/Neville season at the Old Vic in 1956. Seen from the back of the gods, the performances were still mesmerising. The memory of their double Othello/Iago so strong that to this day I have not wanted to direct the play. (Unlike the Brook/Scofield *Hamlet* seen at the same time which only seemed to confirm prejudices.) A folk memory, then, that can be handed down through generations. Arrogant, perhaps, but a genuine desire. 'I saw a production of X once and what happens is . . .' Rather like ESC excursions to Norwich, Sunderland, etc. – rehabilitating an old, half-remembered habit of once going to the theatre. 'Oh yes, I used to do that years ago, but that was BC – Before *Cats*.' Even Plymouth, where we launched *The Henrys*, had not had any Shakespeare in the five years since its opening.

Burton and Neville notwithstanding, I was put off Shakespeare at 'A' level. My English teacher was a marvellous Pickwickian figure who read Chaucer to us, as it would have been read aloud in the fourteenth century. (How did he know? – Anyway none of us ever understood a word.) In between dissertations on the walks of Thomas Hardy and trying to scare us with Edgar Allan Poe ghost stories (tricky, with fifteen-year-old schoolboys), he spent one whole term on just one soliloquy of *Hamlet*. Bored the arse off us. I didn't come back to Shakespeare until I was thirty, declaring that never, if I could help it, would I inflict that kind of torture on people in the name of theatre and particularly in the name of Shakespeare. It distressed and angered me beyond belief to discover that, thirty years on, my son was going through the same torture over *Julius Caesar* for 'O' level. I said so in a *Guardian* interview, much to the wrath of the educational establishment concerned.

How do we release this language in a way that is both exciting, modern, comprehensible and – that most detested of words but surely a most important one – relevant? And how, in particular, do we keep hold of a younger audience diminished by the measly provisions of the new Education Act? In an attempt to remove as many barriers as possible between the audience and the language, I had started, in 1976, to direct in modern dress. (Some would say that this creates a new barrier.) I discovered that the language had a new clarity and meaning, and that young people, in particular, suddenly had an interest and a stake in the characters. They were able to understand immediately the complexities involved. It seemed immaterial to me that one was offering a calculator instead of an abacus, a knife for a sword, a dictaphone for a notebook. We are talking convention here. The suspension of disbelief. The contract that exists between storyteller and listener. The stage makes a contract to pretend and the audience contracts to believe that pretence. If either party breaks that contract, then there is trouble (as there was for myself, when certain members of the audience broke the contract during *The Romans in Britain*). You can't *really* cut someone's leg off on stage, it's against the law. The contract that exists therefore in modern-dress Shakespeare is of that same pretence. The plays could just as easily be performed (and often are) in rubber, moonsuits or togas; set in the Crimea, 1930s Germany, desert islands, *à la* Watteau, Hockney, Disneyland. Again, we are talking convention. In all this ('What of all this, my Lord?') the language is paramount. It is through a desire to release the language into meaning that some of us take what others would see as extreme steps. And, of course, the mark is often overstepped. In my first production of *Richard III* at the Phoenix Theatre, Leicester, in 1975, Hastings had an Avon doorbell – Bing Bong! (It seemed in character at the time.) Stanley, phoning Richmond from a call box, ran out of change. The audience hooted with laughter on both occasions. The moments were gratuitous and the suspension of disbelief impossible.

We learn (sometimes). But, in the final analysis, moments like these are unimportant (though the bell was important enough to one critic for him to devote half his review to it). What is important is the meaning of the language. There seems to be a fear, in some circles, of understanding the plays. That if you can understand it, the production is shallow, simplistic. That the more baffling Shakespeare is, the more interpretations that are possible, the more genuine it is. Nonsense, of course. Nobody – actor, director, or designer – sets out to baffle. We set out to communicate. It is our greatest triumph if we are understood. What joy! We are deeply disappointed and wounded if we are not. We often don't succeed but, by God, we try!

We do not set out to offer ten different interpretations. That would be impossible. We try to advance one personal view of a play and hope it is received as such. The muddiness, the bafflement, the lack of clarity come when we are unsure ourselves of what we are saying, and when the team of wild horses, held in both hands, seems to be straining in different directions and threatening to tear the main body apart. So don't be disappointed if you understood it, chaps. It could be that the people presenting the play have analysed, improvised, discussed in detail, investigated every Quarto, Folio, commentator, debated every syllable, line, every possible etymology: Caucasian, Anglo Saxon, Middle-, High-German derivation – and come up with clarity.

Pennington: Kenneth Tynan wrote rather famously of Laurence Olivier that, between 'good' and 'great' acting, there is 'a gulf fixed . . . Olivier pole-vaults over in a single animal leap.' Labouring in the shadow of Tynan's beautiful metaphor, Michael Billington later devoted a painstaking book to defining the 'great' performances he had seen, seeking to distinguish them from the merely very good ones. Measuring the ground and the size of the drop seems to be an important mission among those who evaluate the craft.

The fact is that it is a waste of time. As everybody in the theatre knows, greatness is everybody's province and there really isn't a lot of time to think about it. There is only quality, high quality, even if nobody quite knows what it is. Ralph Richardson once said (imagine his voice) that acting was a puzzle, being one day like watching your ball soaring cleanly down the fairway, and the next day, hah! Nowhere to be seen. One of the difficulties of the job is that you never know how it's going to go; the essence of it runs through your fingers like water. The same Olivier once stormed off the stage at the Old Vic at the end of a show and shut himself into his room, to the great perturbation of his company, not because he had acted badly, but because he knew he had done wonderfully and didn't know why – didn't therefore know how he could, to his own satisfaction, do it again. And when another time he told an interviewer that every performer has to learn not to take his work home with him to worry over, he must have had in mind not only family wear and tear or living with a sense of failure, but also living with a sense of inexplicable success.

So much for greatness. There is such a thing as perfect acting, however, and everyone can do it, from time to time, for a moment at least. I watched a matinée of *Henry IV Part 2* one day at the Old Vic (when John Dougall was playing Prince Hal). Michael Cronin, as Henry IV, was approaching the celebrated speech in which the beleaguered King, plagued by insecurity and insomnia, implores sleep to come. I knew the performance, the scene, the bloody chair and table – would they last till the end of the run? – too well. But I sat up as if I'd been stung. Michael, not to put too fine a point on it, was acting perfectly. He was utterly sick in his body, and letting us know with the most economical of gestures. Fatigue was in the joints of his elbows and the back of his calves. He had certainly forced Richard II out of his rightful seat all those years ago and for a lifetime had battled to stay in it himself; and his eldest son's profligacy was deepening his illness to death. His brain, meanwhile, alert and political, was still racing, overtaking his body in laps, going over the past, assessing his enemies, imagining the future. In all, he had an utter physical and emotional reality. But what about the verse, that formal enemy that has to be aligned to the truth underneath? The famous speech rolls in waves, like surges of fever in insomnia. The first part of the King's appeal for rest tenses and flows across four lines of verse; the second, filling up with metaphor ('smoky cribs . . . buzzing nightflies to his slumber') takes up six lines, and triggers a sustained, fourteen-line thought that makes up the body of the speech, resolving in its famous last line: 'Uneasy lies the head that wears a crown'. The whole thing is not difficult exactly, but it needs watching, and the formal discipline is absolute. In Michael's hands, the elaborated language seemed simply the only way to speak. The verse, far from being an enemy, was absolutely at his service and was, conversely, providing the very heat in which the emotions were blooming into metaphor. I could see the ship-boy high up in the rigging, nodding off in a tempest fit to wake the dead, and Michael's manner was unpremeditated, passionate and direct. I'm glad we did all this, I allowed myself to think, if it's led to such a moment as this. I tried to say this to Michael afterwards, and he seemed at once modest and unsurprised. Lightning strikes occasionally, and you can't go on about these things anyway. But it was perfect Shakespearian, non-'Shakespearian' acting; and Shakespeare being what he is, it made our work utterly worthwhile.

My point is that there's too much talk about the mantle of greatness and, in pursuit of perfection, far too much 'teaching' aimed at a graduation in Shakespearian acting. Who can teach what to who? Although there are matters of technical interest to be shared, in the end this is a Parnassus that everyone can approach with the same back-pack. Shakespeare absolutely belongs to everyone: the Japanese student struggling with the hieroglyphics, the muttering commuter, the professional actor, the club bore, everybody who quotes him without realising it every day. If a new Shakespearian company has any point, its real gift should be to conceal its qualifications and offer the plays in such a way that its audience may feel that it could go home and do it themselves. All of which is fairly hard work. It is a lot easier if one isn't saddled with definitions of who is 'great' and who is not – or a general celebration of the glorious past – great performances, unmatchable productions – that are most interesting but tend to make you feel inferior even if you're not. Everyone is great for a moment; everything is possible and within our range, for in Shakespeare we are trading in an imperishable common coin.

A Shakespearian actor is only one with a big heart, a brain and an open throat: two out of the three will probably do. So there's nothing posh about it. We belong to one of the few professions where the words 'work' and 'play' are synonyms, and the ESC makes no apology for being popular. In some ways our company is based on the principle of fun. A certain mischief brought it about, and a certain cheek sustains us; these are traceable qualities in the work, for all its deadly intentions and serious verse-speaking. Beneath the searching anatomy of England provided by the Histories lay a certain devilry; I hope audiences are still listening to two men eating pastrami sandwiches in a coffee bar near the Arts Council. Cheek and intellect are not a very English combination; we are regarded in some quarters as not quite serious, and the serious commentators tend to ignore us so far. The English theatre is fashion-conscious, both monolithic and fragmented; its comedy unserious and its tragedy pompous too much of the time. Our best work has come out of a rather unEnglish undermining of expectations. If we lose the fun and find ourselves, as for a moment in Melbourne, dourly contemplating the future with a self-important eye, we'll stop. Meanwhile we hope to see you again very soon.

APPENDICES

1

1986–1987

THE HENRYS

KING HENRY IV PART 1

THE KING'S PARTY

King Henry IV	Patrick O'Connell
Henry Prince of Wales, son to the King	Michael Pennington
Thomas Duke of Clarence, son to the King	Martin Clunes
Prince John of Lancaster, son to the King	John Dougall
Humphrey Duke of Gloucester, son to the King	Charles Dale
Duke of Exeter, half-brother to the King	Morris Perry
Earl of Westmoreland	Michael Cronin
Sir Walter Blunt	Roger Booth
Lord Chief Justice	Gareth Thomas

THE REBELS

Henry Percy, Earl of Northumberland	Hugh Sullivan
Thomas Percy, Earl of Worcester, his brother	Donald Gee
Henry Percy, surnamed Hotspur, his son	John Price
Lady Percy, Hotspur's wife, sister to Mortimer	Jennie Stoller
Edmund Mortimer, Earl of March	Charles Dale
Lady Mortimer, his wife, daughter to Glendower	Eluned Hawkins
Owen Glendower	Gareth Thomas
Sir Richard Vernon	Paul Brennen
Travers, servant to Northumberland	Ben Bazell
Earl of Douglas	Andrew Jarvis
Richard Scroop, Archbishop of York	Darryl Forbes-Dawson
Sir Michael, friend to the Archbishop	Clyde Pollitt

THE BOAR'S HEAD TAVERN IN EASTCHEAP

Sir John Falstaff	John Woodvine
Mistress Quickly, hostess of the tavern	June Watson
Doll Tearsheet	Jenny Quayle
Poins	Charles Lawson
Bardolph	Colin Farrell
Gadshill	Andrew Jarvis
Peto	Paul Brennen
Francis, a drawer	John Tramper
A Vintner	Morris Perry

AT ROCHESTER

1st Carrier	Ben Bazell
2nd Carrier	John Dougall
A Chamberlain	Clyde Pollitt

AT GADS HILL

1st Traveller	Darryl Forbes-Dawson
2nd Traveller	John Tramper
3rd Traveller	Eluned Hawkins
4th Traveller	Roger Booth

THE CONSTABULARY

A Sheriff	Martin Clunes

MUSIC: SNEAK'S NOISE

Ben Bazell   *fiddle/mandolin/banjo/whistle/pipes*
Martin Clunes   *bass guitar/mandolin*
Colin Farrell   *trombone/trumpet/bugle/recorder*
Charles Dale   *acoustic guitar*
Terence Hayes   *keyboards*
Andrew Jarvis   *flute/whistle/recorder*
Dominic Peissel   *drums*

KING HENRY IV PART 2

THE KING'S PARTY

King Henry IV	Patrick O'Connell
Henry Prince of Wales, son to the King, afterwards King Henry V	Michael Pennington
Thomas Duke of Clarence, son to the King	Martin Clunes
Prince John of Lancaster, son to the King	John Dougall
Humphrey Duke of Gloucester, son to the King	Charles Dale
Duke of Exeter, half-brother to the King	Morris Perry
Earl of Westmoreland	Michael Cronin
Lord Chief Justice	Gareth Thomas
Harcourt	Andrew Jarvis

THE REBELS

Henry Percy, Earl of Northumberland	Hugh Sullivan
Lady Northumberland, his wife	Eluned Hawkins
Lady Percy, his daughter-in-law, Hotspur's widow	Jennie Stoller
Lord Morton	Donald Gee
Sir Richard Vernon	Paul Brennen
Travers, servant to Northumberland	Ben Bazell
Richard Scroop, Archbishop of York	Darryl Forbes-Dawson
Lord Mowbray	Martin Clunes
Lord Hastings	Roger Booth
Sir John Coleville	Charles Lawson

THE BOAR'S HEAD TAVERN IN EASTCHEAP

Sir John Falstaff	John Woodvine
His Page	John Tramper
Mistress Quickly, hostess of the tavern	June Watson
Doll Tearsheet	Jenny Quayle
Poins	Charles Lawson
Bardolph	Colin Farrell
Pistol	John Price
1st Drawer	John Dougall
2nd Drawer	Ben Bazell

GLOUCESTERSHIRE

Robert Shallow, a country justice	Clyde Pollitt
Silence, the same	Donald Gee
Ralph Mouldy	Charles Dale
Simon Shadow	Paul Brennen
Thomas Wart	John Dougall
Francis Feeble	Darryl Forbes-Dawson
Peter Bullcalf	Martin Clunes
Davy, servant to Shallow	Hugh Sullivan

THE CONSTABULARY

Fang, a sergeant	Ben Bazell
Snare, the same	Charles Dale

MUSIC: SNEAK'S NOISE

Ben Bazell   *fiddle/mandolin/banjo/whistle/pipes*
Martin Clunes   *bass guitar/mandolin*
Colin Farrell   *trombone/trumpet/bugle/recorder*
Charles Dale   *acoustic guitar*
Terence Hayes   *keyboards*
Andrew Jarvis   *flute/whistle/recorder*
Dominic Peissel   *drums*

KING HENRY V

Chorus   John Woodvine

THE CHURCH

Archbishop of Canterbury   Patrick O'Connell
Bishop of Ely   Roger Booth

THE KING'S PARTY

King Henry V   Michael Pennington
Thomas Duke of Clarence,
   brother to the King   Martin Clunes
Prince John of Lancaster,
   brother to the King   John Dougall
Humphrey Duke of Gloucester,
   brother to the King   Charles Dale
Duke of Exeter, uncle to the King   Morris Perry
Earl of Westmoreland   Michael Cronin
Lord Chief Justice   Gareth Thomas

THE REBELS

Lord Scroop   Ben Bazell
Earl of Cambridge   Paul Brennen
Sir Thomas Grey   Charles Lawson

OFFICERS

Fluellen, a Welshman	Gareth Thomas
Macmorris, an Irishman	Charles Lawson
Jamy, a Scotsman	Ben Bazell
Gower, an Englishman	Patrick O'Connell
Sir Thomas Erpingham	Colin Farrell

SOLDIERS

Alexander Court	Paul Brennen
John Bates	Martin Clunes
Michael Williams	Roger Booth

THE BOAR'S HEAD TAVERN IN EASTCHEAP

Hostess, formerly Mistress Quickly, now married to Pistol	June Watson
Pistol	John Price
Bardolph	Colin Farrell
Nym	John Dougall
Boy, formerly Falstaff's page	John Tramper

FRANCE

Charles VI, King of France	Clyde Pollitt
Isabel, Queen of France	June Watson
Lewis, the Dauphin, their son	Andrew Jarvis
Princess Katherine, their daughter	Jenny Quayle
Alice, a lady attending the Princess	Jennie Stoller
Duke of Orleans	Darryl Forbes-Dawson
The Constable of France	Hugh Sullivan
Mountjoy, a herald	Donald Gee
Duke of Burgundy	Colin Farrell
The Governor of Harfleur	Roger Booth
Monsieur le Fer, a soldier	Charles Dale
A Maid	Eluned Hawkins

Directed by	Michael Bogdanov
Assistant Director	Stella Bond

Settings by	Chris Dyer
Costumes by	Stephanie Howard
Lighting by	Chris Ellis
Fights by	Malcolm Ranson
Musical Director	Terry Mortimer
Company Manager	Graham Lister
Stage Manager	Titus Grant
Assistant Stage Manager	Loretta Bircham
Assistant Stage Manager	Terence Hayes
Assistant Stage Manager	Dominic Peissel
Production Carpenter	Andy Chelton
Production Electrician	Clive Down
Assistant Electrician	Sue Yeo
Administrator	Fleur Selby
Tour Manager	David Hall
Production Assistant	Sue Evans
Press and Publicity	Lynne Kirwin, Mary Parker
Touring Publicist	Chris Taylor
Casting Director	Joyce Nettles
Wardrobe Supervisor	Mandi St Clair
Assistant to Supervisor	Jimmy McCarthy
Voice Coach	Patsy Rodenburg
Dialect Coach	Alan Woodhouse
Prop Buyer	Yolanda Jeffrey
Wigs	Joyce Beagarie
Dance by	Geraldine Stephenson
Production photographs	Laurence Burns
Graphics	Richard Bird Associates
Patrons of the ESC	Dame Peggy Ashcroft and Sir John Gielgud
Board of Directors of the ESC	Jules Boardman, Melvyn Bragg, Victor Glynn, Michael Hallifax, Howard Panter, Peter Stevens

THE TOUR

3–15 November 1986	PLYMOUTH Theatre Royal
17–22 November 1986	CARDIFF New Theatre
24–29 November 1986	NORWICH Theatre Royal
1–6 December 1986	NOTTINGHAM Theatre Royal
8–13 December 1986	BATH Theatre Royal
6–17 January 1987	CHICHESTER Festival Theatre
20 January 1987	LUDWIGSHAFEN Theater in Pfalzbau
22 January 1987	COLOGNE Schauspielhaus
25 January 1987	HAMBURG Deutsches Schauspielhaus
28–31 January 1987	PARIS Espace Jacques Prévert
2–7 February 1987	HULL New Theatre
9–14 February 1987	SUNDERLAND Empire Theatre
16–21 February 1987	LEEDS Grand Theatre
23–28 February 1987	OXFORD Apollo Theatre
2–7 March 1987	MANCHESTER Palace Theatre
9–14 March 1987	BIRMINGHAM Hippodrome
16 March–2 May 1987	LONDON The Old Vic
18 May–27 June 1987	TORONTO Royal Alexandra Theatre

HENRY IV Part 1	78 performances
HENRY IV Part 2	78 performances
HENRY V	79 performances

AWARDS

Business Sponsorship Incentive Scheme
Awarded maximum sum (£25,000) payable under the BSIS (for new sponsorship)

Manchester Evening News Theatre Awards
Best Actor: John Woodvine (Falstaff)
Best Visiting Production: *The Henrys*

Drama Magazine Awards
Special Achievement Award to the ESC for contribution to British Theatre

Laurence Olivier Awards
Best Comedy Performance: John Woodvine (Falstaff)

ABSA (Association of Business Sponsorship of the Arts) Award
for Best Single Project awarded to Founder Sponsor, Allied Irish Bank plc, for their sponsorship of *The Henrys* tour

2

1987 – 1988

THE WARS OF THE ROSES

KING RICHARD II

King Richard II	**Michael Pennington**
Isabel, Queen to King Richard	**Eluned Hawkins**
John of Gaunt, Duke of Lancaster, uncle to the King	**Clyde Pollitt**
Henry Bolingbroke, Duke of Hereford, son to John of Gaunt, afterwards King Henry IV	**John Castle**
Duke of York, Edmund Langley, uncle to the King	**Colin Farrell**
Duchess of York	**Lynette Davies**
Duke of Aumerle, son to the Duke of York	**Philip Bowen**
Thomas Mowbray, Duke of Norfolk	**Michael Cronin**
Duchess of Gloucester, widow to Thomas Woodstock, Duke of Gloucester	**June Watson**
Duke of Exeter	**Ian Burford**
Earl of Northumberland, Henry Percy	**Roger Booth**
Hotspur, Harry Percy, son to Northumberland	**Chris Hunter**
Earl of Salisbury, Lord Marshal	**Ian Burford**
Lord Ross	**John Dougall**
Lord Willoughby	**Charles Dale**
Lord Berkeley	**Stephen Jameson**
Lord Fitzwater	**Ben Bazell**
Bishop of Carlisle	**Hugh Sullivan**
Sir John Bushy	**Siôn Probert**
Sir John Bagot	**Paul Brennen**
Sir Henry Greene	**Michael Fenner**
Sir Stephen Scroop	**John Darrell**
Sir Piers of Exton	**Andrew Jarvis**
Servants to Exton	**Terence Hayes** **Stephen Jameson**
A Welsh Captain	**Barry Stanton**
First Herald	**Andrew Jarvis**
Second Herald	**John Darrell**
First Gardener	**Michael Cronin**
Second Gardener	**John Tramper**
Third Gardener	**Philip Rees**
Lady, attendant to Queen Isabel	**Mary Rutherford**
Servingman, to Duke of York	**Stephen Jameson**
Groom, to King Richard's stable	**Clyde Pollitt**
Keeper, of the prison at Pomfret	**John Tramper**

Other parts played by members of the Company

MUSIC

John Darrell *guitar*
Ben Bazell *violin*
Ian Burford *piano*
Andrew Jarvis *flute*

KING HENRY IV PART 1

THE KING'S PARTY

King Henry IV	John Castle
Henry Prince of Wales, son to the King	Michael Pennington
	John Dougall*
Thomas Duke of Clarence, son to the King	Stephen Jameson
John of Lancaster, son to the King	John Dougall
	John Tramper*
Humphrey Duke of Gloucester, son to the King	Charles Dale
Duke of Exeter, half-brother to the King	Ian Burford
Earl of Westmoreland	Michael Cronin
Sir Walter Blunt	Michael Fenner
Lord Chief Justice	Hugh Sullivan

THE REBELS

Earl of Northumberland, Henry Percy	Roger Booth
Earl of Worcester, Thomas Percy, his brother	Philip Bowen
Hotspur, Harry Percy, son to Northumberland	Chris Hunter
Lady Percy, wife to Hotspur, sister to Mortimer	Mary Rutherford
Edmund Mortimer, Earl of March	Stephen Jameson
Lady Mortimer, his wife, daughter to Glendower	Eluned Hawkins
Owen Glendower	Siôn Probert
Sir Richard Vernon	Paul Brennen
Travers, servant to Northumberland	Ben Bazell
Earl of Douglas	Andrew Jarvis
Richard Scroop, Archbishop of York	John Darrell
Sir Michael, friend to the Archbishop	Clyde Pollitt

THE BOAR'S HEAD TAVERN IN EASTCHEAP

Sir John Falstaff	**Barry Stanton**
Mistress Quickly, hostess of the tavern	**June Watson**
Doll Tearsheet	**Lynette Davies**
Poins	**Charles Dale**
Bardolph	**Colin Farrell**
Gads hill	**Andrew Jarvis**
Peto	**Paul Brennen**
Francis, a drawer	**John Tramper**
A Vintner	**Ian Burford**

AT ROCHESTER

First Carrier	**Ben Bazell**
Second Carrier	**John Dougall**
	Simon Elliott*
A Chamberlain	**Clyde Pollitt**

AT GADS HILL

First Traveller	**John Darrell**
Second Traveller	**John Tramper**
Third Traveller	**Eluned Hawkins**
Fourth Traveller	**Roger Booth**

Other parts played by members of the Company

MUSIC: SNEAK'S NOISE

Ben Bazell   *fiddle/mandolin/banjo/whistle/pipes*
Charles Dale   *guitar*
John Darrell   *guitar/mandolin*
Colin Farrell   *trombone/trumpet/bugle/recorder*
Terence Hayes   *keyboards*
Chris Hunter   *guitar/trumpet*
Andrew Jarvis   *flute/whistle/recorder*

* *Chichester, 10 Feb 88; Nottingham 24 Feb 88.*

KING HENRY IV PART 2

THE KING'S PARTY

King Henry IV	John Castle
Henry Prince of Wales, son to the King, afterwards King Henry V	Michael Pennington
	John Dougall*
Thomas Duke of Clarence, son to the King	Stephen Jameson
Prince John of Lancaster, son to the King	John Dougall
	John Tramper*
Humphrey Duke of Gloucester, son to the King	Charles Dale
Duke of Exeter, half-brother to the King	Ian Burford
Earl of Westmoreland	Michael Cronin
Lord Chief Justice	Hugh Sullivan
Harcourt	Andrew Jarvis

THE REBELS

Earl of Northumberland, Henry Percy	Roger Booth
Lady Northumberland, his wife	Eluned Hawkins
Lady Percy, his daughter-in-law, Hotspur's widow	Mary Rutherford
Lord Morton	Siôn Probert
Sir Richard Vernon	Paul Brennen
Travers, servant to Northumberland	Ben Bazell
Richard Scroop, Archbishop of York	John Darrell
Lord Mowbray	Chris Hunter
Lord Hastings	Michael Fenner
Sir John Coleville	Siôn Probert

THE BOAR'S HEAD TAVERN IN EASTCHEAP

Sir John Falstaff	Barry Stanton
His Page	John Tramper
	Simon Elliott*
Mistress Quickly, hostess of the tavern	June Watson
Doll Tearsheet	Lynette Davies
Poins	Charles Dale
Bardolph	Colin Farrell
Pistol	John Castle

First Drawer   John Dougall
                                                       Simon Elliott*
Second Drawer   Ben Bazell

GLOUCESTERSHIRE

Robert Shallow, a country Justice   Clyde Pollitt
Silence, the same   Philip Bowen
Ralph Mouldy   Michael Fenner
Simon Shadow   Paul Brennen
Thomas Wart   John Dougall
Francis Feeble   John Darrell
Peter Bullcalf   Chris Hunter
Davy, servant to Shallow   Roger Booth

THE CONSTABULARY

Fang, a sergeant   Ben Bazell
Snare, the same   Stephen Jameson

Other parts played by members of the Company

MUSIC: SNEAK'S NOISE

Ben Bazell   *fiddle/mandolin/banjo/whistle/pipes*
Charles Dale   *guitar*
John Darrell   *guitar/mandolin*
Colin Farrell   *trombone/trumpet/bugle/recorder*
Terence Hayes   *keyboards*
Chris Hunter   *guitar/trumpet*
Andrew Jarvis   *flute/whistle/recorder*

* *Chichester, 11 Feb 88; Nottingham, 25 Feb 88.*

KING HENRY V

Chorus   Barry Stanton

THE CHURCH

Archbishop of Canterbury   Hugh Sullivan
Bishop of Ely   Roger Booth

THE KING'S PARTY

King Henry V	Michael Pennington
	John Dougall*
Thomas Duke of Clarence, brother to the King	Stephen Jameson
Prince John of Lancaster, brother to the King	John Dougall
	John Tramper*
Humphrey Duke of Gloucester, brother to the King	Charles Dale
Duke of Exeter, uncle to the King	Ian Burford
Earl of Westmoreland	Michael Cronin

THE REBELS

Lord Scroop of Masham	Ben Bazell
Earl of Cambridge	Paul Brennen
Sir Thomas Grey	John Darrell

OFFICERS

Fluellen, a Welshman	Siôn Probert
Macmorris, an Irishman	Michael Cronin
Jamy, a Scotsman	Ben Bazell
Gower, an Englishman	Michael Fenner
Sir Thomas Erpingham	Colin Farrell

SOLDIERS

Alexander Court	Paul Brennen
John Bates	Stephen Jameson
Michael Williams	Roger Booth

THE BOAR'S HEAD TAVERN IN EASTCHEAP

Hostess, formerly Mistress Quickly, now married to Pistol	June Watson
Pistol	John Castle
Bardolph	Colin Farrell
Nym	John Dougall
	Stephen Jameson*
Boy, formerly Falstaff's page	John Tramper

FRANCE

Charles VI, King of France	Clyde Pollitt
Isabel, Queen of France	June Watson
Lewis, the Dauphin, their son	Andrew Jarvis
Princess Katherine, their daughter	Mary Rutherford
Alice, a lady attending the Princess	Lynette Davies
Duke of Orleans	Chris Hunter
The Constable of France	Hugh Sullivan
Mountjoy, a herald	Philip Bowen
Duke of Burgundy,	Barry Stanton
The Governor of Harfleur	Roger Booth
Monsieur le Fer, a soldier	Charles Dale
A Maid	Eluned Hawkins

Other parts played by members of the Company

MUSIC

Ben Bazell *guitar*
Colin Farrell *trombone*

* *Chichester, 12 Feb 88; Nottingham, 26 Feb 88.*

KING HENRY VI HOUSE OF LANCASTER

FOR THE HOUSE OF LANCASTER

King Henry VI	Paul Brennen
Humphrey Duke of Gloucester, Protector of the Realm, uncle to the King	Colin Farrell
Duchess of Gloucester, his wife	Lynette Davies
John of Lancaster, Regent of France, uncle to the King	John Dougall
Bishop of Winchester, Henry Beaufort, great-uncle to the King	Clyde Pollitt
Thomas Duke of Exeter, great uncle to the King	Ian Burford

Duke of Somerset, John Beaufort	Siôn Probert
Earl of Suffolk, William de la Pole	Chris Hunter
Lord Talbot, leader in the campaign against the French	Michael Fenner
John Talbot, his son	John Tramper
Sir William Lucy	John Darrell
Bassett	Stephen Jameson

FOR THE HOUSE OF YORK

Richard Plantagenet, afterwards Duke of York	John Castle
Edmund Mortimer, Earl of March	Michael Pennington
Richard Neville, Earl of Warwick	Michael Cronin
Vernon	Charles Dale

THE FRENCH

Charles the Dauphin, afterwards King Charles VII of France	Andrew Jarvis
Reignier, Duke of Anjou	Hugh Sullivan
Margaret, daughter to Reignier, afterwards married to King Henry	June Watson
Duke of Burgundy	Barry Stanton
Duke of Alençon	Ben Bazell
Mountjoy	Philip Bowen
Joan la Pucelle, commonly called Joan of Arc	Mary Rutherford

THE PEOPLE

A Lawyer	Roger Booth
Mortimer's Keeper	John Tramper
Sir John Hum, a Priest	John Dougall
John Southwell, a Priest	Ben Bazell
Margery Jourdain, a witch	Mary Rutherford
Roger Bolingbroke, a conjuror	Barry Stanton
Saunder Simpcox	Roger Booth
Mrs Simpcox	Eluned Hawkins

Other parts played by members of the Company

MUSIC

Ben Bazell   *fiddle/mandolin/banjo/whistle/pipes*
Charles Dale   *guitar*

John Darrell   *guitar/mandolin*
Colin Farrell   *trombone/trumpet/bugle/recorder*
Terence Hayes   *keyboards*
Chris Hunter   *guitar/trumpet*
Andrew Jarvis   *flute/whistle/recorder*

KING HENRY VI HOUSE OF YORK

FOR THE HOUSE OF YORK

Richard Plantagenet, Duke of York	John Castle
Edward Earl of March, son to the Duke of York, afterwards King Edward IV	Philip Bowen
George, son to the Duke of York, afterwards Duke of Clarence	John Dougall
Richard, son to the Duke of York, afterwards Duke of Gloucester	Andrew Jarvis
Edmund, Earl of Rutland, son to the Duke of York	Stephen Jameson
Duke of Norfolk, John Mowbray	Ben Bazell
Earl of Warwick, Richard Neville	Michael Cronin
Lady Grey, a widow, afterwards Queen Elizabeth	Lynette Davies
Lord Rivers, Anthony Woodville, her brother	John Darrell
William Lord Hastings	Roger Booth
Sir Robert Brackenbury, Lieutenant of the Tower	Colin Farrell
Tutor, to Rutland	John Darrell

FOR THE HOUSE OF LANCASTER

King Henry VI	Paul Brennen
Queen Margaret	June Watson
Edward, Prince of Wales, their son	John Tramper
John Beaufort, Duke of Somerset	Siôn Probert
Lord Clifford	Ian Burford
Young Clifford, his son	Charles Dale
Earl of Hereford	Hugh Sullivan
John de Vere, Earl of Oxford	Michael Fenner
Sir Humphrey Stafford	John Darrell

William Stafford, his brother	Ben Bazell
Lord Say	Clyde Pollitt
Richmond, as a boy	played by local children
Alexander Iden, a Kentish Gentleman	Roger Booth

THE REBELS

Jack Cade	Michael Pennington
Dick the Butcher	Barry Stanton
Smith the Weaver	Chris Hunter
Michael	Stephen Jameson

THE PEOPLE

Clerk of Chatham	Colin Farrell
A Son, that has killed his father	Chris Hunter
A Father, that has killed his son	Roger Booth
First Keeper	Siôn Probert
Second Keeper	John Darrell
First Watchman	Clyde Pollitt
Second Watchman	Stephen Jameson

THE FRENCH

Lewis XI, King of France	Ian Burford
Lady Bona, his sister-in-law	Eluned Hawkins

Other parts played by members of the Company

MUSIC

Ben Bazell   *clarinet*
Ian Burford   *piano*
Michael Cronin   *clarinet*
Charles Dale   *guitar*
John Darrell   *bass guitar*
Colin Farrell   *trombone*
Chris Hunter   *trumpet*
Terence Hayes   *synthesizer*

KING RICHARD III

THE HOUSE OF YORK

Duchess of York, widow to Duke of York	**Eluned Hawkins**
King Edward IV, her son	**Philip Bowen**
Duke of Clarence, the King's brother	**John Dougall**
Richard, Duke of Gloucester, the King's brother, later King Richard III	**Andrew Jarvis**
Prince Edward, Prince of Wales, elder son of King Edward IV	**played by local children**
Richard Duke of York, younger son of Edward IV	**played by local children**

THE HOUSE OF LANCASTER

Queen Margaret, widow of King Henry VI	**June Watson**
Lady Anne, widow of Henry VI's son Edward, afterwards Queen to Richard III	**Mary Rutherford**
Ghost of King Henry VI	**Paul Brennen**
Ghost of Edward, his son	**John Tramper**

THE WOODVILLES

Queen Elizabeth, wife to King Edward IV	**Lynette Davies**
Lord Rivers, brother to Queen Elizabeth	**John Darrell**
Lord Grey, son to Queen Elizabeth by her first marriage	**Ben Bazell**
Marquess of Dorset, son to Queen Elizabeth by her first marriage	**John Tramper**

CHURCH AND STATE

Lord Cardinal Bourchier, Archbishop of Canterbury	**Clyde Pollitt**
John Morton, Bishop of Ely	**Ian Burford**
Lord Hastings, the Lord Chamberlain	**Roger Booth**
Duke of Buckingham	**Michael Pennington**
Lord Stanley, Earl of Derby	**Michael Cronin**
Lord Mayor of London	**Hugh Sullivan**
Sir Robert Brackenbury, Lieutenant of the Tower	**Colin Farrell**

FOLLOWERS OF RICHARD

Duke of Norfolk	**Ron Donell**

Sir William Catesby	**Siôn Probert**
Sir Richard Ratcliffe	**Chris Hunter**
Sir James Tyrrel	**John Castle**
First Murderer	**Michael Fenner**
Second Murderer	**Barry Stanton**

THE PEOPLE

Tressel	**Charles Dale**
Berkeley	**Hugh Sullivan**
First Citizen	**Paul Brennen**
Second Citizen	**Stephen Jameson**
Third Citizen	**Clyde Pollitt**

THE TUDORS

Henry Earl of Richmond, afterwards King Henry VII	**Charles Dale**
Sir James Blunt	**Colin Farrell**
Earl of Oxford, John de Vere	**Michael Fenner**

Other parts played by members of the Company

MUSIC

Ian Burford *piano*
Colin Farrell *trombone*
Michael Cronin *clarinet*
Andrew Jarvis *flute*

Director	**Michael Bogdanov**
Assistant Directors	Susanna Best, Stella Bond
Original Settings	Chris Dyer
Costumes	Stephanie Howard
Lighting	Mark Henderson
Fights by	Malcolm Ranson
Composer and Musical Director	Terry Mortimer
Fight Captain	Charles Dale
Company Manager	Monica McCabe
Stage Manager	Derek Scriminger

Deputy Stage Manager	Loretta Bircham
Production Assistant	Titus Grant
Acting/Assistant Stage Manager	Simon Elliott
Acting/Assistant Stage Manager	Terence Hayes
Acting/Assistant Stage Manager	Philip Rees
Production Management	Simon Opie and Ted Irwin for Production Management Associates
Additional design by	Colin Peters
Assistant Costume Designer	Tahra Kharibian
Wardrobe Supervisor (production period)	Christine Rowland
Deputy Wardrobe Supervisor (production period)	Lynn Clarke
Wardrobe Supervisor (for the tour)	Petra Bradley
Deputy Wardrobe Supervisor (for the tour)	Annette Heron
Wardrobe/Wig Assistant	Jimmy McCarthy
Wigs	Linda Coolie
Voice Coach	Patsy Rodenburg
Chief Electrician	Andy Grant
Assistant Electrician	Adam Daly
Master Carpenter	Andy Chelton
Properties Supervisor	Rosy Fowler
Chief Sound Technician	Brian Beasley
Technician	David Ogilvy
Production photographs	Laurence Burns
Graphics	Iain Lanyon
Executive Producer	Prudence Skene
General Manager	Kirsten Oploh
Administrative Assistant	Sue Evans
Publicity Officer	Janet Morrow
Accountant	Lynne Ash
Board of Directors	David Kay (Chairman), Melvyn Bragg, Jennie Bland, Patrick Dromgoole, Victor Glynn, Michael Hallifax
ESC Associate	John Winslow

THE TOUR

8 – 19 December 1987	BATH Theatre Royal
11 – 23 January 1988	HONG KONG Centre for the Arts (Hong Kong Arts Festival)
29 January – 13 February 1988	CHICHESTER Festival Theatre
16 – 27 February 1988	NOTTINGHAM Theatre Royal
1 – 5 March 1988	HULL New Theatre
8 – 12 March 1988	BIRMINGHAM Hippodrome
15 – 19 March 1988	MANCHESTER Palace Theatre
22 – 26 March 1988	GLASGOW Theatre Royal
8 – 28 April 1988	TOKYO Globe Theatre
3 – 28 May 1988	CHICAGO The Auditorium (International Theater Festival)
2 – 5 June 1988	CONNECTICUT Stamford Center for the Arts
16 – 19 June 1988	YORK Theatre Royal (York Festival)
1 – 3 July 1988	WEST BERLIN Schillertheater (Cultural City of Europe 1988)

RICHARD II	41 performances
HENRY IV Part 1	27 performances
HENRY IV Part 2	24 performances
HENRY V	26 performances
HENRY VI House of Lancaster	22 performances
HENRY VI House of York	22 performances
RICHARD III	44 performances

AWARDS

Business Sponsorship Incentive Scheme
Awarded maximum sum (£25,000) payable under the BSIS (for
increased sponsorship)

Manchester Evening News Theatre Awards
Best Actor: Andrew Jarvis (Richard III)

*Chicago Tribune's Awards for Outstanding Productions of the
Decade*
The Wars of the Roses

3

1988–1989

THE WARS OF THE ROSES

KING RICHARD II

King Richard II	Michael Pennington
Isabel, Queen to King Richard	Francesca Ryan
John of Gaunt, Duke of Lancaster, uncle to the King	Clyde Pollitt
Henry Bolingbroke, Duke of Hereford, son to John of Gaunt, afterwards King Henry IV	Michael Cronin
Duke of York, Edmund Langley, uncle to the King	Colin Farrell
Duchess of York	Ann Penfold
Duke of Aumerle, son to the Duke of York	Philip Bowen
Thomas Mowbray, Duke of Norfolk	Jack Carr
Duchess of Gloucester, widow to Thomas Woodstock, Duke of Gloucester	June Watson
Duke of Exeter	Ian Burford
Earl of Northumberland, Henry Percy	Roger Booth
Hotspur, Harry Percy, son to Northumberland	Andrew Jarvis
Earl of Salisbury, Lord Marshal	Ian Burford
Lord Ross	John Dougall
Lord Willoughby	Charles Dale
Lord Berkeley	Stephen Jameson
Earl of Westmoreland	Ben Bazell
Bishop of Carlisle	Hugh Sullivan
Sir John Bushy	Siôn Probert
Sir John Bagot	Paul Brennen
Sir Henry Greene	Michael Fenner
Sir Stephen Scroop	John Darrell
Sir Piers of Exton	Jack Carr
Servants to Exton	Simon Elliott
	Stephen Jameson
Welsh Captain	Barry Stanton
First Herald	Andrew Jarvis
Second Herald	John Darrell
First Gardener	Stephen Jameson
Second Gardener	John Tramper
Third Gardener	Philip Rees
Lady, attendant to Queen Isabel	Jenifer Konko
Servingman, to Duke of York	Philip Rees
Groom, to King Richard's stable	Clyde Pollitt
Keeper, of the prison at Pomfret	John Tramper

Other parts played by members of the Company

MUSIC

John Darrell   *guitar*
Ben Bazell   *violin/clarinet*
Ian Burford   *keyboards*
Andrew Jarvis   *flute*

KING HENRY IV PART 1

THE KING'S PARTY

King Henry IV	Michael Cronin
Henry Prince of Wales, son to the King	Michael Pennington
	John Dougall*
Thomas Duke of Clarence, son to the King	Stephen Jameson
Prince John of Lancaster, son to the King	John Dougall
	Robert Hands*
Humphrey Duke of Gloucester, son to the King	Charles Dale
Duke of Exeter, half-brother to the King	Ian Burford
Earl of Westmoreland	Ben Bazell
Sir Walter Blunt	Michael Fenner
Lord Chief Justice	Hugh Sullivan

THE REBELS

Earl of Northumberland, Henry Percy	Roger Booth
Earl of Worcester, Thomas Percy, his brother	Philip Bowen
Hotspur, Harry Percy, son to Northumberland	Andrew Jarvis
Lady Percy, wife to Hotspur, sister to Mortimer	Ann Penfold
Edmund Mortimer, Earl of March	Stephen Jameson
Lady Mortimer, his wife, daughter to Glendower	Jenifer Konko
Owen Glendower	Siôn Probert
Sir Richard Vernon	Paul Brennen
Travers, servant to Northumberland	Simon Elliott
Earl of Douglas	Charles Dale
Richard Scroop, Archbishop of York	John Darrell
Sir Michael, friend to the Archbishop	Clyde Pollitt

THE BOAR'S HEAD TAVERN IN EASTCHEAP

Sir John Falstaff	**Barry Stanton**
Mistress Quickly, hostess of the tavern	**June Watson**
Doll Tearsheet	**Francesca Ryan**
Poins	**Charles Dale**
Bardolph	**Colin Farrell**
Gadshill	**Andrew Jarvis**
Peto	**Paul Brennen**
Francis, a drawer	**John Tramper**
A Vintner	**Ian Burford**

AT ROCHESTER

First Carrier	**Ben Bazell**
Second Carrier	**John Dougall**
	Simon Elliott*
Chamberlain	**Clyde Pollitt**

AT GADS HILL

First Traveller	**John Darrell**
Second Traveller	**John Tramper**
Third Traveller	**Jenifer Konko**
Fourth Traveller	**Roger Booth**

Other parts played by members of the Company

MUSIC: SNEAK'S NOISE

Ben Bazell   *mandolin/mandola*
Ian Burford   *keyboards*
Charles Dale   *guitar*
John Darrell   *bass guitar/harmonica*
Simon Elliott   *guitar*
Colin Farrell   *trombone/trumpet/bugle/accordion*
Andrew Jarvis   *flute/whistle/recorder*
Francesca Ryan   *saxophone/whistle*

---

* *Melbourne, 8 Sep 88; Newcastle, 19 Oct 88; Cardiff, 16 Nov 88; Leeds, 22 Nov 88; Liverpool, 29 Nov 88; Plymouth, 7 Dec 88; Old Vic, 28 Jan 89, 30 Jan 89, 4 Mar 89; Eastbourne, 15 Mar 89; Norwich, 22 Mar 89; Southampton, 29 Mar 89.*

KING HENRY IV PART 2

THE KING'S PARTY

King Henry IV	Michael Cronin
Henry Prince of Wales, son to the King,	
afterwards King Henry V	Michael Pennington
	John Dougall*
Thomas Duke of Clarence, son to the King	Stephen Jameson
Prince John of Lancaster, son to the King	John Dougall
	Robert Hands*
Humphrey Duke of Gloucester, son to the King	Charles Dale
Duke of Exeter, half-brother to the King	Ian Burford
Earl of Westmoreland	Ben Bazell
Lord Chief Justice	Hugh Sullivan
Harcourt	Andrew Jarvis

THE REBELS

Earl of Northumberland, Henry Percy	Roger Booth
Lady Northumberland, his wife	Susanna Best
Lady Percy, his daughter-in-law,	
Hotspur's widow	Ann Penfold
Lord Morton	Siôn Probert
Sir Richard Vernon	Paul Brennen
Travers, servant to Northumberland	Simon Elliott
Richard Scroop, Archbishop of York	John Darrell
Lord Mowbray	Michael Fenner
Lord Hastings	Jack Carr
Sir John Coleville	Philip Rees

THE BOAR'S HEAD TAVERN IN EASTCHEAP

Sir John Falstaff	Barry Stanton
His Page	John Tramper
Mistress Quickly, hostess of the tavern	June Watson
Doll Tearsheet	Francesca Ryan
Poins	Charles Dale
Bardolph	Colin Farrell
Pistol	Paul Brennen
First Drawer	Stephen Jameson
Second Drawer	Simon Elliott
Third Drawer	Ben Bazell

GLOUCESTERSHIRE

Robert Shallow, a country Justice	Clyde Pollitt
Silence, the same	Philip Bowen
Ralph Mouldy	Jack Carr
Simon Shadow	Simon Elliott
Thomas Wart	John Dougall
Francis Feeble	John Darrell
Peter Bullcalf	Michael Fenner
Davy, servant to Shallow	Roger Booth

THE CONSTABULARY

Fang, a sergeant	Ben Bazell
Snare, the same	Stephen Jameson

Other parts played by members of the Company

MUSIC
Robert Hands   *recorder*

SNEAK'S NOISE
Ben Bazell   *mandola*
John Darrell   *guitar/mandolin*
Simon Elliott   *guitar*
Colin Farrell   *trombone/trumpet/bugle*
Andrew Jarvis   *flute/whistle/recorder*

* *Melbourne, 8 Sep 88; Newcastle, 20 Oct 88; Cardiff, 17 Nov 88; Leeds,
23 Nov 88; Liverpool, 30 Nov 88; Plymouth, 8 Dec 88; Old Vic, 31 Jan
89, 1 Feb 89, 4 Mar 89; Eastbourne, 16 Mar 89; Norwich, 23 Mar 89;
Southampton, 30 Mar 89.*

KING HENRY V

Chorus	**Barry Stanton**

THE CHURCH

Archbishop of Canterbury	**Hugh Sullivan**
Bishop of Ely	**Roger Booth**

THE KING'S PARTY

King Henry V	Michael Pennington
	John Dougall*
Thomas Duke of Clarence, brother to the King	Stephen Jameson
Prince John of Lancaster, brother to the King	Robert Hands
Humphrey Duke of Gloucester, brother to the King	Charles Dale
Duke of Exeter, uncle to the King	Ian Burford
Earl of Westmoreland	Ben Bazell

THE REBELS

Lord Scroop of Masham	Jack Carr
Earl of Cambridge	John Darrell
Sir Thomas Grey	Philip Rees

OFFICERS

Fluellen, a Welshman	Siôn Probert
Macmorris, an Irishman	Michael Cronin
Jamy, a Scotsman	Ben Bazell
Gower, an Englishman	Michael Fenner
Sir Thomas Erpingham	Colin Farrell

SOLDIERS

Alexander Court	Simon Elliott
John Bates	Stephen Jameson
Michael Williams	Roger Booth

THE BOAR'S HEAD TAVERN IN EASTCHEAP

Hostess, formerly Mistress Quickly, now married to Pistol	June Watson
Pistol	Paul Brennen
Bardolph	Colin Farrell
Nym	John Dougall
	Stephen Jameson*
Boy, formerly Falstaff's page	John Tramper

FRANCE

Charles VI, King of France	Clyde Pollitt
Isabel, Queen of France	June Watson
Lewis, the Dauphin, their son	Andrew Jarvis
Princess Katherine, their daugher	Francesca Ryan
Alice, a lady attending the Princess	Ann Penfold
Duke of Orleans	John Darrell
Constable of France	Hugh Sullivan
Mountjoy, a herald	Philip Bowen
Duke of Burgundy	Jack Carr
Governor of Harfleur	Roger Booth
Monsieur le Fer, a soldier	Charles Dale
Maid	Jenifer Konko

Other parts played by members of the Company

MUSIC

Ben Bazell *guitar*
Colin Farrell *trombone*

* *Melbourne, 9 Sep 88; Newcastle, 21 Oct 88; Cardiff, 18 Nov 88; Leeds, 24 Nov 88; Liverpool, 31 Nov 88; Plymouth, 9 Dec 88; Old Vic, 2 Feb 89, 3 Feb 89, 4 Mar 89; Eastbourne, 17 Mar 89; Norwich, 24 Mar 89; Southampton, 31 Mar 89.*

KING HENRY VI HOUSE OF LANCASTER

FOR THE HOUSE OF LANCASTER

King Henry VI	Paul Brennen
Humphrey Duke of Gloucester, Protector of the Realm, uncle to the King	Colin Farrell
Duchess of Gloucester, his wife	Ann Penfold
Duke of Bedford, Regent of France, uncle to the King	John Dougall
Bishop of Winchester, Henry Beaufort, great uncle to the King	Clyde Pollitt
Thomas Duke of Exeter, great uncle to the King	Ian Burford
Duke of Somerset, John Beaufort	Siôn Probert
Earl of Suffolk, William de la Pole	Michael Pennington

Sir Humphrey Stafford	John Darrell
Earl of Hereford	Hugh Sullivan
Lord Talbot, leader in the campaign against the French	Michael Fenner
John Talbot, his son	John Tramper
Sir William Lucy	John Darrell
Bassett	Robert Hands
Sir John Stanley	Philip Rees

FOR THE HOUSE OF YORK

Richard Plantagenet, afterwards Duke of York	Barry Stanton
Edmund Mortimer, Earl of March	Stephen Jameson
Richard Neville, Earl of Warwick	Michael Cronin
Vernon	Charles Dale

THE FRENCH

Charles the Dauphin, afterwards King Charles VII of France	Andrew Jarvis
Reignier, Duke of Anjou	Hugh Sullivan
Margaret, daughter to Reignier, afterwards married to King Henry	June Watson
Duke of Burgundy	Jack Carr
Duke of Alençon	Ben Bazell
Mountjoy	Philip Bowen
Joan la Pucelle, commonly called Joan of Arc	Francesca Ryan

THE PEOPLE

Lawyer	Roger Booth
Mortimer's Keeper	John Tramper
Sir John Hum, a Priest	John Dougall
John Southwell, a Priest	Ben Bazell
Margery Jourdain, a witch	Francesca Ryan
Roger Bolingbroke, a conjuror	Jack Carr
Saunder Simpcox	Roger Booth
Mrs Simpcox	Jenifer Konko

Other parts played by members of the Company

MUSIC
Simon Elliott *button accordion*

KING HENRY VI HOUSE OF YORK

FOR THE HOUSE OF YORK

Richard Plantagenet, Duke of York	Barry Stanton
Edward Earl of March, son to the Duke of York, afterwards King Edward IV	Philip Bowen
George, son to the Duke of York, afterwards Duke of Clarence	John Dougall
Richard, son to the Duke of York, afterwards Duke of Gloucester	Andrew Jarvis
Edmund, Earl of Rutland, son to the Duke of York	Stephen Jameson
Duke of Norfolk, John Mowbray	Ben Bazell
Earl of Warwick, Richard Neville	Michael Cronin
Lady Grey, a widow, afterwards Queen Elizabeth	Ann Penfold
Lord Rivers, Anthony Woodville, her brother	John Darrell
William Lord Hastings	Roger Booth
Sir Robert Brackenbury, Lieutenant of the Tower	Colin Farrell
Tutor, to Rutland	John Darrell

FOR THE HOUSE OF LANCASTER

King Henry VI	Paul Brennen
Queen Margaret	June Watson
Edward, Prince of Wales, their son	John Tramper
John Beaufort, Duke of Somerset	Siôn Probert
Lord Clifford	Ian Burford
Young Clifford, his son	Charles Dale
Earl of Hereford	Hugh Sullivan
John de Vere, Earl of Oxford	Michael Fenner
Sir Humphrey Stafford	John Darrell
William Stafford, his brother	Ben Bazell
Lord Say	Clyde Pollitt
Richmond, as a boy	played by local children
Alexander Iden, a Kentish Gentleman	Roger Booth

THE REBELS

Jack Cade	Michael Pennington
Dick the Butcher	Jack Carr

Smith the Weaver	Stephen Jameson
Michael	Robert Hands

THE PEOPLE

Clerk of Chatham	Colin Farrell
A Son, that has killed his father	Stephen Jameson
A Father, that has killed his son	Roger Booth
First Keeper	Siôn Probert
Second Keeper	John Darrell
First Watchman	Clyde Pollitt
Second Watchman	Stephen Jameson

THE FRENCH

Lewis XI, King of France	Ian Burford
Lady Bona, his sister-in-law	Jenifer Konko

Other parts played by members of the Company

MUSIC

Ben Bazell *saxophone*
Ian Burford *piano*
Michael Cronin *clarinet*
Charles Dale *guitar*
Simon Elliott *keyboards*
Colin Farrell *trombone*
Francesca Ryan *saxophone*

KING RICHARD III

Prologue	Barry Stanton

THE HOUSE OF YORK

Duchess of York, widow to Duke of York	Susanna Best
King Edward IV, her son	Philip Bowen
Duke of Clarence, the King's brother	John Dougall
Richard, Duke of Gloucester, the King's brother, later King Richard III	Andrew Jarvis

Prince Edward, Prince of Wales, elder
   son of King Edward IV   **played by local children**
Richard Duke of York, younger
   son of Edward IV   **played by local children**

THE HOUSE OF LANCASTER

Queen Margaret, widow of King Henry VI   **June Watson**
Lady Anne, widow of Henry VI's son Edward,
   afterwards Queen to Richard III   **Francesca Ryan**
Ghost of King Henry VI   **Paul Brennen**
Ghost of Edward, his son   **John Tramper**

THE WOODVILLES

Queen Elizabeth, wife to King Edward IV   **Ann Penfold**
Lord Rivers, brother to Queen Elizabeth   **John Darrell**
Lord Grey, son to Queen Elizabeth by her
   first marriage   **Ben Bazell**
Marquess of Dorset, son to Queen Elizabeth
   by her first marriage   **John Tramper**

CHURCH AND STATE

Lord Cardinal Bourchier, Archbishop of
   Canterbury   **Clyde Pollitt**
John Morton, Bishop of Ely   **Ian Burford**
Lord Hastings, the Lord Chamberlain   **Roger Booth**
Duke of Buckingham   **Michael Pennington**
Lord Stanley, Earl of Derby   **Michael Cronin**
Lord Mayor of London   **Hugh Sullivan**
Sir Robert Brackenbury, Lieutenant of the Tower   **Colin Farrell**

FOLLOWERS OF RICHARD

Duke of Norfolk   **Ben Bazell**
Sir William Catesby   **Siôn Probert**
Sir Richard Ratcliffe   **Stephen Jameson**
Sir James Tyrrel   **Jack Carr**
First Murderer   **Michael Fenner**
Second Murderer   **Barry Stanton**

THE PEOPLE

Tressel	Hugh Sullivan
Berkeley	Philip Rees
First Citizen	Paul Brennen
Second Citizen	Stephen Jameson
Third Citizen	Clyde Pollitt

THE TUDORS

Henry Earl of Richmond, afterwards King Henry VII	Charles Dale
Sir James Blunt	Colin Farrell
Earl of Oxford, John de Vere	Michael Fenner

Other parts played by members of the Company

MUSIC

Ben Bazell   *saxophone*
Ian Burford   *piano*
Michael Cronin   *clarinet*
John Darrell   *bass guitar*
Colin Farrell   *trombone*
Andrew Jarvis   *flute*

Director	**Michael Bogdanov**
Assistant Directors	Susanna Best, Stella Bond
Original Settings	Chris Dyer
Original Costumes	Stephanie Howard
Lighting	Mark Henderson
Fights by	Malcolm Ranson
Composer and Musical Director	Terry Mortimer
Fight Captain	Charles Dale
Company Manager	Monica McCabe
Stage Manager	Derek Scriminger
Deputy Stage Manager	Niki Lawrence
Deputy Stage Manager	Joanna Reid
Assistant Stage Manager	Malachi Bogdanov

Acting/Assistant Stage Manager	Simon Elliott
Acting/Assistant Stage Manager	Philip Rees

Production Management	Simon Opie and Ted Irwin for Production Management Associates
Additional design by	Colin Peters
Assistant Costume Designer	Tahra Kharibian
Voice Coach	Patsy Rodenburg
Chief Electrician	Andy Grant
Assistant Electrician	Edward Moore
Chief Sound Technician and Sound Design	Brian Beasley
Wardrobe Supervisor	Annette Heron
Deputy Wardrobe Supervisor	Joanne Pearce
Wig Master/Wardrobe Assistant	Jimmy McCarthy
Technical Touring Manager	Andy Chelton
Properties Supervisor	Ian Shillito
Production photographs	Laurence Burns
Programme design	Sightlines

Executive Producer	Prudence Skene
General Manager	Kirsten Oploh
Administrative Assistant	Sue Evans
Press and Marketing Officer	Jane Morgan for THEatre GIRLS
Press and Marketing Assistant	Joanna Clift
Accountant	Lynne Ash

Board of Directors	David Kay (Chairman), Michael Bett CBE, Jennie Bland, Sir John Burgh, Patrick Dromgoole, Victor Glynn, Michael Hallifax, Nick Hern
ESC Associates	June Watson, John Woodvine

THE TOUR

2–10 September 1988	MELBOURNE Victoria Arts Centre (Spoleto Festival)

14 – 17 September 1988	BRISBANE Lyric Theatre (World Expo 88)
21 – 24 September 1988	CANBERRA Canberra Theatre
28 September – 1 October 1988	ADELAIDE Festival Theatre
5 – 8 October 1988	PERTH His Majesty's Theatre
18 – 22 October 1988	NEWCASTLE UPON TYNE Theatre Royal
25 – 26 October 1988	UTRECHT Stadsschouwburg
28 – 29 October 1988	EINDHOVEN Schouwburg
1 – 2 November 1988	ROTTERDAM Shouwburg
4 – 5 November 1988	GRÖNINGEN Stadsschouwburg
8 – 12 November 1988	AMSTERDAM Stadsschouwburg
15 – 19 November 1988	CARDIFF New Theatre
22 – 26 November 1988	LEEDS Grand Theatre
29 November – 3 December 1988	LIVERPOOL Empire Theatre
6 – 10 December 1988	PLYMOUTH Theatre Royal
6 – 8 January 1989	HAMBURG Deutsches Schauspielhaus
11 – 15 January 1989	EAST BERLIN Freie Volksbühne
18 – 21 January 1989	FRANKFURT Theater im Scheibebühnenfeld
26 January – 11 March 1989	LONDON The Old Vic
14 – 18 March 1989	EASTBOURNE Congress Theatre
21 – 25 March 1989	NORWICH Theatre Royal
28 March – 1 April 1989	SOUTHAMPTON Mayflower Theatre
4 – 8 April 1989	SWANSEA Grand Theatre

RICHARD II	30 performances
HENRY IV Part 1	29 performances
HENRY IV Part 2	29 performances
HENRY V	28 performances
HENRY VI House of Lancaster	28 performances
HENRY VI House of York	28 performances
RICHARD III	36 performances

AWARDS

*The Mobil Golden Pegasus Award for the Outstanding Creative
Contribution to the Spoleto Melbourne Festival*
Michael Bogdanov for the direction of *The Wars of the Roses*

Laurence Olivier Awards
Best Director: Michael Bogdanov for *The Wars of the Roses*

Laurence Olivier Award Nominations
Best Actor: Michael Pennington for *The Wars of the Roses*
Best Designer: Chris Dyer for *The Wars of the Roses*

4

THE WARS OF THE ROSES

Detail

COSTUMES 600
BOOTS 150 pairs
HATS and HELMETS 100
PROPS 2,500, including 100 swords and guns, 100 red and
white roses, 4 severed heads, 1 crown, 1 throne
FIGHTS 35 hand-to-hand, 6 battles
TRAVEL 4 × 40 ft containers
DUPLICATE SETS 3

Between 1986 and 1989 the Company gave 649 performances.

5

THE BALLAD OF HARRY LE ROY

Come all you good people who would hear a song
Of men bold and men brave, of men weak and men strong;
Of a king who was mighty but wild as a boy,
And list to the ballad of Harry Le Roy.

> *Of a King who was mighty but wild as a boy,*
> *And list to the ballad of Harry Le Roy.*

Thirteen ninety and eight is the year we begin,
King Richard the Second the reign we are in;
Two Lords fought a duel one bright summer's day,
Henry Bolingbroke of Lancaster and Thomas Mowbray.

> *Of a King who was mighty but wild as a boy,*
> *And list to the ballad of Harry Le Roy.*

Both mounted with lances on fire for the fight
Their horses a-flame, brave knight against knight
'Stop the joust' called King Richard, at the very last breath,
'Henceforth you're both exiled upon pain of death.'

> *Of a King who was mighty but wild as a boy,*
> *And list to the ballad of Harry Le Roy.*

One year passes by, Henry Bolingbroke returns,
At the head of an army for vengeance he burns
Defeats and imprisons King Richard alone,
Then murders him shamefully, seizes the throne.

> *Of a King who was mighty but wild as a boy,*
> *And list to the ballad of Harry Le Roy.*

6

THE LADY MORTIMER SCENE

Cyfiethiad

Lady Mortimer. Paid mynd i ryfela, f'anwylyd, paid mynd i
gyflafan ddisynnwyr a ladd gariad ieuanc sy mor ddirodres â
ieuenctid ei hunan. Paid mynd i ryfela!
*Go not to these wars, my love, go not to the senseless slaughter
of a love that is young and green as youth itself. Go not to
these wars!*

Glendower. Paid gofidio, fy merch. Cei di a'th chwaer-yng-
nghyfraith ddilyn eich cariadon.
*Do not fret daughter. Yourself and your sister in marriage will
follow your men.*

Lady Mortimer. Dilyn? I'r rhyfel?
Follow? To the wars?

Glendower. Cewch fod gyda nhw i'w diddanu a'i hanog yng
nghanol y frwydyr.
*You shall be by their sides to comfort them and urge them on
to battle fury.*

Lady Mortimer. Cenedl ydym yn gwastraffu ein bywydau i'n
meistri mewn rhyfeloedd ofer, – mewn tiroedd nad oes gennym
hawl arnynt, – gyda dynion nid ydym yn ei casau. Paid mynd i
ryfela.
*We are a people wasting ourselves in fruitless battles for our
masters. In lands to which we have no claim, with men for
whom we feel no hatred. Go not to these wars!*

Glendower. Fy merch, daw daioni anfodlonrwydd yma!
Daughter, no good will come of this unwillingness.

Lady Mortimer. Fy nhad, mae dyn yn anferth dros fyd bychan,
yn ei dywyllu a'i falchder.
Father, man is huge over the little world, darkening it with
pride!

Glendower. R'oeddem yn genedl, ac ydym eto, pan rown heibio
cweryla am friwsion o dan fwrdd, neu cnoi esgyrn diwylliant
diflanedig. Ail atgyfodwn eto, wedi ein harfogi, ond nid o dan
yr hen drefn.
We were a people, and are so yet. When we have finished
quarrelling for crumbs under the table, or gnawing the bones of
a dead culture, we will arise, armed but not in the old way.

Lady Mortimer. F'anwylyd, cennad y golau a'r bore.
Carcharwyd fi hyd nes y daethost attaf. Dy lais oedd yr allwedd
a agorodd y clo anferth o anobaith. A agorodd y drws i'm
gollwng i, neu, i dy adael di i mewn?
My love, my herald of the light and the morning – I was in
prison until you came; your voice was a key turning in the
enormous lock of hopelessness. Did the door open to let me out
or you in?

   D'oes dim amser i fyw a llai i farw, felly gyda'm holl ewyllys,
ond yn erbyn dymuniad fy nghalon, ymwahanwn ein dau yn
awr, ni ddywedwn nad oes gobiath – ymddengys mor bell i
ffwrdd.
   No time there is for life and even less for death. Then with
all my will, but much against my heart, we two now part. We
will not say there's any hope. It is so far away.

   Rho dy ben, f' anwylyd, ar fy nghôl a chanaf gân i leddfu dy
fryd anesmwyth.
   Then rest your gentle head upon my lap and I will sing a
song of love to soothe your troubled mind.

   Mae holl feddyliau, dagrau a llygaid ddoe yn aros gyda ni, ac
yna yn symud i ddiflannu mewn breuddwydion.
   And all the thoughts and tears and eyes of yesterday stay with
us and are gone in the same world of shared memories.

Cân Y Gaeaf (Song of Winter)

Otid eiry, gwyn y cnes,
Nid â cedwyr, i'w neges,
Oer llynnau, eu lliw heb des.

Otid eiry, toid ystrad,
Dyfrysynt, cedwyr i gad:
Mi nid af, anaf ni'm gad.

Otid eiry, gwyn goror mynydd,
Llwm gwŷdd, llong ar fôr,
Mecid llwfr, llawer cyngor.

> Anonymous. From the *Oxford Book of
> Welsh Verse*, ed. T. Parry, Oxford
> University Press, 1962.

Snow is falling, white the soil.
Soldiers go not campaigning.
Cold lakes, their colour sunless.

Snow is falling, cloaks the valley.
Soldiers hasten to battle.
I go not, a wound stays me.

Snow is falling, white the mountain's edge.
Ship's mast bare at sea.
A coward conceives many schemes.

> Translated by Joseph P. Clancy. From the
> *Oxford Book of Welsh Verse in English*,
> ed. G. Jones, Oxford University Press,
> 1977.

7

PROLOGUE: RICHARD III

Narrator:

THE LATE KING HENRY VI.
Deposed by Edward IV, imprisoned in the Tower, then
murdered by Edward's brothers Richard and Clarence. Only a
few months earlier, Henry's only son had been stabbed to death
by Edward, Clarence and Richard at the battle of Tewkesbury.

EDWARD IV, KING OF ENGLAND, THE SUN IN SPLENDOUR, AND
ELIZABETH HIS QUEEN.
By overthrowing and murdering Henry VI, Edward has settled
an uneasy peace on the houses of York and Lancaster.

GEORGE DUKE OF CLARENCE, BROTHER TO THE KING AND RICHARD.
Joint murderer with Richard of Henry and Henry's only son.

RICHARD DUKE OF GLOUCESTER, THE BOAR.
Brother to the King and the Duke of Clarence; his father and
his younger brother were murdered by Henry and Henry's
queen, Margaret.

EARL RIVERS.
Brother to Queen Elizabeth. Later he will be executed.

LORD GREY.
Son of Queen Elizabeth (by her first husband). Later he will be
executed.

THE MARQUESS OF DORSET – HIS BROTHER.
He will escape execution and fly to France.

THE DUKE OF BUCKINGHAM.
Richard's confidant and right-hand man. Peer of the realm and
a politician at the heart of the struggle for power. Later he will
be executed.

LORD HASTINGS, THE LORD CHAMBERLAIN.
Supporter of King Edward IV, arrested, released, arrested again
and finally executed.

LORD STANLEY.
Supporter of those in power. Supporter of Henry VI, Edward
IV, Richard of Gloucester and the Earl of Richmond. He will
live to a ripe old age.

And now the ladies.

MARGARET, HENRY VI'S WIDOW AND FORMER QUEEN.
Her husband was murdered in the Tower. Her only son was
stabbed to death at the Battle of Tewkesbury.

THE DUCHESS OF YORK.
Mother to Edward, Clarence and Richard. Her husband, three
of her sons and her two grandsons are murdered.

LADY ANNE.
Her father, father-in-law and her husband were all killed by
Richard of Gloucester. Later, she herself will be killed by him.

The sons and heirs to the throne – THE PRINCE OF WALES AND
THE DUKE OF YORK

THE ROYAL BROTHERS – Edward, Clarence and Richard.

THE WOODVILLES, related to the Crown through marriage, not
blood.

THE LADIES IN MOURNING:

MARGARET, mourning her son and her late husband, King Henry
VI.

LADY ANNE, mourning her late husband and her father-in-law, the late king.

THE DUCHESS OF YORK, mourning everybody.

And there you have it.

THE POLITICIANS, THE LADIES, THE WOODVILLES, THE PLANTAGENETS.

Simple.

8

Chronology of English kings, 1377–1485

Richard II *1377–99*
Henry IV *1399–1413*
Henry V *1413–22*
Henry VI *1422–61 and 1470–71*
Edward IV *1461–70 and 1471–83*
Richard III *1483–85*

Chronology of Shakespeare's Wars of the Roses *plays* (several dates conjectural)

1590–91   *Henry VI Part 2; Henry VI Part 3*
1591–92   *Henry VI Part 1*
1592–93   *Richard III*
1595–96   *Richard II*
1596–97   *Henry IV Part 1*
1596–97   *Henry IV Part 2*
1599   *Henry V*

9

Torquay, Devon, 11th November 1986

The Rt Honble Richard Luce, M.P.
Minister for Arts and Libraries
House of Commons
Westminster

Dear Mr Luce,

I wish to protest in the strongest possible terms about the performances being given by the English Shakespeare Company, advertised in the enclosed leaflet, which I saw last Saturday at Plymouth, and which are being funded by the Arts Council. In particular, the production of *Henry V* is of such a low standard as to be quite unacceptable. For instance:

1. In the embarkation scene at Southampton a crowd of 'football hooligans' is suddenly revealed on a gantry. They unfurl a banner with 'Fuck the Frogs' in large letters. The three traitors, denounced by King Henry and ordered to be taken into custody, are shot in the back by soldiers in modern battledress as soon as his back is turned.

2. 'Pistol' drops his trousers and bares his bottom to the audience (squeals of girlish teenage laughter) and then sits over a sandbagged trench ostensibly to relieve himself whilst talking to the incognito King – then bares his bottom to the audience again when he gets up.

3. The pathos of the murder of the young boys in the baggage train is completely lost, making King Henry's line 'I was not angry since I came to France until this moment' quite meaningless as he is only looking at one adult soldier on a British Rail luggage trolley.

4. We have to listen, in silence, to Falstaff relieving himself

(off-stage) before he appears in the Boar's Head Tavern (where
'Doll' is attired in scanty black leather and there is a creature
with a Mohican hair-do).

5. There is quite gratuitous and unnecessary violence to the
French officer wounded on the field at Agincourt – repeated
kicking in the groin by a supposed Medical Orderly (in modern
battledress), who also violently robs three bodies (three
dummies cast about, who were presumably supposed to be the
murdered boys). What an odious example to set to young
people! Pistol and Nym go for each other with flick-knives
produced out of trouser back pockets.

6. There are constant vulgar hand signals throughout.

More general criticism:

The scenery is almost non-existent, consisting of two metal
'TV' masts with the aforesaid gantry on top which can be raised
or lowered. Other props include two luggage trolleys which are
pulled about, a shopping cart on which the wounded French
prisoner is removed from the battlefield, a modern double divan
bed, odd tables and a modern office desk and twelve office
chairs.

The costumes are a curious mixture of medieval and modern,
and assorted military uniforms. For instance at the battle of
Agincourt the French are in immaculate white pantaloons with
pale blue, reminiscent of Napoleon's time, whilst the British are
in modern flak battledress with berets, with rifles which are
shot indiscriminately. At the final peace meeting, the French are
in lounge suits whilst the English are in dress uniform, around
the aforesaid office desk. By contrast, the Queen of France and
Princess Katherine are in long black plain calico – no expense
here, as the same dresses were worn by Lady Northumberland
and Lady Percy. The Dauphin is completely bald and looks
older than his father. In fact, the whole thing is completely
unbelievable.

I do beg you to send someone to view this subversive and
indecent production before further harm is done. The leaflet is
advertising for school parties, but in my opinion no children
should be allowed near it – they would come away with an
extraordinarily muddled view of history, and the impression
that it is all right for British soldiers to shoot prisoners in the
back, rob the dead, use foul language and behave like hooligans

– and that in fact this is what the British Army does. How dare the producers equate the heroes of Agincourt with football hooligans? And why should they be allowed to destroy our culture by knocking down our historical heroes? This is just a travesty of Shakespeare misused as a vehicle for modern pornography. If allowed to go to Canada as threatened it cannot fail to give offence to French Canadians, and at home it must offend our neighbours across the Channel (fellow members of the EEC), thus undoing many hours of patient diplomacy by the FCO.

I strongly object, personally, to any part of my taxes being used to fund such an obscene and degrading performance. At the very least it should be stated in the advertising that it is a 'modern version' and 'after Shakespeare', so that playgoers like myself, expecting a pleasant evening of the real thing, can avoid being offended. As it is, it smacks of obtaining money by false pretences.

I do believe Mrs Thatcher's aim is to uphold our cultural values, and so I do hope that better control can be exercised over what is funded by taxpayers' money through the Arts Council.

Yours sincerely,

Mrs A. N. Butler

Office of Arts and Libraries, London, 16th November 1986

Mrs A N Butler
Torquay
Devon

Dear Mrs Butler

Thank you for your letter of 11th November, addressed to the Minister for the Arts. I have been asked to reply.

The Minister's relationship with the Arts Council and with

other funded bodies is such that he does not seek to guide them in their artistic judgements; it would be wrong to do so. We have all seen where governmental direction of artistic decisions can lead. It happens that one of the Minister's officials did see the production of *Henry V* to which you refer. I was there myself, more or less by chance; I was attending the conference of the Theatrical Management Association in Plymouth that weekend. I must say that I enjoyed the play – not that that is in any way an answer to your criticisms – and that the majority of the audience appeared to enjoy it too. Since the Minister does *not* take it upon himself to direct the artistic policy of companies which, like the English Shakespeare Company, are partly funded by the Arts Council, I don't know that it would be profitable to discuss your criticisms point by point – but as the Minister's representative, I was pleased to see that the producer had had some regard to economy. Time will tell whether the English Shakespeare Company succeeds in attracting audiences with its style of portraying Shakespeare; if it does not, it will no doubt either go out of business, or change its interpretation.

I have sent a copy of your letter to the Arts Council's Secretary-General, Mr Luke Rittner, 105 Piccadilly, London W1, and asked him if he would like to let you have his comments.

Yours sincerely,

Derek Lodge

West Norwood, London SE27, 1st March 1989

Dear Friends,

After spending so many hours in your company last weekend, that seems the proper way to address you. My daughter Dorothy (who's fifteen) and I had the great pleasure of sitting in the middle of the front row of the Upper Circle on Friday

Saturday and Sunday, as part of the excellent and responsive animal that your audience became, while the plays unfolded before us. Lit up by the truth of your response to the script and the ingenuity and inventiveness of your presentation of it. I reckon Shakespeare would have loved it. We certainly did. Thank you, the people we saw and the people we didn't.

Yours,

Ann Watkins

London W12

Dear Michael Pennington,

I spent a magical day in the Old Vic on Saturday 25th February. I couldn't leave it at that, and feel that I want you and the rest of the company to know . . .

So often it isn't like that and one leaves the theatre disappointed with a hollow feeling, slightly cheated, because what one has seen is somehow not relevant at all to one's own life and the way we live now. Not so with the three magnificent productions that we saw on Saturday!

We felt enriched – stimulated – we had spent a day that we'll remember all our lives.

Many many thanks to you and the rest of the cast.

With best wishes and good luck for future productions.

Yours sincerely,

Nicolette Baylis

Madison, Wisconsin 53705, USA, 17th May 1990

Dear ESC,

It was exactly two years ago this week that I first encountered the English Shakespeare Company at the International Theater

Festival in Chicago. I do not think I am exaggerating in the
least when I say that this experience changed my views on
Shakespeare forever. I had always enjoyed the plays, but I never
realized the full depth, the spirit, or the excitement they could
contain until I saw *The Wars of the Roses* . . .

I think the world would be a poorer place without the
Company. I wish you the very best of luck now and always.

Sincerely,

Diane L. Balmer

Globe Theatre, London WC1, 20th February 1988

Dearest All,

Last night, with *Richard II*, I completed the *Wars of the Roses*,
albeit in a somewhat hotch-potch order! And this is simply to
say thank you to you all for approximately 24 hours of truly
remarkable theatre! It's a monumental achievement to mount
and perform seven plays as you do, and your combined talent,
stamina, courage, commitment and spirit is very moving indeed.

There are countless memories that will, I know, live with me
now forever; many moments that illuminated and enriched those
plays I am familiar with and a thrilling introduction to the
Henry VIs and *Richard II* which I did not know at all. It is a
unique and astonishing experience for us as audience and for
you as performers and, shattered with exhaustion as you must
be, you must also feel very, very proud. I do, to have seen you!

These are not my words, but I wish they had been: *Great
theatre is a catharsis. It purifies and when you come through to
the end there is real fulfilment and elation in the survival.* Belief
too!

Many, many congratulations and love and I wish you huge
success with the rest of the tour.

Sara Kestelman

Department of English, University of Leicester

Dear Michael Bogdanov and/or Michael Pennington,

... It was the one totally successful example of modernisation I have ever seen, and made me feel that I never want to look at a pair of purple velvet galligaskins again ...

Yours sincerely,

Lois Potter
Senior Lecturer in English

Retford, Notts

Please accept the enclosed cheque towards your appeal. Your work is far too important to sink into oblivion ... if companies like yourself do not tour, what will tour and arrive at Theatre Royal Nottingham? ... Present the plays on a bare stage, with the actors in their rehearsal clothes, but please keep your operation alive ... What is half a million over two years to the Arts Council?

Please do not acknowledge the cheque. Well, it is a small saving.

Best of luck,

Peter Sutton

Wellington, Telford, Shropshire, 15th May 1990

Dear Mr Bogdanov and Mr Pennington,

Enclosed is a cheque for £50. I do hope you are successful in raising the money you need.

The marathon in York was wonderful. It was a revelation to see a Shakespearian production where every word spoken by every actor made sense. In Swansea I sat next to a schoolteacher who said, 'We teach the kids that Shakespeare's wonderful. They'd believe us if every production was like this.'

The ESC must go on.

Yours truly,

Jeanne Fielder

INDEX

'God Say Amen': Andrew Jarvis (Photo: John Tramper)